Pelican Books

D0715643

OF BREAD AND GUNS

Nigel Harris lives in London with his wife and two children. He teaches in the University of London and also works extensively in the developing countries. He is a founder member of the Socialist Workers' Party, and former editor of *International Socialism.* His earlier works include *Beliefs in Society* (1967), *Competition and the Corporate Society* (1972), *India-China: Underdevelopment and Revolution* (1974), *The Mandate of Heaven: Marx and Mao in Modern China* (1978), *Economic Development, Cities and Planning* (1978).

OF **BREAD** AND **GUNS**

The World Economy in Crisis

Nigel Harris

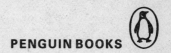
PENGUIN BOOKS

Penguin Books Ltd, Harmondsworth, Middlesex, England
Penguin Books, 625 Madison Avenue, New York, New York 10022, U.S.A.
Penguin Books Australia Ltd, Ringwood, Victoria, Australia
Penguin Books Canada Ltd, 2801 John Street, Markham, Ontario, Canada L3R 1B4
Penguin Books (N.Z.) Ltd, 182–190 Wairau Road, Auckland 10, New Zealand

First published 1983

Made and printed in Great Britain by
Richard Clay (The Chaucer Press) Ltd, Bungay, Suffolk
Bungay, Suffolk
Set in VIP Times

CONTENTS

PREFACE

This is a book about the world economy. The aim in writing it has been to describe for the ordinary reader in as simple a fashion as possible some of the elements of how the system works, its central dynamics and important features. It has not always been successful in this attempt, and the text is still regrettably burdened at various stages with those awful terms with which economists frequently try to disguise their thought.

The world system described here is seen as a geographical system of production and finance, not primarily as a set of relationships between countries. This is not how people normally see it. Nor is the account concerned with where the majority of people live. We are preoccupied with production, not consumption, with the forces that produce change and with those areas and activities with the greatest influence over the rest. It accordingly pays much more attention to the industrialized core of the system than to the territories of the world where the majority of people live.

It is, at best, a cartoon of the system, or rather, a set of cartoons. The idea of a cartoon is a bit misleading. Normally we can check our drawing against the politician's nose to see if it really portrays it. But the world system has no easily recognizable noses. It is only a set of abstractions. We can check the information against the cartoon, check the speculative connections between the facts, but we still have enormous room to be very wrong. Nevertheless, the risk is worth taking. Although we may make many errors, part of the argument of the book is that we do need to understand the world system if the people living in any part of it are to be able to thrive; there is little possibility now of the survival of any part independently of all the rest.

There is another difficulty. The available facts seem clear and unambiguous. They are not. There is an infinity of facts which we could have, but only a small selection available. The selection exists because we have particular assumptions about the world, theories, which in turn embody purposes not our own. Somebody had to think up the idea of Gross National Product before facts could be collected to illustrate it, and in doing so, fed in to the idea all sorts of assumptions which we might want to say are just plain wrong. The passage of time and new research turn what we see as 'facts' upside down. In this account, we have dodged any discussion of the reliability of the facts – whether they are accurate, whether they indicate what they are supposed to show, whether they leave out more than they include. It is a sort of philistinism, but cannot be helped if we are to stick to the aim of making a cartoon that can be understood by other than the professionals.

For the same reason, the text has been purged of most of its references. The book nibbles information like a magpie, here and there, without thanking or acknowledging those who have provided sustenance. We can only apologize.

Another apology is due. The book is written in one place and at one time. Try as we may, we cannot escape the prejudices and preoccupations of that point of reference. The view from London, Britain and Europe, at the low point of slump, provides endless opportunities for confusing wood and trees.

To keep matters simple, the text in general avoids those thickets of initials that are nowadays popular. Some of the better known ones are included here and there, but more often names are written in full; the clutter of the text is less onerous than having to check what the acronyms mean. The dollar occurs all over the place; it is, characteristically, that of the United States. When it occurs in billions, that also follows the American style, meaning thousands of millions.

The structure of the book is as follows. First there is an introduction about the approach, a chapter which can be skipped by those keen to get to the substance. The immediate past of the system is laid out, then an overview of the seventies. Two chapters then describe some of the more important features of the system today. Chapter 6 looks at the Eastern Bloc, and Chapter 7 at two important sectors of activity. An Appendix to Chapter 7 then sums up the argument to that point, before the last two chapters examine the current proposals to restore the world system.

The text is the result of work and discussion with many people over several years. It is impossible to list and thank all of them. However, particular thanks are due to those who, under duress, agreed to read and comment on the manuscript – Tirril Harris, Duncan Hallas, Chris Harman, Michael Kidron, Tony Cliff, Christopher Scott and Bill Kaye. We did not always agree, but without their efforts the text would be much worse. I would also like to thank Mary Williams for shouldering so much of my normal work while this book was being written. Faults and errors are all my own work.

London
August 1982

ONE A WORLD OF VILLAGES

Everything should be as simple as possible, but no
simpler.[1] [In an epoch of social revolution,] just as our
opinion of an individual is not based on what he thinks of
himself, so can we not judge of such a period of
transformation by its own consciousness; on the contrary,
this consciousness must be explained rather from the
contradictions of material life, from the existing conflict
between the social forces of production and the relations
of production.[2]

The world economy is a miracle of collective organization. When it
works well, the needs of millions of people are met on a daily, on an
hourly, basis. For people in London, the corn that has gone into the
breakfast cornflakes was harvested in Tennessee or Brazil. The wood for
the table was cut in Malaysia. The sugar, the tea or coffee, the formica
table top, the oil that powers the kitchen light – each detail concludes
such an enormous and complex world division of labour that no single
person can comprehend it. The world economy is not some external
phenomenon far away: it is present in each kitchen.

Furthermore, this vast process takes place without any conscious
direction, without a single intelligence guiding it. Hundreds of millions
of people unknowingly collaborate to make it all possible. It is a system –
like the classical theory of capitalism – which has no guiding State, no
planning instruments, only a market and competition. If there is an
'invisible hand' – as Adam Smith, the economist, suggested – it moves
the world in directions no one discovers until long after it has arrived.

The operation of the world economy, despite a plethora of facts, is
almost as obscure a subject as was the human body in ancient times. We
interpret obscure shadows on the wall. Yet despite the mystery, the
world economy is decisive for all that is most important for the inhabitants of the globe. Men and women lose their jobs in Detroit and
Calcutta because of some unknown event thousands of miles away.
Babies cry with hunger in Peruvian fishing villages because news of the
harvest of soya beans arriving in Chicago has depressed the price of their
fathers' anchovy catch. A Brazilian shoemaker in the Rio Grande do
Sul, or another in Taiwan or Naples, take their lives because Europe has
limited the increase in shoe imports. We rarely glimpse the terrain
through the fog. We may note that the sugar price is high, but we don't

see the Caribbean family that briefly starts eating meat again as a result. The spoonful of tea you pop in the pot does not cry out because the Tamil fingers that plucked the leaf in Sri Lanka were weak with malnutrition. Fortunately, commodities are mute.

Let no one tell you that this is all merely 'economics' – that the things of the spirit transcend mere material livelihood. Without bread or rice and many other mundane things, there can be no poetry, no music, indeed, neither laughter nor joy.

The problem of understanding is not simply that the right information is lacking. Indeed, there is too much information. What we most often lack are the right questions to ask. Our concepts are usually inappropriate. The preoccupations with which we have been instilled militate against understanding. In particular, a problem of incomprehension arises because we live in a world of self-enclosed villages, or rather, the illusion of self-enclosed villages, of separate States.

Villages of the mind, or 'common sense'

It is part of conventional wisdom that you should believe the evidence of your eyes. Undoubtedly, for those things that can be seen, there is much sense in having a careful look. But in our world, you cannot see the most important things, for they are abstractions, concepts. You cannot *see* 'Britain' or 'China', the population of Zambia, a gross national product or a steel industry. You may see illustrative details of each. But each detail only makes sense because you already have a concept that you cannot see, except as a word on a piece of paper. You may see a steel plant, a line of workers queuing to clock on, the glow of furnaces in the night sky, but it is only a detail of the 'German steel industry', a detail meaningful because we have conjoined three concepts – 'Germany', 'steel' and 'industry'. It is a 'theory' that these three elements can be so related. In a rough and ready way, the theory works – it allows us to understand something, and, what is ultimately the point of understanding, it allows us to act.

The common wisdom of 'seeing is believing' most accurately fits a small locality, a village, a unit that is, in the main, economically self-sufficient. What is most important for the life of the villagers can be seen. Today, people are still in the main brought up in one place – in a family, on a particular street, in a small locality. The furniture of the mind of the growing child is still related to tangible elements that can be seen, touched, heard, smelt and tasted. For quite a lot of people, these tangible elements remain central to their perception, and they are too busy living a given life to wonder how these elements came to exist and what are the factors that cause them to change. Quite often, in any case, they are powerless to change them or to prevent them changing, so that there seems to be no point in understanding them. Their world is governed by events that seem to be accidental – rains fall, the sun shines, as if random acts of an unknowable God. It is understandable if the theory created to accommodate these random happenings is superstitious – all forces are turned into human beings, either nice or nasty, and efforts made to placate them with bribes or sacrifices.

Today, the area of tangible familiarity is for many people no longer one place. People move, and their minds collect several localities, spots of light in a map of darkness. The spots can span the globe. A migrant from Melbourne lives in a London street, and puts together two places thousands of miles apart. A Mexican garment worker in Los Angeles conjoins a network of American streets and the narrow alleys of a village far to the south.

These spots of light are not simply experiences; they are elements in the person's identity – perceptions fashioned and remembered relative to the person's interests and purposes. At least in principle – but almost never in practice – it is possible to stay at this level. But the moment we need to understand something new, we must create distinguishing concepts, or rather, we must borrow on a cultural tradition which offers a confusing myriad of concepts. The clerk in a bedsitter in Earl's Court in London can then become an 'Australian', supposedly distinguished in important respects from those around him or her, 'British' or 'Welsh' or 'Jews' or whatever. As with the 'steel industry', we assume such groups have a real existence – for we cannot see them, only particular illustrations of each.

These concepts – of groups – are part of a theory, and one which is rarely set down coherently so that it can be examined. Indeed, most people so take the theory for granted that they might deny it exists at all. *Of course*, they say, 'Australians' are different, it is common sense, and they will quote endless examples to illustrate the point, even though the examples *merely* illustrate: they do not prove the existence of the group, and indeed, the illustrations only illustrate if we presuppose the group exists. The concept makes sense if we assume people are fundamentally distinguished by groups, which in turn are created by some common place of origin or ancestry. There is a theory that differences of 'blood', genetical inheritance, or 'culture' separate humanity into clear groups.

Most people do not choose the theory; they assume its validity, and, in some cases, spend a great deal of time illustrating the peculiarities of 'Australians' and so on. A compound of fragmentary information, of rumour and invention goes to make up the notions of Australians as sporting giants, Welsh romantic poets, military Germans, merry Africans and spiritual Indians. If people soberly considered their real experience – if they took 'seeing is believing' seriously – they would find the attributes were nonsense. Maybe as many Australians are small and poetic as sporting, as many Welsh practical, Germans pacifist, Africans melancholic and Indians materialist.

But because the concepts exist, they are not refuted by particular examples. They have a life of their own, sustained by practical needs in the individual. Some Australians in London find migration so disturbing, the local inhabitants so different, that they need a concept to identify that feeling of differentness (other Australians have no such need – 'Australian-ness' is merely part of their past biography, not their present existence). In other cases, the reaction is defensive. Black people in white societies usually have no option but to identify themselves by colour, for it is their colour which is nailed on them by the rest of society: whatever they do, it is a 'black' person who does it, not a young factory worker or an old age pensioner or any of the other available distinctions.

If the world economy is mysterious, then explaining events is a field day for the mythology of group identities. When the British economy grows, that is attributable to the wonderfulness of the British: when it declines, it is the result of the low cunning of foreigners – they work too hard, they cheat, they are too efficient, have low wages, and so on. The fact that the people who inhabit Japan or Germany or Hong Kong are chained to the same machine, running automatically at the same speed to produce an identical output, is lost in a welter of moralizing.

It is true that the universality of the human condition is expressed through thousands of peculiarities, of unique differences which are infinitely detailed and concrete. But the differences do not correspond to the groups identified. What creates the myth that groups are composed of similar sorts of people is the institution of political authority. The modern State dragoons its population into what can be presented as some sort of uniformity. The interests of the dominant power are drilled into each soul: what is in fact uniform is not common personal characteristics but a common subordination, stiffened by a standardized education, a common military service, a common law. At the end, even those subordinated become nationalistic, demanding that newcomers adopt the same outward forms of culture, religion, dress, roles. The totalitarianism implicit in all States produces the myth of uniformity within in order that the differences without may be enhanced. Then, as Marx puts it in discussing Ireland: the English worker 'feels himself a member of the *ruling* nation and so turns himself into a tool of the aristocrats and capitalists *against Ireland*, thus strengthening their domination *over himself* ... It is the secret of the impotence of the English working class, despite their organization. It is the secret by which the capitalist class maintains its power. And of this that class is well aware.'[3]

The State inherits, reinforces and transforms the concepts of the tangible village. It does so in part by creating prototype families or individuals to stand as the symbol of unity, symbols which overshadow the rest of the people. How is one to understand such oddities as: 'Winston Churchill won the Second World War', 'Joseph Stalin transformed Russia', 'Mao Tse-tung created modern China'? The village elder, Chairman of the Parish Council, decrepit though he may be, now completely displaces the village. He must do so to give a tangible reality to the concept, the abstraction, the State, to hold together the manifest contradiction of interest. For where 'our land' is distributed between a landowner and a mass of landless, the concept has to hold together rich and poor: 'our property' is mine and not yours; the millionaire and the pauper do not equally possess 'our wealth'.

People become exhausted by the concepts. They need to protect their tangible humanity from the ravages of abstract identification. One way of doing so is to invent a compensating sanctuary, 'personal life'. It is in this secret corner that one is to be consoled. But the world will not leave to itself the secret corner of 'the personal'. It returns to structure it with the fantasies which will sell goods. Hoardings of brown blondes in white cars or knights on horseback peer into the hermit's secret corner, beckoning him or her to embrace the public symbols of private joy. The personal becomes reduced to consumption. An inhuman public existence does the producing, and the role of 'human beings' is simply to consume, to become reduced to an insatiable mouth, ear, eye or loins. The world is not 'outside' the individual at all, any more than it is outside the national village. It is inside. The great debates are not in Parliament, but in our own heads. It is our minds which are part of the world, our work which sustains it, our actions which create it.

The village is not simply the village of the lord, but the village of the villagers, who by their work create and sustain the lord. Even the culture the State creates to maintain its power can be turned inside out – 'It is a free country so you should continue to work at the wages I pay', says the lord: 'It is a free country and therefore we will not work', can be the reply.

The State is the agency people see as governing their lives, not the world economy. People discuss shifts in government policy endlessly in the press and television, seeking to identify exactly 'what the President meant', what are the true intentions of the Chancellor. It all assumes that there are answers to such questions – the President knows what he meant, the Chancellor has true intentions – and that the answers matter. Yet there is sufficient evidence to show that while some States have greater power than others to influence events, States neither control the world nor create what happens. They cannot determine boom and slump, how many will work and how many will go hungry. It is only their pretension that all triumphs are of their making, all disasters the result of nature or foreigners. States are only one type of the many agencies and institutions operating in the world; they are, like all the others, as much victim as master of what happens.

Nonetheless, it is difficult to keep hold of sense when the air is filled with the din of States, declamations of fantasies and vanities. A dutiful press plays back the images, smooths their savageries into charities, their barbarisms into civilization. Preparation for world war becomes the maintenance of peace, pure banditry 'the legitimate defence of legitimate interests' (when the State invents the law, its actions can never in any ordinary sense be 'legitimate'); its lies become truth in the defence of 'security', and its anarchic chaotic internal structure 'the united will of the nation'.

At the level of society, common sense, often so wise in its local tangible origin, is converted to nonsense, serving only to forge the links that bind us all to the State.

The world

The real world is a global system, not a village, and accessible as a system only through the impersonal, through abstractions. It is dominated not by concerns of consumption, but by those of production – or rather, of the profit that can be made from production. It is a geographically distributed system of production, linking sources of raw material to the endless complexity of processing and to a global market. Since it is geographically distributed, activity entails vast movement – of goods, of finance, of information and of labour. But the movement of these elements is not the central cause of activity. Trade and money are the results of connecting geographically dispersed units of production to each other.

The existence of such a system presupposes the partial conquest of geographical space: the elimination of distance as a decisive factor in production costs. The S.T.D. telephone which, within seconds, connects Los Angeles to Tokyo, Munich to Hong Kong, is a condition for unifying geography in a nearly instantaneous system. Air freight is less instantaneous, but with each decade, the gap in time between producer and user narrows. A stock short-fall at a New York garment store can now, with the aid of telex and air freight, be met within twenty-four hours by the manufacturer on the other side of the globe in Taiwan. For some commodities, the exchanges now scarcely close – video flashes London's closing gold prices to New York in time for the opening of the exchange, and New York's are flashed to Hong Kong at the close of day; when the market is feverish, the bullion broker never sleeps.

The distribution of production is, as everyone knows, highly dispro-portionate. There are the great zones of world manufacturing – the 'golden triangle' between Frankfurt, Amsterdam and Paris; the New York–Baltimore area, the Great Lakes and California; Osaka to Tokyo; with dozens of smaller zones scattered over the surface of the globe, some no more than industrial estates. Between the zones lie great areas, at best able to service the manufacturing zones with raw materials, or to provide homes or food or holidays both for those privileged to be chained to the world's industrial machine and those, the majority, excluded from it.

The system has a myriad set of technical interrelationships straddling geography – for example, from iron to pig iron to steel to, by a long complicated jump, cars. The men – and some women – who make the decisions concerning this process have no particular attachment to one place rather than another (that would be part of their secret 'personal life'). Costs govern their decisions, or rather profit rates at different levels of costs. So the technical relationships are not stable geographi-cally – if the relative price of iron ore between Venezuela and India and Brazil changes, the buyers move their orders from one to another, without even noticing. Indeed, they, like the users of iron ore, may not even know the source has changed, for commodities have no nationality, no distinguishing marks of identity. Only the jobless iron miners have that distinction. Nor are the technical relationships technically stable; they are constantly transformed, rendering parts of the linkages redun-dant. The changes make whole ways of life redundant, and create, in virgin locations, new ways of life. For the participants, all seems bound by necessities imposed upon them from outside.

'Division of labour' suggests a stable distribution of complementary work, a cooperative effort that spans the world. It does not suggest change, nor does it suggest how such a system could be created in the first place. The dynamic element, the spirit that puts life in the machine, is the direct opposite of cooperation: competition. The steelmaker would not change technology nor necessarily expand his output (it would depend upon what level of output and price produced the highest rate of profit) if it were not that other steelmakers threatened to capture his markets. It is competition, the struggle to survive by growing, which drives the system to such frenetic self-transformation, and competition which introduces such powerful elements of growth, instability and decline. It is competition which makes it impossible to plan or even to guide the world system. The world blunders on, only discovering where it has arrived long after it has already left that place.

There is a third element, predicated by the second. Power is unequally distributed within the system, between sectors of world production, giant companies and States. None is willing simply to permit market forces to operate unimpeded, trusting to the justice of whatever is the outcome. Each agency, company or State, tries to use its relative power to twist the terms of competition in its favour – whether it is General Motors buying up the Los Angeles tramways to force people into cars, Lockheed buying a clutch of prime ministers and presidents to force the sales of its aircraft, or the States, Washington and Moscow, undertaking covert or open warfare to control a segment of the globe. Such activities do not determine the world; they presuppose the sources of movement come from elsewhere, but, on the margin, the outcome can be influenced. The occurrence of such activity, much of it secret, cautions us against accepting without qualification the simple justice of either a set of technical relationships, the division of labour, or a unified world market that none can control.

Competition and cooperation, the twin polarities, must coincide in constant and mutual antagonism to make possible the existing world system. Competition is the precondition for growth in capitalism, itself the basis of the power of the rivals. But if there were nothing else but competition, the social order would disintegrate, dissolving all into competitive buyers and sellers. Anarchy would reign, each snatching what he or she could where they could, and making off with the loot. But what would the 'loot' be? There could be no money, for there could be no State to enforce the accepted value of its pieces of paper. Without money, there could be no loot of any size, for mere goods need to be sold to give power. Pure gangsterism could not rise to the towering heights of modern capitalism, where loot is measured in trillions of dollars.

Cooperation is required for stability, the precondition for competition between capitals. Cooperation makes possible families – the stable reproduction of a labour force of requisite skills – and ethnic groups, classes, States, alliances of States, and even *détente* between Washington and Moscow. But, though it may curb the excesses of competition, to eliminate competition would be to end the system as it currently exists. When the President of the United States kisses the worn cheeks of the

Chairman of the Praesidium of the Supreme Soviet, each has one hand behind his back, one finger hovering over the button that unleashes mutual annihilation.

The metaphor fits the world order. The world is ruled by a class of people, cooperating through great companies and States, but also competing. Each fears the other, and, unless obstructed by the urgent need for collaboration, seeks their destruction. They have as it were divided up the territory in patches, countries, each governed by a sub-section of the world ruling order, and each sub-section being composed of another loose coalition of cooperating and competing elements, yoked into a single discipline – when they are so yoked – by a State, the institution they have created to embody their territorial power. The coalitions form and reform. They are not a tribe or caste, granted by birth the role of kingship (although families, like companies and States, try to ensure that their role becomes hereditary, competition and change ensure they can never finally succeed). Nor does the right to rule invariably unite them all. There are civil wars within the national patches, between groups within the ruling order who seek to batter their rivals into submission.

So it is with the global order, where civil war becomes the great spectacle of world war. Now competition, that chain that binds subjects, lowliest and mightiest, becomes a scourge to whip them. The polite phrases of the undying friendship between 'our peoples' gives way to overt efforts to slaughter each other. Like economic crisis, slump, war is part of the costs of production, a 'regrettable' excess of competition, but an excess which, at least in the past, assisted the destruction of rivals and the concentration of capital and power.

Thus, one economic system creates and sustains a single social system. The international social system may be reconciled with local circumstances in many different ways, but ultimately one world market constantly disciplines each part, enforces conformity.

It is the same within each national patch, each country. Ancient and venerable cultures are subverted from within. Here is a country whose people were divided into many tribes, living originally in different circumstances with different cultural traditions. In so far as they survive within a State, it will be by some manner of accommodation (which may include forcible suppression). The elders, the brokers between the local and the national, may inhabit two cultural worlds, changing from robes to suits as they move from the tribal homeland to the capital. But in time, the habits of the capital will undermine those of the tribe.

The elders of the world's tribes reveal the unification of the social system in the astonishing uniformity of their consumption patterns; or

rather in the acceptance by all the world's rulers of the cultural style of
the dominant section. Once the suit was the mark of Europe's tribes. But
now even the Saudis increasingly don them abroad; they have long
driven the same cars. At home, the same extended leafy suburb, with
spacious houses and rolling green lawns (even where desert is the norm
for everybody else) – designed and laid out by the same architects and
landscape designers, or at least, members of the same school – gives
uniformity to Westchester County, to the hills high above Kingston,
Jamaica, to Wimbledon and Santiago de Chile, to select neighbourhoods
of Calcutta, Lagos, São Paulo and Tokyo. At work the world of power is
the same, the same desk in the same air-conditioned office, the same
telephone to bark command, the same gadgets, the same potted plant
and discreet secretary. At leisure, they bask on the same beaches, golf on
the same links, and hob-nob in the same air corridors that link their
homes dispersed round the globe, carrying them high above the intervening areas of darkness.

Indeed, we might say that in the last half of the twentieth century, the
world has become governed more totally by Europeans than ever
before. Physically the Europeans come in many sizes, shapes and
colours, but that was always partly so. Today, some are black, brown and
yellow. They speak at home, in their 'personal lives', a variety of
tongues, but they are one class. By contrast, the majority of people in
Europe and America are not 'Europeans' at all – like the majority of
people in Africa, Asia and Latin America, they are not part of that circle
of world power, membership of which alone qualifies people to be
'European'. The Europeans of Africa may seem to be black, but in
reality, by reason of their membership of the great club, they are white.
And most of those who are under the illusion that they are white are, by
the symbols of the time, black.

The world ruling class, wherever it is its fortune to serve in the world,
has homelands: in Western Europe, in North America, and now in
Japan. When there is civil tumult, when the mass of the population is
sullen or grumbles at its lot, it is to those places that the rulers flee for
safety. It is there that the prudent dispatch part of their fortune as a
safeguard against expropriation 'at home', and perhaps buy somewhere
to live. For all his supposed love of Iran, the late Shah kept form with
palaces in Switzerland, France, Britain and the United States – and then,
copying the American rich, even in Acapulco. The recent collisions in
Poland have revealed similar customs – a high State official is discovered
to own a villa in France.

It is the homelands of the world ruling class that are the destination for
the 'flight of capital' when there is local trouble. It is there that the rulers

send their children to school and university, that their wives go to shop, and that they retreat to repair their souls for the harsh tasks of district officering the far-flung extremities of the world empire. And in the event of dangers, it is there that they retire to wait, in the hope that they may once more be summoned to rule.

Mapping the world order

To understand the system we need concepts. But there is a difficulty. We have information on the sectors of world production – the world engineering industry, world wheat production – but constructed not so that we may understand the technical relationships concerned, but merely to exhibit the respective shares of different sections of the world ruling order: 'German engineering' or 'United States wheat production', etc. The statistics may tell us something about the relationships between States, about the distribution of activity by patches of territory, but not about the all-important production relationships.

Alternatively, we ought to be able to look at the world as a set of relationships between competing companies, some large, but most small, some owned by States, some not. But the statistics do not exist, and the company's need for secrecy to protect its competitive power will ensure that they will not be created.

Perforce, we are left with a world as seen through the distorting mirror of the interests of States. Indeed, in many studies of what is called the world economy, we are not at all concerned with a global production system, only with the *external* transactions of a set of States. The statistics are dragooned into illuminating the States, and the mystery thereby compounded. For it becomes almost impossible to explain what happens, or rather, each explanation is driven conceptually to 'explain' what happens as if it were no more than the product of the decisions of States. 'Policy', the public intentions of governments, then becomes the only explanatory variable, even though only with great difficulty can policy be identified as the cause of what happens.

For the advanced industrial powers, the commodities they claim as their own are in fact produced internationally. This is not simply because there is a creature called the 'multinational' corporation which produces goods in many countries. Even the small manufacturing firm depends upon imports to produce. Intra-industry trade has been the core of the growth of world trade since the Second World War – that is, trade between the same industry in different countries, each producing specialized inputs to the other. The label 'Made in X' only indicates where the finished article last came from, not who made fundamental contributions to its making.

It is for this reason, among many others, that States, the political form of world control, cannot provide the explanation for world production. Although States may have privileged access to the surplus produced by that part of the world economy which happens to be located within their patch of territory, it is the world economy which determines what that part is, what the local level of incomes and employment are. Only in the mythology of the State is the country an economic island, self-sufficient and alone, that chooses or not to establish links with other islands after the needs of the local inhabitants have been satisfied.

In practice, the officials of the State know this. From their viewpoint, they see only the constraints on their power, the imperatives imposed by internal and external necessities. It is the same with companies, who see themselves as reactive, responding to necessities generated external to themselves, created by a market within which they are only one participant. Of course, the largest companies and the richest States have greater room to manoeuvre, more options for compensating losses in one area from gains elsewhere, but even then they cannot control the world nor guide it to suit their purposes. No one controls it.

There are other reasons for scepticism about a view of the world which sees it as simply interacting 'national economies'. For one thing, the units of measurement are so grossly unequal. In terms of people, the core of the world is Asia, with 56 per cent of the inhabitants of the globe. Another 18 per cent live in Europe (including Russia), and the same proportion in Africa and South and Central America; 6 per cent live in North America. But the 180 or so States of the world in no way correspond to this distribution, let alone possess comparable shares of the couple of thousand billion U.S. dollars of trade swapped each year, or the half a thousand billion dollars-worth of other business. Some of the States are Lilliputian, not much more than medium-sized cities of half a million people: others are Gullivers, with inhabitants running into hundreds of millions (and China topping them all with a billion or more). Each, in economic terms, encompasses a unique configuration of activities, and with therefore an appropriately unique set of relationships to the rest of the world. For scientific purposes, the categories – 'United States', 'New Zealand', 'Pakistan' – can only increase confusion.

The confusion is partly acknowledged by trying to group States. But the appearance of manageability is only illusion, for the categories highlight only one set of relationships at the expense of all the others, and impose a spurious homogeneity on each group identified. Thus, we have the 'rich', the advanced capitalist countries, the 'more developed' or 'industrialized' countries, the market economies, the O.E.C.D. group (that is, the twenty-four members of the Organization for Economic Cooperation and Development, mainly industrialized countries but also including – for military needs – Turkey and Greece), or 'the first world'. This is contrasted with the 'poor', the 'Less Developed Countries', the old 'Group of 77' created by the U.N. Conference on Trade and Development, the 'South', or the 'Third World'. The variety of terms indicates the divergent political – as opposed to scientific – purposes for which the phrases were invented. We are obliged to use them for want of the data fitting a more useful set of categories, but in doing so we must be fully aware of the tyranny of concepts diverting our attention in irrelevant directions.

The ambiguity of the 'Less Developed Countries', covering two-thirds of the world's peoples, is the most extreme case. The phrase is all that unites Argentina, a relatively prosperous and advanced country, with India or Papua-New Guinea. The problems are acknowledged by inventing a number of sub-groups – the oil exporting countries (a term only partially coincident with the oil cartel, O.P.E.C., but at least having a functional utility) as opposed to the Less Developed Oil Importing Countries. Then there are the newcomers, the Newly Industrializing Countries (N.I.C.s), a term invented to embody the ferocious suspicions of the industrialized States of the export capacity of others. (Who the N.I.C.s are has no standard answer, but in most groupings occur South Korea, Taiwan, Hong Kong, Singapore, Brazil, Mexico; in other lists, India, Yugoslavia and others appear). Yet another division within the Less Developed is sometimes made, between 'Low Income' and 'Middle Income' States (the first with below 250 U.S. dollars, the second above, in terms of income per head in 1976), but again it is not clear what this statistical benchmark – the national income divided by the population – indicates.

Finally, there is that product of Cold War obsessions, the 'Centrally Planned Economies', the 'Socialist countries', the Eastern Bloc, the Communist Powers. But even here, what seems a politically coherent entity turns out not to be so when we note the political standpoints of Yugoslavia, China and North Korea, not to mention, in different ways, Romania and Poland.

The groups identified may have political significance, but this need not at all be matched by an economic dimension. The divisions highlight particular rivalries between competing segments of the world ruling order, not the most useful economic classifications. But the categories have effects, for they shape our minds. In particular, the great divide between 'rich' and 'poor' conceals the poor of the rich countries – the slums of Belfast, the *bidonvilles* of Paris, the decaying cabins of mining families in the Appalachian mountains, malnutrition in Am Grauenstein in Cologne or the backstreets of Naples. Equally, it conceals the palaces of the rich in Calcutta or Manila.

Even if we accept the myth of a world composed of no more than competing States, any consistent approach tends to break down the coalitions. What States command the largest shares of world production? Let us assume that the official figures for gross product are correct, and ignore the fact that different historical rates of inflation and the nervous standing of different national currencies distorts the gross national product figures (in particular, the unconvertible currencies and lower rates of inflation in the Eastern Bloc considerably understate their real economic weight).

In 1978, the money value of world production was put at something over seven and a half thousand billion U.S. dollars (or in American terms, 7.5 trillion). Of this total, about 28 per cent was claimed by the most powerful single section of the world order, the ruling class of the United States. Four States, together, claimed nearly 60 per cent of world production: in order of size, the United States, the Soviet Union (with, on these figures, about 46 per cent of total U.S. production), Japan (with about 40 per cent), and West Germany (with about 28 per cent).

The second tier of States – those with gross products valued at between 4 and 500 billion dollars – included France and the People's Republic of China. The third (2 to 300 billion dollars) covers three: Britain, Italy and Canada. The fourth has five: Brazil, Spain, Poland, Australia and India. And finally, the fifth covers a scatter of seventeen countries (with production valued at between 40 and 100 billion dollars): in order of size, East Germany, Belgium, Sweden, Mexico (80–100 billion); Switzerland, Czechoslovakia, South Africa (60–80 billion); Austria, Yugoslavia, Turkey, Argentina, Denmark, Indonesia, Nigeria, South Korea, Venezuela, Saudi Arabia.

These thirty-two States – of the world total of 180 or so – claim some 88 per cent of world production, and 64 per cent of the people of the world. The pecking order in terms of absolute size of product thus indicates that East and West, rich and poor, are jumbled. Of course, different – more realistic – assessments of the value of national product, what are known as 'purchasing power parities', might change the distribution. Nor does absolute size indicate the surplus available to the State concerned to prosecute its interests – China in the second tier, and India in the third, would be brought down the list precisely because much of their product is consumed to keep their giant populations alive rather than build the military means to deter other States. Nonetheless, the exercise, using the estimates made by the World Bank, indicates one anomaly in the categories normally employed to identify the world economy.

Structuring the world economy according to the interests of one type of competitor, States, is not an error of judgement. For the ultimate sanction in the maintenance of the share of world production held or claimed by a particular ruling order is war, and here, for most of the time, the State is paramount. In part, the State's domestic power resides in its capacity to oblige the share of the world's labour force that lives within its frontiers to go out and slaughter the inhabitants of other territories, to destroy the segments of world production held by rival States. It can do so in the hour of crisis only if, at other times, it has been able to dragoon people into manning the local segment of world production, obliging them to produce the surplus which makes armies and arms possible (or alternatively, if it can raid the surplus produced in the territories of rival States).

It is the State which survives the cataclysm of war with enhanced power. Americans may die in droves, but the 'United States' has its hidden fortress in the Iron Mountain.[4] The State makes the law and is therefore above it; it is constrained only by political necessities and economic limits. Its security takes precedence over all other considerations, including the survival prospects of the population inhabiting its territory.

The other side of the coin to the lawlessness of States is their inability to master their rivalries, to secure an effective international order which will ensure that production, employment and incomes steadily advance. The integration of the world economic system demands political unification. But the institutions thrown up by the States to implement collaborative action remain shadows, either mere forums for periodic declamation or simply instruments of one or a group of States. The United Nations, the International Monetary Fund, the World Bank, C.O.M.E.C.O.N., the General Agreement on Trade and Tariffs, and all the others, ultimately rest upon the sharp rocks of the egoism of States. It is still the case that in the world order only conquest or subordination of one State by another can secure full 'cooperation'.

How did such a political system come about? The modern State arose in Europe as an institution for the collective management of the affairs of the ruling class of a particular territory, and as the unified power of the rulers of one territory against those of another. It was transformed by the development of capitalism. In a society governed by competition, the competitors will only conform to a common collective discipline by the use or threat of force, the forcing of a class identity that is threatened by the disunity induced by the market. Thus, one of its tasks was to hold together the political and economic ruling order, and thereby make possible the subordination of everybody else and, in particular, to make them work. Its third function became the seizure of the territories and peoples of other parts of the world, the competitive imperialisms of the nineteenth century. In defence, the rulers of threatened territories were obliged to copy the aggressors and build States themselves, build defensive bulwarks against the invaders. All the world's territory thus came to be appropriated in defined patches, owned by a particular ruling order and its State – much as the common land of Britain was appropriated earlier through its parcelling up among a class of private owners. In the process, all free lands and free men and women were corralled in one or other pen. By now, the division of the globe is so all-embracing, the fences that divide each national garden built so high, that its sheer novelty in human history is no longer apparent.

Once the boundary is beaten and troops posted round the perimeter, the State undertakes to colonize all within, to drill all the inhabitants who find themselves trapped behind the fence with an invented common inheritance of loyalty, supposedly to a common culture or way of life, but in practice to a particular State. Increased nationalization of life within the national patch thus parallels the obverse phenomenon, increased 'internationalization' – that is, increased interaction between increasingly colonized national patches.

The appropriation of territories and peoples by the States – whether as political empire or, as in our own day, as independent States – is a competitive phenomenon. States compete and are driven to expand or subvert by competition, not by some internally generated force of aggression. In the twentieth century, two world wars bear witness to the now extraordinary power of some States to compete. But war has another effect. It obliges the State to encompass even greater areas of activity within its territory, to absorb part of what had hitherto been independent activity. What began as the administration of the affairs of a class, increasingly absorbs part of that class. Production may not be overtly expropriated, but large parts of it are either absorbed by the State or survive only because the State so wills it. State capitalism – whether in solitary isolation as in the Eastern Bloc, or in collaboration with a class of still private capitalists – has become the norm in our own times.

Yet simultaneously a reverse process has been occurring. Indeed, the growth of State capitalism is not only the product of the rivalries between States but also a reaction to the growth of forces outside the control of the States. The startling pace of general expansion in the postwar period has forced the growth of the 'non-States' sector. The internationalization of capital undercuts the power of the territorial State, and opens a new contradiction between its political and economic interests. On the one hand, the *raison d'être* of the State is its territory, and the share of world production (and population) it holds; this is the primary basis of its power. It needs therefore to retain the loyalty of its citizens, and the basis of that loyalty is the belief that this State is better than any other, that it can master its domestic environment. But at the same time, the economic system integrates the local segment of production to the point where it has no national autonomy; it cannot be determined by State fiat. The State becomes in economic terms a local authority. Its political needs require it to act economically, but each act of economic nationalism jeopardizes both the world order and domestic economic needs.

Slumps and booms

Each surge of growth expands the capital base of the world system, the capacity to produce abundance for all. The expansion is produced by accident, not by intention. It is the by-product of the search for profit. Variations in activity – boom and slump – are similarly by-products of variations in the profit rate. Increases in profit rates induce businessmen to invest, and thereby – the theory says – expand employment and so the expenditure of the incomes earned in employment. Decreases in profit rates induce the reverse process: declining output and employment, down to the point where the 'return to capital' stabilizes.

In the real world, the simplicities of theory have the merit of directing our attention at particular phenomena. But only religion has the capacity to explain events without examining them at all. Assessing what happens to the average profit rate does not tell us why at one time the profit rate rises, why at another it falls. In any case, in the real world it is extraordinarily difficult even to measure the world profit rate, so that it is no wonder that the theory has so frequently become almost as mystifying as events. The profit rates that businessmen perceive vary by sector, by company, by country, by commodity and from day to day. Even in a slump, there are highly profitable activities, and capital is in constant movement to find them.

To raise the profit rate when it is low requires a change in the ratio between the 'surplus' – what is added by labour to products in the process of manufacture after all costs have been covered – and the total capital stock, a change in the relationship of labour and capital. In theory this could be achieved in a number of ways: by an expansion of the system to include new labour at lower costs (thus changing the ratio between the total labour cost and the capital stock); by reducing the absolute cost of the existing labour employed (which could be achieved by laying off workers, cutting wages or other labour costs, but without lowering the existing level of output); by cutting other costs on a scale sufficient to affect existing average profit rates; or by collapsing the value of the capital stock itself (for example, through bankruptcies, which include the wiping out of debt and the scrapping of machinery, or through war and the destruction of capital). In practice, capitalism has ultimately found a combination of methods in the past to offset declines in the profit rate, but not without considerable 'boom–bust' cycles in the nineteenth century, and long periods of stagnation in the twentieth.

Cycles are exaggerated by the type of structure operating. Assume that there are only two sectors which can be distinguished – one producing the means of consumption (which keeps labour alive and reproduces the new labour force), and one which makes the equipment to produce the means of consumption. Second, assume that the first sector experiences a decline in profit rates. This will prompt businessmen in sector one to cut their 'investment'; that is, suspend their orders from sector two and make do with what equipment they already have. Sector two slows down, or, if the reduction is sharp enough, shuts down altogether. The workers of sector two are either unemployed or on short time; that is, their purchases from sector one decline sharply – which in turn produces another wave of contraction. The limit to contraction is the maintenance of some consumption.

The example is highly simplified, but it shows how the interaction between sectors can exaggerate the upward and downward movement, and why often slump is so much more severe in heavy industry (industries which provide basic equipment), and slighter in light industry. The more advanced the world economy, the greater is the share of investment and output concentrated in heavy industry; thus, other things being equal, the more difficult is a resumption of growth after a decline. This is part of the case for Marx's theory of the inevitable long-term decline in the rate of profit. Furthermore, the simple example indicates the importance of investment – the purchase of new equipment as well as the opening of new production – in resuming growth. Industries, companies or countries where investment remains relatively high during a downturn stand the greatest chance of commanding an increased share of any upturn.

The immediate source of change is thus investment, itself the result of

both an average profit rate for the system as a whole, and, in its disproportionate growth, in the different profit rates of different sectors,
companies and countries. It is a matter of indifference theoretically
whether we assume that slump or boom is the 'normal' state in order to
understand why there is movement from one to another, or why on
occasions the system remains suspended between the two – 'stagnation'.
Boom is by no means the 'natural' state of the system, and even when
there is boom, it is far from encompassing all equally. So far the system
has never succeeded in fully employing the world's labour force, let
alone employing all who wish to work at a tolerable wage.

Different forms of social and political organization are frequently
associated in part with the different phases of growth and contraction. In
a slump, the needs of the ruling order for political stability collide with
the economic needs of a profit-making system. In theory, bankrupting a
large enough sector of capital (and scrapping the equipment) would help
restore the average profit rate. But allowing the financial collapse of
New York City or British Leyland raises major political problems for
any government which undertakes such a strategy. On the other hand,
subsidies to such important segments of unprofitable capital can only
reduce the profit rate or at least restrain its rise – the rest of capital has to
pay for the subsidies, for the sake of political security. The introduction
of import or immigration controls raises similar paradoxes. Cheap
imports will lower the costs of domestic production both by cheapening
the inputs to manufacturing and cheapening the diet of labour, so
making possible a lowering of real wages (or a cut in money wages while
real wages stay the same); low-paid immigrants similarly could be used
to lower labour's share of the costs of production. But in both cases, a
government can only do these things at the cost of jeopardizing its
political rationale as protector of its 'own people' – imports may displace
employment at home, and immigrants may displace local workers. On
the other hand, blocking imports and immigrants can then produce
another phenomenon – foreign companies set up subsidiaries inside the
State that inhibits their trade, and domestic companies set up plants
abroad to utilize cheaper labour. Increased competition is thus
generalized, not at all contained by the State.

Economic crisis is the central theme of this book, but its children are
political, social, cultural, psychological. These areas, the most important
in the direct experience of the inhabitants of the world, are left on one
side, not because they are unimportant, but because to be manageable a
work must stick to one already highly simplified theme. The method by
which capital seeks to 'rejig' its relationship to labour is a continuing
preoccupation in the pages which follow. Our initial concern is with what

has been hitherto the main engine of world economic growth, the O.E.C.D. group.

The national village and the world inhabit two separate sets of minds. The majority of people, for much of the time, are kept so busy working to survive that there is little point or leisure to lift their eyes beyond the village. There may now be holidays for some which take them beyond the parish boundary; for the older generation, there was soldiering; and the popular newspapers occasionally refer to wars and coups and famines beyond the horizon, as if to stress how fortunate the villagers are to escape the particular disaster described. The great world is so often no more than a daydream, half forbidden pleasure, half nightmare. The mystifying images hide the fearful thought that all the world's peoples are much the same: although cultures, languages, customs vary enormously, people are concerned with very similar things – their triumphs and tragedies are comprehensible to all. Above all, they are all chained to work as the condition of existence.

The minority, on the other hand, runs the world, and knows that the world is the condition of survival of each national village. Their 'personal life' may include all sorts of absurd prejudices, but prejudice does not govern the system – collaboration and competition are too important to be left to mere sentiment.

But this is only a half truth, one dimension. The opposite dimension is that the village, the concrete realities facing people, sustain them as human beings. It is from the tangible village that the imperative arises that you should not kill other people, even if the survival of capital so requires it. From the village, it seems that people ought not to starve, particularly if the granaries are full: from the world, the famine is merely 'maintaining normal market incentives'. Thus, the isolation of the village alienates the villagers from knowledge of reality, the world, but simultaneously ensures that they remain focused on the real, on humanity. Without that, there could be no hope for the world.

Notes to Chapter 1

The debts in this chapter will be self-evident to some readers. To Marx for superficial renderings of his core conception; to Lenin – and his forebears – for the philosophy of *State and Revolution*; to the Bukharin of *Imperialism and World Economy* (Moscow, 1917; English translation, London, 1972) and *The Economics of the Transformation Period* (Moscow, 1920; English translation,

New York, 1971); and to L. D. Trotsky, who identified 'the world economy, not as a sum of national parts but as a mighty and independent reality, which has been created by the international division of labour and the world market, and which in our epoch imperiously dominates the national markets' (*The Permanent Revolution*, trans. John G. Wright, London, 1962, p. 22).

1. Albert Einstein, source unknown.
2. Karl Marx, *Critique of Political Economy*, included in *Selected Works of Marx and Engels*, Vol. I, London, n.d., p. 356.
3. Karl Marx, letter to Meyer and Vogt, 9 April 1870, in *Correspondence of Marx and Engels 1846–1895*, trans. and ed. Dona Torr, London, 1935, p. 289 (stress in the original).
4. Iron Mountain was said, in the 1960s, to be a vast underground nuclear shelter for the senior officials and archives of hundreds of large U.S. corporations and of government; see *Report from Iron Mountain, On the Possibility and Desirability of Peace*, with introductory material by Leonard C. Lewin, Macdonald, London, 1967.

> The bourgeoisie, during its rule of scarce one hundred
> years, has created more massive and more colossal
> productive forces than have all preceding generations
> together. Subjection of Nature's forces to man,
> machinery, application of chemistry to industry and
> agriculture, steam navigation, railways, electric telegraphs,
> clearing of whole continents for cultivation, canalization of
> rivers, whole populations conjured out of the ground –
> what earlier century had even a presentiment that such
> productive forces slumbered in the lap of social labour?[1]

Marx's admiration for the achievements of the capitalism of 1848 appears now only quaint. For the triumphs of the years that followed dwarf all that came before. It is not merely the pinnacles of achievement – men landing on the moon, cameras snooping on the lifeless wastes of Mars or Jupiter or Saturn, harnessing microbes, constructing intelligence as robots, creating the means to annihilate more millions of people more quickly than ever before – these are impressive, or frightening, enough. It is the transformation of the base of production, the astonishing expansion of labour productivity – which makes possible these achievements – which is dazzling, the centralization of the muscles and brains of the world in one gigantic endeavour.

Let steel stand as surrogate for these changes. Modern raw steel production began in the 1870s. It took some fifty-seven years for the world to produce its first 100 million tonnes of output (1927), and another twenty-four years to reach its second (1951). But it was only eight years more before the third, in 1959. By 1973, more than 700 million tonnes poured from the world's steel mills, and by now – despite world contraction – the total is something over 800 million tonnes. Since 1951, the world has increased its output of steel four times over. And production has spread. Now the orange glow in the night sky can be seen by peasants in India, Korea, Mexico, Brazil, Indonesia; from the rooftops of Cairo; from fishing boats off the coast of Anshan in China.

Impressive though the rate of growth might be, 800 million tonnes of steel is still puny beside the scale of human need. Countless millions of the world's inhabitants have neither a pin nor a needle, let alone access to those miracles of ingenuity (already present in Marx's day), a bicycle or a sewing machine. The world's industrial revolution has only just begun, and there are many miles to go before the achievements can be thought adequate.

The achievements were nonetheless solid enough. By the mid 1970s the world's gross product was some two and a quarter times larger than that of 1950. In twenty years, agricultural production increased at a rate of between 2 and 3 per cent per year, almost always ahead of the increase in the number of mouths. Industrial production increased at nearly three times this rate, and international trade just under four times. In volume, world manufacturing output per head of world population doubled in the fifteen years preceding slump, and world trade in manufacturing trebled.

In statistical history – fading gently into the mists of spuriously accurate guesses – there had never been such a time. Only the thirteen years before the First World War came near comparison – a rate of growth in industrial production of 4.5 per cent per year (compared to 5.5 per cent in the great boom). But in comparison to the period from 1950 to 1970, the pre-1914 period started from a tiny productive base, so that the absolute figures of output were puny by comparison.

Output grew in three great surges – in the first half of the fifties, in the sixties, and the early years of the seventies. The pace of growth in each spurt tended to increase. In the seven years up to 1970, world production increased 44 per cent, and trade 50 per cent. In the three years up to 1973, output increased by a third, and trade by 40 per cent. When the world system was geared to grow, it grew with spectacular speed.

Nor was it simply the dull figures of production. Consider the life and expectations of an English couple born around 1900. The moment of heroism inspiring the man's teens was the task of killing Germans, as the task of killing Englishmen was the inspiration of his peers across the water. Perhaps he survived intact, and was lucky enough to get work in his and the century's twenties, but he probably lost it in the fearful giddiness of world slump in the early thirties. By 1938, the couple would take for granted a world dominated by the search for work. Perhaps they might congratulate themselves a little on their modest triumphs – keeping the children fed, with a decent change of clothes; a motor cycle, perhaps an annual holiday in Blackpool, perhaps keeping a small rented flat. They would fear for their sons as their moment of teenage heroism approached in 1939. For such a couple, the 1960s would have seemed a world beyond dreaming – for many the problem had become to eat less, to close the wardrobe door on all their grandchildren's clothes, to service the car at the weekend, to prepare for a fortnight's paid holiday in Spain, to keep up the mortgage payments on their own house.

The change might seem dramatic, but it was less so than that affecting others. The Japanese couple increased their purchase of clothes (1955–69) by 9 per cent each year, of food by 6 per cent, and of durable goods by another 6 per cent. The improvement in their children's diet was making them bigger and bigger each generation; the parents' school desks no longer fitted the bulging knees of their children. The French or Italian couple bought 10 per cent more durable goods each year, and the Dutch pair more than 10 per cent.[2] Throughout the industrialized countries, the great world boom could be measured in the tangible realities of the village.

However, these tangible realities were only superficial signs, important though they may have been for those who experienced them (and the process, real enough, did not by any means encompass all who lived in the industrialized countries). Much more impressive was the improved level of livelihood of more people in the world than ever before. This was not measured in terms of the bric-à-brac of the system, 'consumer durables', but in basic diets, in the new capacity of mothers to survive childbirth and produce children who lived. The health status of thousands of millions of people steadily improved, a change which showed up in the transformation of the figures for average expectation of life at birth. A United Nations guess has it that, in the 1930s, people in the backward countries (two-thirds of the world's inhabitants) possibly had an expectation of life of thirty-two years, a standard that had probably not changed much since the time of the Roman Empire.[3] In just three decades, roughly seventeen years have been added to this. Table 1 shows the figures, broken down by continent.

1. Life expectancy at birth, in years[4]

	1935–9	*1950–55*	*1965–70*
South Asia	30	41	49
East Asia	30	45	52
Africa	30	36	43
Latin America	40	52	60
All less Developed Countries	32	42	49
All More Developed Countries	56	65	70

The change is one of the most important single triumphs in the history of human beings, and certainly the most spectacular achievement of the world boom in capitalism. It could not have been achieved simply by changes in medical technology or improvements in public health – very often, these facilities did not reach the rural areas where many of those affected by the change live. A large part of the change must derive from improved diets: fewer mothers suffered the cumulative effects of protein deficiency; the body weight and the diet of the newborn improved. One of the greatest sources of permanent anguish throughout the ages, the death of children, was curbed.

It takes a system like ours to snatch defeat from the jaws of victory. That more babies survive now becomes a source of panic – the world is being 'swamped' by people; there is a 'population explosion', and all the world's troubles are to be laid at the door of the stubborn resistance of the young to dying. By implication, people must be tailored to fit the system, not vice versa.

Capitalism produced as no one in 1945 thought it could. It had produced in war on a spectacular scale, but no one thought that could be sustained. No one foresaw the boom, no one planned or directed it. It happened, as always, as an incidental by-product of other concerns. Indeed, there is still no agreement on why it happened, so there can be no agreement on why it came to a close. However, without pretending to an authority which does not exist, let us look at some of the factors that might account for the unprecedented growth of the system.

Sources of the great boom

The First World War was the culminating achievement of nineteenth-century capitalism. As a system, it was economically a much more 'national' one than that which exists today, or rather, an imperial one, for the dominant powers each controlled geographical areas beyond their frontiers. Capital still had a structurally vital relationship to the State, although in retrospect we can see already the beginnings of internationalization. The world system depended upon a dominating role by Britain, the largest source of capital, mediator of trade, the largest market for exports, and containing the quasi central banker for the globe. Military, naval and territorial power was the result and the condition for that role.

The First World War both ended the dominant role of Britain and brought to a close the role of the great 'basic industries' which had been the content of the Victorian economy. Europe had been the manufacturing heart of the world system; three countries – Britain, France and Germany – supplied 60 per cent of the world's exports of manufactured goods (and 75 per cent of Europe's manufacturing exports). War vastly 'over-expanded' the basic industries, without – as happened in the Second World War – destroying a major part of them. Nor did the slow war reorganization of the combatant national economies allow the same radical cut in labour's share in the production process. Terrible disorganization there was, but when the gunsmoke cleared from the trenches, when the daunting overhang of debt was counted, Europe found itself trapped in stagnation.

Nothing had happened to raise the profit rate; everything conspired to lower it, and to hold it down. In no way could it support the revival of investment on a scale capable of long-term expansion. The poor profit levels only exaggerated the squabble of the national powers to hold what they had or to grab more, even to the point of dismembering the German economy – but without destroying German capital values. Efforts were made during the 1920s to cut labour's share, but what was politically possible was trivial in comparison with the overall problem. In the 1930s, the 'write-off' of capital was accelerated, but again not on a sufficient scale to compensate even for the damage caused by the mutual paralysis of the leading powers, to break the deadlock and re-order the standing of the rivals. The business of 1914 remained unfinished.

The agony which dominated the interwar years was that of the 'basic industries' – coal, iron and steel, shipbuilding, textiles. Their contraction gave the tone to the whole of society. There were booms in other sectors. For example, British vehicle output increased ten times over between 1913 and 1930. Expansion was a continuing feature in electricity generation, the production of rayon, aluminium, radio and telecommunications equipment, aircraft, and so on. But although the expansion might produce relative prosperity in some areas and affect national investment and gross national product figures, in sum it could not affect the domination of the old industries. Both capital and labour remained locked in the inherited structures, even though seepage out continued all through the years up to 1939.

Perhaps also – judging with the benefit of hindsight – the scale of output for many of the growth industries already required international markets; perhaps the industry possible within the narrow boundaries of the European countries was too small to generate economies of substance. Without large-scale exports, output remained high-cost and sluggish in innovation, monopolistic or oligopolistic. Perhaps the dynamics of growth were already technically appropriate to international scales of production. The rivalries of the dominant States – their struggle to prevent imports and restrict the movement of private capital – rendered impossible the restoration of international trade (except as supervised by cartels, more concerned to guard existing markets than to run the risks of expansion). For the old empires, Britain and France, there was a safe but stagnating market for old-fashioned goods, a factor encouraging obsolescent methods of production without lifting the profit rate high enough to produce a boom.

The demands for political stability, for the defence of the State – presented always through the hypocrisy of 'protecting national employment' – were the product of the low profit rate. Low profit rates make for the cowardice of capital. The maintenance of political stability in turn made it more difficult to restore profit rates. Thus, quite separately from the source of the low profit rate, political priorities added to mass unemployment. They also demarcated the world in ways that made war necessary. By the end of the thirties, the global economy was divided into mutually hostile economic empires, with negotiated political relationships between them – the British, the French, the Japanese, the American and the German (covering much of Eastern Europe).

Why was the same sequence of dispiriting events not repeated after the Second World War? Certainly, many prominent people expected a re-run of the interwar years.[5] The justification for much of the planning and welfare structures, for large public sectors, which were introduced in Europe was the need to stabilize society on the assumption that long-run unemployment would characterize the postwar years. National autarchy was taken for granted. For some of the imperial powers, autarchy entailed a fierce fight to prevent the loss of their imperial possessions – the French in Vietnam and later in Algeria, the Dutch in Indonesia.

There were at least two important factors which were different in 1945 in comparison to 1918. Europe's capital structure had been radically reduced. In particular, Germany, the dominant industrial power in Europe, had been devastated by years of war, by bombing, and the damage of foreign occupation. France, the Netherlands and Italy were capable of only half their prewar output.[6] Furthermore, the war – with rationing and a great shortage of consumer goods – had substantially lowered the real return to labour. At least, potentially the profit rate could have been relatively high – if capital could have been induced to set the machine going.

Then there was the existence of the United States as, by now, overwhelmingly the dominant industrial power of the world. The size of its market permitted the development of scale economies which dwarfed those of Europe; and war, supplying the Allied powers in Europe and the Far East, had produced a vast expansion in industry, a war-fuelled investment boom, and waves of industrial innovation. Unlike Europe, American industrial capacity was intact; the weight of its capital structure could, in the absence of other factors, only crush the profit rate and precipitate slump. American industry needed external demand, needed Europe's thirst for industrial goods – if a means could be found whereby impoverished Europe could buy. Europe's capacity to buy was severely limited, and it was not clear that what could be bought would produce not merely some measure of reconstruction but a sustained investment boom. The European instinct was to return to defensive autarchy, to restore national egotisms, a system which presupposed political instability sufficient to deter any bravery by capital. The United States might have the overwhelming power of victor, but short of direct military conquest, it could not force the battered European States to gamble on their political survival by opening their domestic markets.

A fourth factor was needed. Between 1945 and 1947, the U.S. government decided that the war had settled nothing – the unfinished business of 1918 was, it seemed, still unfinished in 1945. The threat Germany was supposed to have constituted might have been removed, but that removal had only exposed the existence of an even greater danger, that of the Soviet Union. We can use the word 'decided' since it was a decision, not an inevitable development. European Conservatives – for example, Winston Churchill – might try to attract American subventions to their respective States by reiterating that Red divisions, panting along the Oder–Neisse line, waited only to seize Western Europe, and that would bring the northern bear to the brink of the Atlantic. But until 1947 Washington was not impressed; indeed, it was embarrassed lest such lurid fears endanger the close relationship with Moscow, then the foundation of postwar peace. The Americans wished to retain the option of cultivating either Western Europe or the Soviet Union or some combination of both.[7]

Whether it was the need to ward off the expected slump of U.S. manufacturing by creating export markets in Europe, or the need to defeat a perceived threat of Russian rivalry, in 1947 the conclusion coincided. Germany was not to be punished more for disturbing the American peace, not to be raided as had happened in the 1920s, but rehabilitated as the defensive bulwark of American power in central Europe. The change – from 1944 to 1947 – was one of the swiftest and most remarkable in modern times. The Russian ally was recycled as enemy.

During the war, Washington had assisted its allies through Lend-Lease. Although that programme was terminated in 1945, American contributions to relief funds – for example, those of U.N.R.R.A. – did something to help sustain European demand for American goods. But they could hardly make up for the effects of the rapid decline in U.S. spending upon its own armed forces in Europe, even though that spending came to be concentrated upon the most devastated area, Germany. Washington, from its position of unrivalled strength, was concerned once and for all to prise open Europe and its empires to American exports. The interwar depression in the States need not happen again if external markets for U.S. manufactured goods could be found and kept. It was this which underlay the creation of a new financial order, formulated at Bretton Woods in July 1944, and a new set of institutions to embody this order – the International Monetary Fund, and what became known later as the World Bank and the General Agreement on Tariffs and Trade. Of course, the institutional changes could not create the dynamic required to make them work. Nor could U.S. efforts to secure American markets in Europe work, unless Europe could also enter into an exchange with the United States, by finding markets in America. That was something Washington steadfastly opposed. And since U.S. private capital showed no inclination to undertake the hazardous business of investing in politically unstable Europe, the dearth of dollars in European hands became the main obstacle to sustaining U.S. industry and restoring Europe.

By 1947 the problem was becoming severe. The ending of direct U.S. assistance to Europe, major cuts in U.S. military spending overseas and at home, the exhaustion of European reserves, were all tending to reduce Europe's dollar purchases and precipitate the expected American recession. It was in this context that Washington launched a temporary funding scheme, which became known as 'Marshall Aid' (June 1947), properly justified in the first public murmurings of the Cold War (the 'Truman Doctrine'). It gave immediate relief, although it was not substantial enough in itself to produce a European investment boom. Nevertheless, in European terms, it was important – from 1947 to 1950, the U.S. government financed a quarter of Western Europe's total imports (and two-thirds of its imports from the dollar area[8]). Funds added power to American political leverage now that it had been decided who were friends and who enemies; the beneficiaries, Europe's conservatives, were able to beat off the postwar challenge of the Left, to divide Europe's labour movements so that the Communists were isolated, and to undertake a purge of radicals in almost all important institutions.

The character of Marshall Aid made it no more than an *ad hoc* arrangement, and the U.S. Congress ensured that it could not be made permanent. Exporters to Europe might rejoice, but American business as a whole counted the tax cost of subsidizing the Europeans who, after all, had brought the war upon themselves. The only way of vindicating a transfer to Europe of sufficient size and permanence would have been a political threat so overwhelming that business would feel America's very survival was at stake, particularly if the sacrifices demanded were sweetened with a boom. The Cold War resolved both the short-term political problems and some of the long-term economic ones.

Despite Marshall Aid, U.S. recession hovered on the edge of reality through much of 1948. What might seem large in Europe, was insufficient to sustain the American giant. This was particularly so since the United States insisted on running an export surplus on its trade across the Atlantic, and excluded imports from Europe. Rates of investment started falling in 1949, and unemployment rose from 5.9 to 7.6 per cent in early 1950. A wave of devaluations in Europe – and the second major sterling crisis – were symptoms of a fundamental imbalance.

Meanwhile the bricks required to build the new international order were being fired on both sides of the Oder–Neisse line. Russia, perhaps increasingly nervous at the drift of events, sought to make pre-emptive gains, to secure its frontiers against a feared threat. The 'fall of Czechoslovakia' was one sign of this, and the Russian detonation of an atomic device. Furthermore, outside Russian control, the Chinese Communist Party completed its long climb to power in 1949. In 1950, the United States and the Soviet Union decided to make events in Korea an issue of their new open world rivalry. From retaining its nuclear programme intact – and initiating the development of the hydrogen bomb – Washington moved to general rearmament. Between 1949 and 1953, United States military spending increased from an annual figure of $13 billion to $50 billion. Now the State injected liquidity into the U.S. economy and into Europe's rearmament: American industry was lifted to a new height, stimulating a massive demand for raw materials from the rest of the world, producing the first great boost to an underemployed world. Europe might still not be able to get its manufacturing exports through the minefield of restrictions round the American market, but it could at least resuscitate the prewar division of labour – selling manufactured goods to Asia, which in turn exported raw materials to the United States, which in turn exported goods and funds to Europe.

The change of gear was not achieved without difficulty. European States had to reverse the tide of social reforms that had been the reward for the wartime deprivation of Europe's working classes. In Britain and France, the return to rearmament required special sacrifices in the new world of peace won at such cost. The British Labour Government doubled military spending in three years, in an economy impoverished by war, thus re-beginning that process of making impossible sufficient modernization of British capitalism to make it an effective competitor. The rearmament of Germany – a shocking proposal so soon after 1945 – caused considerable difficulty, even though it was necessary to integrate Germany in the new structure of N.A.T.O. (the North Atlantic Treaty Organization, the funnel for U.S. military power in Europe) in order to ward off the dangers of any 'Ost-Politik', a German relationship with the Soviet Union (in response to Russia's persistent offers to re-unify the two parts of Germany in return for a guarantee of German neutrality).

The creation of a permanent arms economy in time of peace[9] supplied the first massive boost to economic growth in the core zones of the world system, and its effect was maximized because it had a disproportionate effect on the capital goods industries. The effects could be so dramatic because of the peculiar conditions of Europe at that time – collapsed capital values of a partially devastated and depreciated industrial structure, collapsed value of labour but a labour force whose skills were still intact, and all alongside an American economy with, potentially, much spare capacity. Expanded arms spending was not a conspiracy to save the American economy; the economic effects were not the secret of remilitarization. Nor, indeed, were the full effects of increased arms spending envisaged; few, except in retrospect, could see what would be the effect of the spending on the peculiar structure of the 1945 Atlantic economy. The relationship of capital to labour was rejigged for what was then the core of the world system, the United States economy, incorporating cheap and skilled European labour in a newly, if only semi, integrated Atlantic system. The political change which produced the military effect operated on the margin; it acted as a spark to set the engine running. It was not simply a reconstruction boom, for military spending continued, producing a self-generating boom in the exhausted and damaged European investment industries.

By contrast, these basic conditions were lacking in the 1920s. Both the United States and Europe were depressed by the great overhang of war-expanded capacity and debt. The structure of the 1970s Atlantic economy was also quite different, for, before the onset of slump, capacity world-wide was stretched to its limits and the world profit rate in decline. The position of great relative power which permitted the United States to create the Atlantic economy in the fifties had gone; other contenders blocked its way, and the rejigging of the relationship between capital and labour through the Atlantic economy incorporating the globe could not be achieved.

Arms spending had other effects. It tended to offset some of the fluctuations in economic growth, in much the same way as general government spending had been seen by Keynesian economists. Furthermore, it had an even more important characteristic. Arms were not sold as commodities except in what was at that time a quite marginal phenomenon, the arms trade. Arms were 'thrown away', sterilized by destruction. Thus the growth in the capital stock could take place without, to the same extent, jeopardizing the profit rate. At least, that was theoretically the case; but in theory, for arms spending to play the role of stabilizing capitalism it would have had to be increased steadily at the same or a higher rate than total investment. Boom – sustained high profit rates – could continue until all gross investment was absorbed in armaments production and the economies collapsed.

The absurdity of this outcome indicates some of the problems. Arms are produced from the surplus generated in the civil economy. The more arms production encroached on the civil economy, the more it limited the surplus and so civil capacity to compete. There were also practical political problems. American businessmen might tolerate the diversion of resources from civil to military investment, provided all competitors bore the burden equally – net civil investment was lower, but no individual capitalist suffered disproportionately. The moment that businessmen appeared who did not bear the burden, who could use a greater proportion of the annual surplus for civil investment, then U.S. business would become much less tolerant. The rivals – German and Japanese businessmen in the main – could then capture a larger share of the markets of the world and drive back the Americans. Germany and Japan, like the whole world economy, benefited from U.S. arms spending through the stabilization of world profit rates; but they gained disproportionately relative to their American competitors so long as German and Japanese arms spending remained low. The rise of the major rivals to U.S. manufacturing capital is thus also the decline of the 'permanent arms economy'.

There were other factors which militated against the maintenance of the originally high levels of U.S. military spending (high, that is, in comparison to the U.S. gross product). The concentration of resources in arms production produced dramatic increases in productivity and advances in technology; a stable proportion of the national income permitted disproportionately large increases in military output. It was unnecessary to increase arms spending proportionately, particularly given the many pressures to lower it. Moreover, high levels of military spending increasingly distorted the civil economy to the loss of American competitiveness in civil production. Military spending did produce important technical 'spin-offs' for civil production – in aircraft, radio and radar, in computer technology and new synthetic materials – but at a high cost, and only accidentally related to the most pressing needs of market output.

These considerations were fairly remote in the 1950s, the brief age of Pax Americana. What at the time was seen as the massive productive surplus of the American worker, assisted through a variety of mechanisms by the rest of the world, seemed so stupendous that it could sweep all before it; the U.S. economy could achieve unprecedented levels of domestic prosperity, a world military role, and a global American empire.

The sustained boom which allowed the potentially high profit rate in Europe to be realized, to sustain American profit levels and later make possible high profit levels in Japan, was thus, in terms of the conscious intentions of the leading participants, the result of a series of 'accidents'. Once begun, however, the boom utilized all those factors which in retrospect were seen as favourable (but which, on their own, could not have created sustained growth) – the spreading of new technology from advanced America to backward Europe, the new institutions available for increasing liberalized trade, and so on. The momentum was sustained by its uneven character – high profits in some sectors and geographical areas were then superseded by high returns in others. The necessary fluctuations in output generated in different regions of the world were not synchronized through much of the period, so downturns in some areas were compensated by booms in others. The increasing ease of trading and capital movements stabilized the growth pattern at the same time as it integrated the system; it also, in time, increased the degree of synchronization between regions.

By the late fifties, the new world order was constructed. Europe was rehabilitated, but its labour costs were still low and its capital structure thirsty for funds. U.S. capital was now brave enough to venture after the U.S. State, and the developments of a more liberal trade system at long last gave European goods some access to American markets. However, the Europeans did not fully embrace an American world of free trade. They settled, at least in the first instance, for free trade in one region, the European Economic Community (1957), a market thought to be large enough to support companies of a size comparable to the giants of the United States. Nor were the Europeans consistently enamoured with a world incorporated in the dollar zone. Originally, it had been necessary to accept the terms of a dollar world in order to gain access to the United States for manufactured goods, foodstuffs, raw materials and arms – by 1949 the United States had acquired, as a result, three-quarters of the world's gold. But from the time of the Korean War, the United States moved into external deficit – dollars flowed out of the United States. When the Europeans made their currencies convertible (1958), some of them began to demand settlement of the U.S. deficit in gold, to claw back some of the gold lost earlier to Washington. In 1960, Washington safeguarded its position by offering to take back 'surplus' U.S. dollars held abroad in return for U.S. Treasury bills – that is, asked foreign governments to re-lend their dollars to the United States. France refused what was in effect yet another measure to oblige the rest of the world to subsidize U.S. military and political ambitions overseas.

By 1968, the U.S. gold stock had declined to 10 billion from 22 billion dollars in 1951. The United States deficit had become a permanent mechanism to draw on world production, a means to make up for the growing relative weakness of the United States compared to its ambitions. In return for production, Washington offered its paper, the main world currency. No one could refuse it without establishing some other medium of exchange, although all tried to get rid of the dollars as soon as feasible – producing in passing the giant Eurodollar market. If foreign governments refused to accept dollars, their exchange value would decline, and as a result, U.S. exports would be cheapened; if they accepted, they sustained the dollar at a value higher than otherwise, so cheapening foreign assets to the gain of U.S. capital searching for outlets abroad.[10]

The financial dispute was only one of many recurrent irritations between the powers. It symbolized the relative equalization of the European and American economies in comparison to the great imbalance between them earlier. The equalization was part and parcel of integration between the two, and as a result, synchronization of their business cycles and standardization of profit rates. Perhaps after the great surge of growth in the early sixties, all would have converged in decline in the second half of the sixties without one last throw by the American State to re-establish by military means its lost hegemony. The Vietnam war had the hallmarks of an act of despair.

U.S. military spending now heavily depended not simply on its domestic base of production but on the world system as a whole. The world system did not have surplus capacity waiting only to be drawn into production. Thus, the massive increase in international liquidity that followed from U.S. military intervention drove the world into synchronized boom. High inflation was caused not simply by the expenditure on the Vietnam war – war spending was, as it were, the last straw. Severe bottlenecks, particularly in raw materials, as well as the general pressure of labour to sustain or advance real incomes, were part of the basic structure on which increased international liquidity worked.

Nowhere was the process more frenetic than in East Asia. Japan was propelled into a world power, dragging behind it a clutch of 'miracle' economies along the Pacific seaboard. But for the United States, the war was economically disastrous. It accelerated the increasing depreciation of the American capital stock relative to its rivals; it fuelled a domestic revolt, which culminated in challenges so severe that the war had to be drawn to a close. The Europeans were increasingly resistant to paying the bills that flowed from the war, and that hostility was an important factor in their refusal to save the Bretton Woods international financial system when it came under threat in the early seventies (indeed, they themselves produced that breakdown by refusing to hold dollars).

The war left a legacy of unprecedented inflation. Perhaps it also expanded the world capital stock to the point where profit rates in the investment industries began to fall sharply; it did not prevent a further sudden sharp boom in 1972–3, but that boom did not lift world heavy industry investment. It was fitting that an age inducted by the American State should have been ended by it, by a *coup de grâce* – the temporary ruin of American military power and the indictment of the President for a sordid and petty history of lying and fraud.

The great increase in military spending which had, at the end of the 1940s, reacted on the peculiar structure of the postwar Atlantic economy and precipitated the momentum and stability for long-term growth, resulted, in the circumstances of the late sixties – with the world at the limits of productive capacity – both in producing a new permanent propensity to high rates of inflation and in preparing the way for the collapse of the world profit rate. The proportionate increase in military spending in the late sixties was much smaller than in the earlier period, but the structure of the world economy was quite different.

The resulting decline of the dollar, in turn, broke the Bretton Woods monetary order, no longer elastic enough to contain both the unbridled rivalries of the dominant powers and, even more important, the new giant, the uncontrolled Eurocurrency market. Currencies now became rivals, or rather, symptoms of rivalries which exaggerated competition and added a further dimension of instability to the world trading system. Wild movements of speculative finance illustrated the fact that no State or combination of States could any longer govern the private market for funds; States could command neither the world economy nor their own domestic part of it.

The new capitalism

The long boom did not leave the system unchanged. Important shifts of structure took place.

First, the long process of changing the output of the system was completed. The nineteenth-century economy had been based upon extractive and relatively primitive processing industries; it was an 'extensive system' (that is, increases in output were secured by roughly commensurate increases in capacity, raw materials and labour). The twentieth-century economy came to be based on an increasingly complex system of manufacturing, employing far greater quantities of equipment, changing technically much faster, an 'intensive system' (increases in output could be secured with declining increases in inputs). Manufacturing came to dominate industry, and within manufacturing, metal-working (engineering) and chemicals proved the most dynamic postwar sectors. By way of one illustration of the process, consider the changes in West European manufacturing output (Table 2).

2. *Percentage shares of the value of manufacturing output, current prices* [11]

	1901	1913	1937	1955	1958–60	1968–70
Food and drink	27	19	15	13	13.4	11.4
Textiles	20	18	12	8	7.5	5.6
Basic metals	7	10	10	9	8.3	7.3
Metal working[a]	16	24	28	34	36.3	38.2
Chemicals[b]	5	6	10	14	9.5	14.5
Other	25	24	25	22	25.0	23.1
	100	100[c]	100	100	100	100[c]

a: includes metal products, electrical and non-electrical machinery, transport equipment.
b: due to changes in definitions, the post-1955 figures are not strictly comparable to the earlier ones.
c: columns may not add up to 100 exactly, because of rounding.

The categories mask the full nature of the change, for each term covers a vast and shifting set of goods; nonetheless, some important trends emerge – the rise and decline of 'basic metals', and the enormous increase in metal-working and chemicals.

Within the industrial sector, world heavy industry expanded most rapidly. About 59 per cent of the world's industrial output was classified as 'heavy' in 1955, and about 66 per cent in 1970. In the industrial core of the system, the comparable figures were 64 and 67 per cent; for the Less Developed Countries, 33 and 47 per cent.[12]

In the postwar period, trade between the industrialized countries provided the main core of world trade, and world trade the main inducement to expansion. Between 1950 and 1959, the volume of manufacturing imports of the industrialized countries increased by 9.5 per cent per year, and between 1959 and 1971 by 13–13.5 per cent. In the case of the middle range of poor countries, the 'semi-industrialized' increased their manufactured imports from an annual rate of 2 per cent in the fifties to 9 per cent in the sixties. The largest industrialized countries had the highest rates of growth in imports.

Thus, while the volume of manufacturing trade tripled in the last twelve years of the period, the volume of manufacturing output only doubled – a much more rapidly increasing proportion of output was being traded internationally. What was being traded also changed (Table 3).

3. *Percentage composition of world trade (in current U.S. dollars)*[13]

	1913	1953	1973
All commodities	100	100	100
Agricultural products	45	36	21
Mineral products (including fuels)	8	13	14
Manufactured goods	44	49	63
Machinery and transport	7	18	33
Textiles and clothing	14	6	6

Thus, the raw materials and food component of world trade fell from over half the total on the eve of the First World War to just over a third in the early 1970s. Manufacturing came to dominate the trade total, and within manufacturing, machinery and transport. In the sixties (1959–71), the period of highest growth in world trade, the leading sectors among the exports of the major industrial countries were: chemicals (12.9 per cent per year increase); transport equipment (12.5 per cent); machinery (10.3 per cent); textiles and clothing (9.6 per cent).

It was an increasingly concentrated system. World trade was increasingly concentrated in the exchanges between industrialized countries, in the flows between giant companies and giant plants.[14] By the late sixties, about a third of the West German labour force was employed by just 123 groups, producing just under three-quarters of Germany's industrial output. In the British export trade, 87 companies produced half the exports, 260 companies two-thirds. The growth in size of units yet further blurred the concept of ownership, for such giant enterprises could be 'owned' only in the loosest sense. Shareholders – apart from a group of institutional owners – exercised scarcely any power over companies. The 'capitalist' in the old nineteenth-century sense became a rarity. By the mid 1970s, a third of British equity was held by insurance companies and pension funds, and at the then current rate of acquisitions by such institutions, it was reckoned they would own between 69 and 84 per cent of all equity within twenty-two years. Half the London stock exchange listings were held by institutions (in comparison to a fifth in the mid 1950s) – individual holdings had declined from two-thirds to under a third. In some cases, the pension fund had come to exceed its parent in size, and vastly to exceed the value of assets of major manufacturing companies. In the Japanese case, individual ownership of total shareholdings declined from 46 to 30 per cent between 1960 and 1979; the share of financial institutions increased from 23 to nearly 37 per cent. Finance capital had grown even faster than the value of manufacturing capacity.

The capital stock grew rapidly – by, for example, 4 per cent per year in the United States in the sixties. The capital per worker grew even more rapidly, producing increases in labour productivity that would have earlier seemed utopian – from Japan's annual average for the sixties of just under 10 per cent, to Italy's 7 per cent, and the 5–6 per cent of France and West Germany.

Necessarily, the labour force of the industrialized countries was also transformed. The characteristic worker of the nineteenth century, the unskilled manual worker – the source of the images of 'the working class' – became almost as rare as the capitalist, the nineteenth-century employer. In 1950, nearly 30 per cent of the O.E.C.D. labour force was still employed in agriculture – it had been 40 per cent forty years earlier. By the mid seventies, the share was down to 12 per cent. In the United States, one of the great agricultural countries of the world, one in three workers had been employed in cultivation in 1910; by 1950, the farmers and their hands were 12 per cent of the labour force; and by 1973, 4.1 per cent. The same was true for other workers employed in the harsh tasks of extracting raw materials. In 1913 Britain employed one and a quarter million workers in mining and quarrying; it was three quarters of a million by 1961; and 364,000 by 1973.

The great legions who worked as domestic servants in Victorian times all but disappeared. There were nearly one and a half million employed in Britain in 1911 as 'indoor' domestic servants. By the 1950s the numbers were so small that they were no longer separately recorded (and the *au pair* girls, who temporarily substituted, were not counted in the native labour force).

Manufacturing industry might be the most expansive element in the generation of the gross product of the industrialized countries, but increasingly it was not the fastest growing element in employment. All the industrialized countries expanded their manufacturing labour forces in the fifties, but most reached a peak thereafter, and manufacturing employment began to decline, either proportionately or absolutely. Only Japan and Italy continued to expand their manufacturing share of the workforce after the sixties, and in both cases, their proportions were for much of the time below most of the other major industrialized countries – the 13.5 million Japanese manufacturing workers of 1975 constituted just under 26 per cent of the labour force, compared to 30 per cent of the British workforce employed in manufacturing; Italy's 6.1 million manufacturing workers in 1975 were just over 32 per cent of the workforce. For the rest, a declining proportion was engaged in manufacturing after the peak in the sixties or early seventies – from 9 million or 34.7 per cent in West Germany in 1961; 5.9 million or 28 per cent in 1974 France; and 27 million and 32.5 per cent in the United States of 1973. It was a phenomenon that became known as 'deindustrialization'. Like arms spending, it was not important if it affected all equally; but it seemed to have particularly marked effects in Britain and the United States.[15]

The categories – 'manufacturing' or 'services' – were increasingly misleading; they showed little of how the system worked in reality. Nonetheless, it was the great ragbag of jobs, 'services', which seemed consistently to generate more employment. The high and increasing productivity of labour in modern manufacturing required an increasing proportion of the labour force to work in services to make manufacturing activity possible. By 1982, more than twice as many people sold McDonald's hamburgers in the United States as made steel; there were more people employed in retail and wholesale trade than in the whole of manufacturing. Even within manufacturing itself, it was 'non-production' activities which increased most rapidly; in United States manufacturing, the 18 per cent employed in 'non-production' in 1950 had reached 28 per cent by the late seventies.

The growth of service employment for the six leading O.E.C.D. countries is shown in Table 4.

4. *Per cent of the labour force employed in services*[16]

	1954	1957	1973
Italy	28.0	29.1	38.6
West Germany	–	35.7	43.0
France	33.0(1950)	37.9	48.5
United Kingdom	48.0(1951)	46.4	54.5
United States	53.0(1950)	55.2	64.2
Japan	30.0(1950)	39.0	49.4

In the British case, between 1961 and 1976, about 2.3 million jobs were lost in agriculture, mining, manufacturing (1.2 million), construction, gas–electricity–water, transport and the distributive trades; while 2.4 million jobs were created in insurance, banking and finance, professional and scientific services (1.4 million), public administration and defence, and 'miscellaneous services'; or, to oversimplify, there was a more than one million job shift between manufacturing and 'professional and scientific'.

There are different threads of possible explanation here. The technical nature of production implied that a far larger number of technically qualified workers were required to service the rest. With higher household incomes, spending on services tended to rise relative to that on goods; thus, American households used 36 per cent of their spending for services in 1960, 43 per cent in 1978. The size of units, public and private agencies, the maintenance of work disciplines at much higher levels of productivity, generated enormous bureaucracies. They were both supervisory, and engaged in what was increasingly a core activity in the system, the gathering, analysing, exchanging and storing of information. One estimate has it that there are eight file drawers of information (each drawer containing some 18,000 documents) for every American white-collar worker; some 72 billion documents are produced each year, and 300 billion filed; the rate of growth is about two new file drawers per office worker per year. And while busy filing these documents, American office workers make 100 billion telephone calls at a cost of 15 billion dollars per year.[17]

The State itself grew as part of this process, adding an increasing array of functions to the public sector. In the 1960s, public sector employment in the industrialized countries increased on average at 3 per cent per year (when the labour force was increasing by one per cent annually), and in the early seventies, at 4 per cent per year. For a time in the sixties, seven out of ten new jobs in Britain and Sweden were in the public sector. Public employment in the United States increased from just under 9 per cent of the civilian labour force in 1950 to 14 per cent in 1970; in France from 6.5 to 11.4 per cent. Of course, the figures must be treated with care, for the boundaries of the 'public sector' were rarely clear or comparable.

Other service sectors were equally growth-oriented. Finance and banking, for example, showed sustained increases in the sixties. But in the seventies, mechanization tended to curtail the growth – in Britain, bank transactions increased by 8 per cent annually in value terms from 1972 to 1979, but bank employment only by 3 per cent. Retailing and hotels – 12 million workers in the United States and 2.5 million in

Britain – expanded rapidly. More people had more money and less time to cook, and many more people moved more than ever before – part of the 280 million tourists of 1979.

The people who did the jobs also changed beyond easy recognition of what had once been a 'worker'. For one thing, many more of them attained levels of education that had in the past been associated only with their betters. Fewer men worked, and many more took higher education. The growth was particularly marked in the sixties. Enrolments in French higher education increased by nearly 10 per cent annually; in the United States, by 7.5 per cent; in Japan by 7 per cent; in West Germany and Britain by 5 per cent. The prerogatives of the old bourgeoisie were eroded; smart clothes became the mark of the working class, shoddy clothes of the rich.

There was a remarkable increase in the employment of women. The 38 per cent of American women who took jobs in 1950 had increased to 58 per cent by 1978; in Britain, the number of employed women grew from 2.7 million in 1951 to over 6.5 million in 1976. The proportion of married women at work showed the most rapid increases – in the industrialized countries as a whole, the proportion increased from about a third in the early sixties to between 40 and 47 per cent in the mid seventies. Women went to work as the family declined and the State increasingly took over primary responsibility for the 'reproduction of the labour force'; they were driven to work by the increasing need for income to support the costs now thought to be necessary for the much reduced family.[18]

Work also changed: from the use of muscles in the back to those in the fingers. Hours worked weekly fell from the 70 or so worked a century ago in Britain to 46 in 1951 and 40 twenty years later; in the United States, from 39 to 35, and in Japan, from 48 to around 40. By the early eighties, Norwegian men worked 31 hours and women 26, and at the other extreme, South Korean women worked 54 and men 53 hours. British hours, for manual workers, had fallen to 39½. Annual paid leave increased, to the top score of eight weeks in Australia, and three or four in most of the other industrialized countries. There was more earlier retirement, and the aged, with less destructive working lives, lived longer. Part-time work – especially for women – increased. In 1975 some 17 per cent of jobs in Britain were part-time (and some 40 per cent of all working women were engaged part-time); 30 per cent of jobs in retailing and hotels were part-time. In the United States, 15 per cent of registered workers worked under 30 hours a week.

The workforce was continually upgraded. Officers and N.C.O.s outstripped soldiers, and gaps appeared in the ranks. The gaps were an illusion, for outside the boundaries of the industrialized States, soldiers – workers – were plentiful, and desperate to sell their labour. In the last half of the fifties and the first half of the sixties, employers turned beyond the boundaries to recruit. By 1970, the core zone of the Common Market had officially recruited over 6 million workers from six countries of southern Europe (Greece, Italy, Portugal, Spain, Turkey and Yugoslavia) and two of the north (Finland and Ireland). Italy's remarkable growth in the sixties sucked some of its workers back, but there were thousands more eager to replace them – from north, central and west Africa, from the Middle East. In the United States, the flow of workers was drawn from central America, and from across the Pacific – from the Philippines, Korea, China. The tip of southern Africa drew workers from as far away as central Africa, and later, in the seventies, the oil-producing countries of the Gulf area drew labour from all over south Asia and the rest of the Middle East as well as from Korea and the Philippines. The loss of labour to sending areas was sometimes considerable – northern Portugal, like parts of southern Ireland, was depopulated; in 1970 the proportion of the African labour force abroad ranged from 6 per cent in Morocco, between 11 and 12 per cent in Algeria and Tunisia, 13 per cent in Malawi, 14 per cent in Botswana, to 21 per cent in Lesotho.[19] Since quite often the workers came from particular districts in a country, the local impact was even greater than the figures suggest.

The movement did not simply provide replacements for the disappearing unskilled manual worker. It was an important addition to the technical and professional cadre of the industrial heartlands. As with the loss of workers in general in sending countries, the loss of those with rare skills imposed particular costs; the departure overseas of Thai doctors equalled two-thirds of those medically qualifying each year, and roughly a fifth of those graduating in India, the Philippines, Turkey, Haiti and Nicaragua.[20]

The absolute numbers of those moving internationally – both officially and illegally – were large, possibly even 30 million or so. But they were small as a proportion of the world labour force, and also relative to those who moved within national frontiers. Regional concentration of activity and population was one marked product of the great boom, particularly where incomes – and therefore commuting possibilities – were low. The 70 cities with one million inhabitants each which dotted the globe in 1950 had become 180 by 1975 (and the 170 'half-million population' cities of 1950 had become 399).[21] The poor countries concentrated population more rapidly than the industrial core zones, producing urban giants that began to overshadow their puny predecessors in Europe and the United States. The citizens of Mexico City increased from under 3 million in 1950 to nearly 9 million in 1970 and 12 to 14 million by 1981; and Brazil's great industrial centre, São Paulo, increased from 2.5 million to over 10 million. People already spoke of cities of 20 and 30 million. For the rich, it was fearful and dramatic, breeding the illusion that riches could be produced without creating such monsters; as always, the victims were blamed – immigrants were abused for producing squalor, not praised for their contribution to gross product and profits.

In the industrialized countries, the pattern was different. The population began to disperse over larger and larger areas. In some cases – in the United States and Britain – industry trickled away from the old cities into the countryside; the workers pursued work to the villages and the green fields. There was almost a hint of the ending of the ancient division between town and country. But in the interim, the wrecked hulks of the old cities remained, the 'inner city crisis'.

The movement of many millions of workers, legally and illegally, from where they were raised to where the world's work was done, was not because jobs were intrinsically immobile. On the contrary, the world's production base was in continual movement both within the core region and between there and elsewhere. But the demand for work and the demand for workers were only accidentally connected by the profit rate. Capitalism does not simply shed its old skin, staying in one place. Like the locust, it moves on. The great centres of nineteenth-century industry in the industrialized core of the world system, the central element in the long-term stagnation of the interwar years, were partly abandoned; they became 'the regional problem'. The heart of industrial Germany under the Kaiser, the Ruhr, decayed; from the mid sixties to the mid seventies, 400,000 jobs disappeared, over 300,000 workers left the area, and still the regional unemployment rate was double the national average. Northern Ireland, Scotland, the north of England, stagnated, sustained only by public subventions and outmigration. In the seventies, blight came to the cities of the north east and north centre of the United States, while the old Deep South, Texas and Georgia, boomed.

Where governments pitched themselves against localized backwardness, the results could be important for local consumption, but rarely in terms of jobs. Southern Italy, receiving up to 27 per cent of national investment over the best part of two decades, increased its industrial employment at only slightly above the national average. Despite the 4–5 million people who left the south in the fifties and sixties, at the first chill wind of contraction in 1975, southern unemployment rates rose to two and a half times the national average.[22]

The change in the industrial geography was not simply within the old core regions. Japan rose with dizzy speed to become part of the core. In the sixties, a number of backward countries also began to edge into the category of 'industrial'. Manufacturing employment in the Less Developed increased at 4.2 per cent per year (1960–73) in comparison with 1.3 per cent in the More Developed. China, India, Brazil, Mexico built industrial capacity of world standards. Almost everywhere new working classes were created, but remained unseen until they struck or rioted. Electronic production leapt the Pacific from San Francisco's Silicon Valley to capture cheap labour in East and South-East Asia; in Brazil and the Caribbean, Iran and Mexico, the same nimble-fingered girls as those in Korea were set in competition with each other to precipitate 'the micro electronic revolution'. Hong Kong, Taiwan and South Korea became major producers of clothing, of television sets, and of radios. Volkswagen became Brazilian.

The world changed with dizzy and unpredictable speed, but very often, some of the villagers scarcely noticed. They had the illusion of stability. But nonetheless, all villagers felt some change, and although in the managed heartlands of the system it was supervised, change was an acid to inherited prejudice.[23] In the sixties, even as the wave was beginning to founder and the world was stunned by the familiar barbarities of the Vietnam war, the 'permissive society' in the West seemed to herald the end of old constraints. The relations between men and women, between adults and children, between those historically dominant and those subordinate, all seemed to be qualitatively changing. The relief of some – or even many – of the scarcities in the industrialized core that had scarred earlier generations produced some increase in compassion at home, an unwillingness to take for granted discriminations inherited from the parents of the sixties generation. The death sentence, that act of unequivocal barbarism so firmly enshrined earlier, was abolished. Abortion, drugs, long hair, symbols both important and trivial which still had the capacity to drive some to fury, became half tolerated. At its peak in San Francisco, the flower was to replace the gun.

Doors needed, of course, to be pushed – by American blacks in the first instance, followed by women, homosexuals and others. But what was astonishing was not that they pushed, but that the door could be pushed, that there was a door at all in the seamless bomb-shelter of past social mores. It was no less astonishing that the changes in public ideology (and one could not assume that changes in behaviour exactly paralleled the changes in public expression) could be reversed once slump chilled the bright hopes. Nonetheless, some of the moral corsetry – like corsets themselves – that had been the uniform of an earlier slump and of world war were unwound. Tight-lipped parents could no more stem the tide than they could stop the growth of capitalism; many hardly noticed that the old soldiers faded without even a fight.

Liberation was the vanity of the age – sexual liberation, ethnic liberation, gender liberation, national liberation. But all without liberation from the lynch-pin of diverse ills: work, subordination as labour, the brute maintenance of world labour discipline from which flowed that monster governing all people, the State. Nonetheless, the atmosphere lightened temporarily, helping to put more heart into a heartless world. Even though the effects were limited by geography, by social class and age, just as the world's gross product had very unequal effects for the same groups, nonetheless the changes spread. Hastings Banda of Malawi might ban the outrage of mini skirts; Singapore's Lee Kuan Yew might give public sanction to a drive against those with long hair, decree the death sentence for drug-carrying, but they could have no more permanent success than enraged parents.

The change was international in a different sense. The black people of the United States were inspired by the nationalism of Africa, decolonization and the establishment of new independent black regimes; the women of Europe followed the lead of their sisters in the United States. The struggle to end the Vietnam War inspired student rebels round the globe. And China's Cultural Revolution, despite a quite different domestic significance, scattered a shower of sparks in Paris in May 1968. It seemed as if things had returned to the first century of capitalism – when revolutions inspired each other across Europe in 1789, 1848 and 1871 – but now it spread across the entire globe.

There were changes, but not as many as people thought, nor were they often of such substance as to resist the erosion of time. The black people of the United States in the early eighties could have little illusion that everything had changed – black median income, as a proportion of white, was 63 per cent in the sixties, 56 per cent in 1981. The 'permissive society' provided in the seventies a convenient explanation for slump – 'the erosion of the social underlay of a stable capitalist order (or more generally of any market or contractual society) set in train by the values of market society'.[24] The characteristic fever of 'new capitalism', inflation, seemed to prompt such thoughts in conservatives. 'Inflation is a moral as well as an economic crisis,' the *Daily Telegraph* solemnly intoned, '. . . what we are suffering from, as a nation, is greed'.[25] It meant the greed of workers, not the greed of capital, not the greed of an institutionalized order of society.

Even permissiveness itself was a half truth. It somehow excluded the long trail from a Korean War to a Vietnam War, from Seveso to Soweto, from Derry to Watts. Neither the State nor capital had been displaced.

The State

All had the impression that the inexorable growth of the State was one of the prime characteristics of the system of New Capitalism. Growth there had been. In the 1950s, government spending in the industrialized core was in real terms nearly 75 per cent above that of the 1930s. By the 1970s, it had increased by another 20 per cent. But part of this increase was illusory, for it measured transactions flowing through the hands of the State, not direct State expenditure. Between 1965 and 1972, for the O.E.C.D. group as a whole the increase in share was relatively small. By 1974, public expenditure (including transfers) for the O.E.C.D. group had reached 35 per cent of the combined gross products, having increased by 0.4 per cent per year over the preceding decade.

The uniformity of the process suggested common factors were at work, independent of local political fashions. In practice it was more difficult to assess, since there was no agreement on how 'public expenditure' was to be determined. Take three measures – taxes as a proportion of gross product, social security as a proportion of gross product, and government current spending (excluding transfers) as a proportion of gross product – in order to compare those with the highest levels in 1965 and 1972. On the first, taxes, France, Sweden and Austria headed the list in 1965 (34–36 per cent); Norway, Denmark and Sweden in 1972 (44–45 per cent). On the second, social security, France, the Netherlands and Luxemburg were at the top in 1965 (10–13 per cent); the Netherlands, France and Italy in 1972 (12–15 per cent). Finally, government current spending: in 1965, the leaders were the United States, Sweden and Britain (around 17 per cent); and in 1972, Sweden, Denmark and Canada (19–23 per cent). Only Japan of the O.E.C.D. group diverged markedly from the common pattern.

Slump and stagnation in the seventies, at least initially, exaggerated the process. Between 1973 and 1979, the increase in government spending in the industrialized countries was on average 30 per cent faster, so that public expenditure as a proportion of Gross Domestic Product increased from 30 to 37 per cent – in Europe from 36 to 44½, most of the increase concentrated in 1974 and 1975. However, the increase was not an expansion in public purchases of goods and services – that remained roughly constant at around a fifth of Gross Domestic Product. The increase was in 'transfers and subsidies' – increasing, as a proportion of Gross Product for all the industrialized countries, from just over 8 per cent in 1965 to 14 per cent in 1979 – with a large increase in the small component, 'interest payments'. The change of the seventies was a response to slump, a mark of the rigidity of earlier programmes (that could not be scaled down in slump) and the high price of political stability.

The growth of the State was not continuous over the years, nor was it peculiar to one State or another. The causes of the growth were complex, but it was most frequently associated with the needs of war and the permanent preparation for war that characterized the post-1945 years. War was part of the competition of States for domination – or to protect an existing position from threats. But there were other areas of competition, not least in the field of the maintenance and upgrading of the quality of the labour force (producing vast growth in publicly provided educational welfare and medical services), and in spurring research and innovation. In Europe, the State entered directly into production. In some cases, immediately after 1945, nationalization was a means to divert demands for more radical social change and to ensure a stable decline in the industry concerned. In others, it was a means to mobilize major investment resources for an industry when the profit rate in the private market did not warrant the expenditure (but the State conceived of the industry as vital for its economic survival, and was unwilling to replace its products with imports). Yet other elements of public incorporation were intended to force the pace of technical change and ward off threats from competitors overseas. In practice, however, nationalization tended to make the industry concerned part of political debate, and subject it to numerous political interventions. In turn, this tended to affect balance sheets and therefore the political view of the economic viability of State industry.

The discussion was frequently clouded by the assumption that whatever the State willed, it could bring about. It was said that the nationalized industries were not 'subject to market disciplines', as if this were in principle ever possible. British coal could have no such illusion, as its share of the market was squeezed by oil; nor public railways and air, as private road transport pressured them; nor public steel, as private steelmakers, imports and alternative materials nibbled at its market. Even where effective monopolies existed, there was competition between them – as, for example, between public electricity and public gas. The problem for State industries was not that they lacked market competition, but that on top of that they were required to keep prices down in the interests of counter-inflationary policies, prevented from borrowing without public sanction, required to maintain loss-making operations, and so on. The State wobbled between treating State industries as private corporations of which it was no more than the commercial shareholder, and using them as instruments of government policy. In general, it was the market that won.

The State expanded in another area of increasing importance – in education, welfare and health. Again, the competition of States involved the respective quality of labour forces. In boom, when ambitions rose, standards were pitched at high levels as part of the process of matching or exceeding levels of productivity abroad. Discussion of the output of graduates in the United States or the Soviet Union as proportions of their respective labour forces became, in Britain in the early sixties, part of the political debate on British relative economic decline. And when Labour returned to power in 1964, the same figures were the rationale for a major expansion in higher education. Similar observations could be provided for other areas of public sector services – they were determined not merely by abstract assessments of need, but by what levels of service were required to maintain existing or projected output. Inevitably, the State made major errors of judgement in an area where there were few clear guides, errors compounded by the competitive complexity of different public agencies and the pressures of private beneficiaries of public contracts.

State intervention imposed a rigidity upon society which, in the seventies, intensified some of the problems of slump. Take, for example, the reproduction of labour. In the family, economic fluctuations in the past could be reflected in the wage-earner's pay packet, and so in the family's standard of living. But when public expenditure was used to establish a minimum of 'reproduction' – infant welfare and medical services, educational and training systems, etc. – the standard could be varied relative to business cycles only through open public debate and political competition. The governing party had to submit itself to possible political defeat in order to 'vary minimum reproduction costs' in public expenditure.

The rigidity in the welfare–health–education sector was only one aspect of the attempt to create a 'managed' national economy. In that context, the attempt to remove employment and wages from the market, to remove their variation, was the centrepiece. Governments, explicitly or not, in the immediate postwar years were dedicated to prevent the downward variation in employment, and accepted an increasing rigidity in the wage system so that wages also could not be varied downwards (in the case of the incomes policies which subsequently became popular, the aim was the opposite – to prevent upward movement of aggregate wages). It seemed as if governments had striking success in this endeavour (Table 5).

5. *Unemployment rates, variation between seven major industrialized countries*[26]
(United States, Canada, France, Germany, Britain, Japan, Sweden)

1920–29:3.2 to 6.3 per cent
1930–38: 5.6 to 18.2 per cent
1950–60: 1.7 to 4.5 per cent
1961–73: 1.3 to 5.2 per cent

National economies could apparently be managed to reduce unemployment to the lowest level. A new technique of management had been discovered, associated with the name of the economist, Keynes, which made it possible to reduce fluctuations in activity and run economies at that point where output and employment were maximized. A whole ideology was created around this new technique which purported to explain why old capitalism had failed and new succeeded. The 'euthanasia of the rentier', as Keynes put it, or rather, the reduction of the shareholder interest in favour of the State, and the 'managerial revolution' had removed the old capitalist in favour of a new quasi-public-servant businessman whose interest was less in profits, more in the public welfare. Science could now be brought to bear to control and guide the market, and in so far as science was successful, argument became unnecessary: the 'end of ideology' and of classes had arrived. Since a common technical basis propelled different societies along the same path, Moscow and Washington were both tending towards 'People's Capitalism'.[27]

The environment was unusually stable, and the ideology of 'managed capitalism', planning, accordingly flourished; it became as fascinating for the Establishment as was liberation for the young. Large companies became enamoured with plan and projection, and the fashion spread to almost all States, producing a further technical field, futurology. The fashion was one thing; obdurate circumstance another. India's brave first Plan in 1951 might offer 'maximum production, full employment, the attainment of equality and social justice'.[28] There might be large public sectors, major public heavy industry programmes, incorporation of trade unions and private business in State plans, but still the rains and the balance of payments could unhorse the rider in the Less Developed Countries; in the More Developed, for much of the time, they eschewed formal targets and thus nominal failure. States were careful to protect their dignity, their infallibility, to place anomaly well on the margin. The return of the market in, for example, the growth of private medicine and education in Britain, were not to affect the public status of the Welfare State.

The State grew during the boom. The content of what the State did also changed. Often the symbols of public power concealed a content of the private, and much that was thought to be private survived only because of public initiative. The distinction grew blurred and semi-fictional.

The world

However much the State seemed to grow, there was one section of private activity which seemed to grow much faster and was entirely beyond the merely national power of the State: the fully international area of activity. Indeed, on balance, the world seemed to witness not a steady expansion of State capitalisms so much as a resurgence of a reprivatized world economy beyond the fiat of States. If slump had enervated old capitalism, driving it back into its territorial corners, boom drove new capitalism out into the open, into a world become in principle less, rather than more, governable.

Three features of the world system stood out – the growth and nature of trade, the character of capital and the integration of finance. We will take each in turn.

The growth of world output (real gross product) – 4.7 per cent annually between 1950 and 1960, and 5.6 per cent from 1960 to 1973 – was much slower than the rate of growth of trade, the exchange of goods and services across national boundaries. But the exchanges were heavily concentrated in certain regions; indeed, the world changed in this respect less than might have been expected, and remained tied to four major zones of power – the Mark, the Dollar, the Rouble and the Yen. In the most dynamic sector of world trade, manufactured goods, two-thirds of the increase between 1955 and 1973 was within Western Europe and the United States; trade between these two regions and Japan was under a quarter of the total increase, and between More and Less Developed countries, about 11 per cent. By 1974, the industrialized countries – with 40 per cent of the world's manufacturing labour force employed to manufacture 66 per cent of manufacturing output – accounted for 85 per cent of the world's manufacturing exports. In terms of regions, West Europe's 27 per cent of world output contributed 56 per cent of manufacturing exports, and Japan's 8 per cent, 11 per cent of exports; by contrast, the United States' 26 per cent of world manufacturing output provided only 14 per cent of manufacturing exports. The Less Developed contributed 14 per cent to production, 7 per cent to manufactured exports (and the Eastern Bloc, 20 and 8 per cent). For the Less Developed, the categories are suspect, for only ten countries produced 75 per cent of the combined manufacturing exports of the Third World.[29]

The comparison between European and American figures was misleading. For what is 'domestic trade' in the great land mass of the United States became 'international trade' among the smaller powers of Europe. The Common Market, that cartel of States, had not withdrawn its family affairs from the 'international' category.

Each major power had become through this process of trade growth more dependent upon imports and exports for the maintenance of domestic output and incomes. Only Japan seemed to have partially preserved itself from this process (Table 6).

6. *Growth of manufacturing imports (percentage of imports in domestic supplies of manufactured goods, large industrial countries, 1950–71)*[30]

	1950	1959	1963	1971
Britain	4	6	9	16
France	7	6	12	19
West Germany	4	7	9	17
Italy	8	8	13	15
United States	2	3	3	8
Japan	3	4	4	5

In the British case, the growth in proportional terms was no more than a return to the share at the end of the last period of trade growth, up to 1913. In 1913, 17 per cent of British domestic supplies of manufactured goods came from imports (but then Britain was still the largest trading country, at the centre of the world economy). The Japanese case, however, was reversed; in 1913, 34 per cent of Japanese domestic manufacturing supplies were imported.

The figures conceal considerable changes in the pecking order of States in trade terms. Of the total exports of the twelve leading manufacturing powers (1950 to the 1970s), the British share declined from 26 per cent in 1950 to 16 per cent in 1960 and between 8 and 9 per cent in the mid seventies. The share of the United States declined from 22 to 16 per cent. On the other hand, West Germany's share increased from 15 per cent in the early sixties to over 20 per cent in the mid seventies; Japan's from 9 to over 15 per cent.

Trade in primary commodities represented a different picture. Before the First World War, the European powers had, through imperial controls or market power, secured almost monopoly access to the raw material supplies of much of the world. By the 1970s, Western Europe was much more heavily dependent upon open market purchases, in competition with many other equally powerful buyers. On the other hand, part of the dependence had been reduced by the great growth of primary production within the industrialized countries – by the late 1960s, the industrialized countries exported nearly double the volume of food and raw materials exported by the Less Developed. The United States showed one of the sharpest changes in this respect. Although American agricultural exports had increasing dominance in world markets, the United States became increasingly dependent upon imports; export and import of goods and services were equal to what was, in American history, the unusually high figure of 10.2 per cent in 1965, to 15 per cent by 1973, and 19.1 per cent by 1977 (oil imports, just over a fifth of U.S. consumption in 1965, were nearly a half by 1977).

Trade was only one dimension. Britain and the United States maintained much stronger positions in what is known as 'invisible trade' – dividends and interest payments on capital and loans made abroad, returns on banking services, shipping and commerce, tourism and migrant remittances. Between 1961 and 1973, income from 'invisibles' expanded nearly as fast as that from merchandise trade, and in some of the years of the 1970s, faster. In the late seventies, the American surplus on invisible trade – some 70 billion dollars – was about half the size of its visible exports; the same was true for Britain. Japan and West Germany, however, had considerable deficits in invisible trade.

The growing integration of the more industrialized zones of the world system in terms of trade was a growing integration in terms of production. This was particularly true for the most dynamic sectors of world trade, those in engineering goods and chemicals. Within engineering, the character of trade was increasingly not between industries, but within industries – 'intra-industry trade', an exchange of 'intermediate goods' (that is, 'manufacturing inputs into manufacturing, excluding machinery and equipment that is produced as final demand as investment goods'). The exchanges indicated increased specialization by country, and decreased capacity to cover the entire range of output of a particular industry. For example, 'the United States exports large printing machines to Europe for high production in long runs, while it imports smaller and more versatile machines from Europe'.[31]

The trade statistics, dealing in crude sectors like 'metal products' – even when refined – only with difficulty revealed the integration of production – the part manufacture in one country of goods further manufactured in another, and yet further processed in a third. What appeared as 'exports' and 'imports' of a particular State might in fact be no more than intermediate stages in a continuous manufacturing process straddling several countries; in the process, quite a large part of what were classified as 'exports' might turn out to be no more than former imports, and a large part of imports, former exports. Perhaps that was part of the explanation for the fact that, in Britain, those industries with the highest propensity to import were also those which exported most (Table 7).

7. British engineering, by selected sub-sector, 1976[32]

	Imports, as percentage share of domestic market	*Exports, as percentage share of output*
1. Instrument engineering	53	55
2. Electrical engineering	32	37
3. Shipbuilding and marine engineering	42	34
4. Vehicle production and components	31	44

Intra-industry trade – bilateral exchanges within the same product group – already accounted for 63 per cent of the trade of the O.E.C.D. group by 1967. It was particularly important in manufacturing, especially in chemicals. It was the sector of trade which expanded most rapidly in the 1960s. The share of intermediate goods in engineering exports in the Common Market increased from 35 to 45 per cent between 1959 and 1965; and for Britain, from 42 to 48 per cent between 1963 and 1971.

Something comparable happened in a number of other sectors. For example, a large part of the so-called 'textile exports' of the Less Developed Countries consisted of earlier imports from the More Developed – synthetic fibres, buttons, dyes, spun materials and so on, without enumerating the machines on which the textiles were manufactured, or the capital employed. Thus, Third World garment exports necessarily promoted exports from the industrialized countries which partly offset the first; between 1960 and 1974, the first increased in value from 0.7 billion U.S. dollars to 8.4 billion, but the net textile import deficit of the industrialized countries increased only from 1 billion to 2.7 billion dollars. In the same period, exports of textile machinery from the industrialized countries increased from 0.3 billion to 2.4 billion dollars.

Many factors were involved in the redistribution of the production system. One was the very rapid fall in transport costs, as well as the changed weight of what was transported – from bulky raw materials to lighter manufactured goods. Another was perhaps the change in the scale of production – the market in any one country no longer provided demand sufficient for a company to realize the full economies of scale. Specialization in one part of the process of manufacturing a product could lower costs of a unit of output by permitting greater standardization of output, longer production runs (machines did not have to be rejigged for small runs of output), and so on – but specialization was only possible with an international market. With diversified outlets for production, exports to several countries, production in one country became more stable; thus, internationalization increased the stability of production. It also increased the uniformity of output, for all goods tended towards using the same set of standardized inputs; governments might continue to speak of 'Japanese' or 'German' cars, but as matters of perception, they had become quite indistinguishable.

The great boom thus tended to wash away what had hitherto been seen as the clear national identification of production. It was becoming more difficult to speak accurately or unequivocally of 'British' exports and imports where both were only stages in the interdependent flows of an international system of production, where exports always involved a majority contribution from imports, and imports turned out to have been formerly exports. The categories broke down, even if State accounts continued to perpetuate the fictions.

In capital, the situation was even more extreme. For a major part of world capital, it was becoming increasingly difficult to identify its nationality. The criteria disappeared – was it ownership of stock, location of headquarters, nationality of personnel, or something else which determined the national identity of a company? As the significance of the ownership of assets had weakened, as the distinction between 'public' and 'private' activities began to disappear, so also did the distinction between 'British' and 'French' and the rest.

The statistics were of little help, for the complexities disappeared into simple criteria: ownership of 10 per cent or more of the assets of a company abroad by a company registered in the United States constituted 'U.S. capital overseas', even though there could be, on the same basis, ten companies from ten different countries each owning 10 per cent of the stock of the company in an eleventh, and each claiming the whole company as its own. Furthermore, the calculation was based upon 'U.S.-registered company', not on who owned the company or a significant part of it; if 10 per cent ownership were enough, then many 'U.S.-registered companies' would turn out to be 'foreign-owned', and then in turn they might recur as partly 'American', and so on. The problem was not the facts, but the concepts, the categories: they could no longer encapsulate the complexities of the real world.

As in the case of the integration of production, it was not a phenomenon peculiarly associated with a new form of company, the multinational or transnational corporation. In production, the integration proceeded on the same basis even where the companies were small; for example, in machine tools, specialized small companies in different countries became technically interdependent.

It remained no less difficult for people to discuss a non-national issue in a world drenched in concepts of nationality. It was supposedly 'American' capital which 'invaded' Europe in the 1960s, and 'American' companies which overwhelmingly predominated in the new fashionable entity, the multinational corporation; its armaments rolled, in the prose of Servan-Schreiber, who endeavoured to express the fears of Europeans, 'from Naples to Amsterdam with the ease of Israeli tanks in Sinai'.[33]

The figures seemed daunting – in the 1960s, the combined sales of multinationals were said to average 500 billion U.S. dollars, or a sixth of the world output of goods and services. The majority of the companies maintained their head offices in the United States, and were therefore identified as 'American'. In the 1960s, of the hundred largest companies in the United States, eighty-one earned a quarter of their annual income overseas, and eleven more than half. The flow of capital continued eastwards to Europe into the 1970s: by 1977, the cumulative total of 'U.S. investment overseas' was put, on one estimate, at 310 billion dollars; the U.S. Department of Commerce, using the criterion of 10 per cent or more of a company overseas owned by a U.S.-registered company, put the book value of American capital in Europe at 50 billion dollars in 1975, out of a world total of U.S. investment overseas of 133 billion dollars. The U.S. Tariff Commission estimated that 'U.S. majority-owned' firms in European manufacturing in 1970 employed 195,000 people in France, 715,000 in Britain; French and British estimates of the same figures for 1973 and 1971 were: 280,000 and 605,000.[34] If the divergence in estimates could be thought to encompass the appropriate range of possible variations, it might still be possible to comprehend the phenomenon, but there could be no such assurance.

The preoccupation was with 'foreign capital'. In fact, multinational corporations had been identified somewhat differently – as international companies manufacturing interdependent parts in several countries. The crudity of the figures gathered by States did not permit any such refinement, any distinction between mere 'foreign' capital and multinationals. So the estimates for the first were used as if they described the second, and used as if the distinction between foreign and native described a real phenomenon. Native capital, it seemed, was decent and loyal to the local State; foreign must be disloyal. In fact, the moment of European panic in the 1960s about 'the flood of American multinationals' tended to die down in the 1970s. For by then, 'European capital' was invading the United States, and there was even a modest crop of 'multinationals' emerging from the Less Developed Countries and bidding successfully for, in particular, international construction contracts. It seemed that the Europeans complained when they felt robbed, but were indulgent when they in turn robbed.

Despite the fears – either of national expropriation by 'foreign' capital or of the expropriation of all nationalities by a new force, a non-national company – international companies still required a geographical location to produce. The need for territory entailed the necessity to relate to a particular State governing a territory and normally offering active assistance, support, a context of political and financial stability, a supply of services and appropriately trained labour. The forms of value – money, shares, bonds, deeds, etc. – that were the preconditions for the realization and transfer of profits were alone legitimized by States; assets were defended alone by the police and army of particular States. Thus, the international company continued to be dependent on the State; or rather, dependent on one State, even if it did not need to be the one governing the territory where the company was originally founded. In a world of competing States, companies could 'shop around'; they were not necessarily dependent on any particular State. Once production was located, they became very dependent; the internationalization of production increased their vulnerability, increased the diversity of contradictory political loyalties which they might have to reconcile.

Part of the fear was also that multinational companies had a common interest, a common attitude to the State. It was as much a myth as that 'native' capital had a common loyalty to the local State. Loyalties were the product of profit rates and inducements to capital. States paid increasingly highly to induce capital to stay in or enter their territory. The competition between States bid up the going rate to astonishing levels in terms of 'cost per job created' figures. That phenomenon emerged in the 1970s in the More Developed in slump, but it had equally afflicted the Less Developed Countries earlier. The structures of national protection, maintaining tariffs and quotas round an economy, as part of the 'import-substitution programme' of industrialization, brought monopoly profits in those companies operating inside the barriers, and very high cost production to the country concerned. The World Bank estimated, for example, that in 1965 the Less Developed Countries expended 2.1 billion U.S. dollars to manufacture domestic automotive products of a world market value of 0.8 billion dollars; the 'loss' of that 1.3 billion dollars roughly equalled World Bank aid to the Less Developed during the twenty-three years of its existence.[35]

The economic strength of large foreign companies was frequently related to their cumulative lead in technology. This in turn derived from their activities in the largest world markets and their sustained expenditure in research and technology. That factor was related to those governments which made the greatest expenditure on 'R and D', research and development, which was itself partly a function of defence preoccupations. For much of the 1950s, the Federal Government of the United States funded two-thirds of American R and D, and the U.S. spending as a whole was three times larger than the combined total in West Europe. However, real growth in R and D declined from some 12 per cent per year between 1953 and 1964, to 3 per cent between 1964 and 1971, and to zero up to 1975 (this partly reflected the rapid rundown in the Federal space research programme). In any case, it seems R and D, regardless of its level, became less productive of technical change.[36] U.S. and British spending stagnated in the 1960s, while the West German, French and Japanese expanded, only then to level off with the onset of general economic stagnation. Uncertainties over the future of profits cut into civil R and D, without military spending making up the difference. If it were still true in the 1960s that the position of the industrialized countries derived from 'an almost impregnable monopoly of advanced technology that comes from the concentration of research and development in the world's industrial heartlands',[37] in the 1970s far cruder and more old-fashioned factors were reintroduced by slump.

To the integration of production and the complexity of capital ownership was added yet a third factor, even more extreme than the first two. The growth of international finance in the 1960s rapidly overtook the growth of the combined activities of the industrialized States, and did so as an 'offshore' phenomenon (that is, outside the control of any particular State or any combination of States). The flows of finance became even more important than intra-company transactions, and they could not easily be identified by company or State. The flows were 'denationalized', flowing through national territories without gathering any moss of national sentiment. Temporary crises produced 'flights of capital'. Oil price increases generated more. Speculative flows wrecked official attempts to stabilize the international monetary order by the most powerful States. In the world of finance, all distinctions were dissolved – between public and private liquidity, between the liquidity of different States, between domestic and international liquidity. Fixed exchange rates of currencies defined the distinction between the internal monetary system and the external; they defined the size of national reserves. Floating rates blurred matters; the capacity of States to borrow added an unknown increase to reserves, and fluctuating currency values varied the value of official reserves. A group of conservative economists described the situation thus:

> ... the limits of reserve creation have become ill-defined and fluid, being set now by the private market's judgement of the credit-worthiness of the system as a whole ... In this sense, the private market has taken over the functions and responsibilities that used to be thought more appropriate to national and international authorities, and the international monetary system has taken on some of the characteristics of a domestic credit system without a central bank.[38]

Even before the ending of fixed exchange rates, however, the growth of the Eurocurrency market increasingly circumscribed the external monetary power of States. Furthermore, in so far as domestic banks participated in the international market, the distinction between domestic and external transactions for the industrialized countries became equally 'ill-defined'. External transactions offered an 'escape hatch',[39] and a basis of power to the banks to resist policies of governments they disliked.

The growth of financial activity should not be understood as the increased domination of banking agencies. Increasingly, large companies came to operate as independent financial agencies. Just as they had diversified between countries, so also changing profit rates between sectors forced them to diversify between sectors and markets – sectors of manufacturing, of finance, of commodity or currency trading, of different services. It became almost impossible to identify the specific orientation of a company, simply because of the diversity of activities and the rapid change in that diversity. The dominant operators on the Eurocurrency market were, the banks said, manufacturing companies, and if twenty or thirty of the largest moved together – the giants of car, oil or chemical production – they could move the market, move currency values and interest rates. The oil major, B.P., maintained world-wide currency trading that was larger than that of the Bank of England, larger than the value of its annual oil trading; its London dealings in the first quarter of 1982 were put at £4.3 billion. Volkswagen was said to overshadow most major banks in the Eurocurrency market. Poor profits in manufacturing pushed idle funds into the financial markets, and international trade necessarily obliged big companies to engage in large-scale currency dealing. Companies reorganized their management divisions appropriately, for more could be made (or lost) by currency or interest rate fluctuations than could be made in a whole year of selling manufactured goods.

The growth of barter trade – by 1982, fully a quarter of world trade was said to be by barter, a reflection both of the severe shortage of convertible currency in the hands of buyers and the desperate drive to increase sales – forced a different kind of diversification on companies. If machine makers swapped their goods for apples, perforce they were required to become sellers on the apple market. In a famous case, a Control Data computer was exchanged in Moscow for paper products, including a major shipment of Russian Christmas cards. Large companies set up special buying and selling divisions for goods outside their normal range, paying close attention to potential currency gains involved in shrewdly timed deals.

In sum, the boundaries between sectors and agencies became blurred. Publicly owned national banks became simple private operators in the world market. Banks, through the increasing number of potentially bankrupt manufacturing companies, came to supervise and even manage manufacturing companies. Supposedly manufacturing companies came to operate as international banks, as commodity and currency dealers. A wide range of what were supposedly separate markets became fused in one world market, and its activities increasingly disciplined all participants.

The evolution of the structure of the world system undermined the power of States – or rather, the power of those, the most powerful group of governments, who controlled the most industrialized regions of the system. The appearance of the steady growth of State power was a plausible one only from within a given country; outside, in the world system, the growth of the essentially private system (even if State-owned companies also operated there) was more impressive. Governments might bend all efforts to bribe, bully or charm the elusive 'international capital', but ultimately, the world profit rate rather than the behaviour of States determined the trend. For capital, national loyalty was strictly contingent, a bargain based upon a profit rate which, although influenced by State behaviour and subsidies, was ultimately not determined by it. Indeed, the world system that stood revealed in the 1970s had a closer resemblance to the classical theory of a capitalist system than any that had existed before – a mass of competing units, none of which was large enough to influence the market's outcome, and lacking official governance in the interests of all competitors. The international market was the nearest thing to the economist's dream, a 'perfect market'.

While the great boom persisted, these were at best merely idle observations. But the ending of sustained growth, the growth of unemployment, revived the necessity of States to control more closely their domestic patches. The new structure, however, severely limited their capacity to do so; efforts to do so threatened to damage both the world system and thereby each 'domestic economy'. The remedies of 1931 looked increasingly utopian: the State, as an *economic* agency, was becoming obsolescent.

The great boom ended in 1973–4. It became a myth with great speed, enshrined in a revival of the fifties Rocking generation, in the nostalgia of the sixties generation. The accomplishments of the boom were substantial, but so also were the items the myths omitted – the terrors of Cold War, the dead and maimed of Korea and Vietnam; in Northern Ireland and Palestine, in the defeated struggle of America's black people, of the workers of Budapest, Poznan and Berlin, and countless other places. Even with all the economic factors most favourable, capitalism could neither resolve the ancient wrongs of society, nor even forbear to add to them. The States of the industrialized regions might, by sleight of hand, redefine capitalism as no more than their own little patches, so that the wealth they there accumulated could be matters of self-congratulation. But exiling all the rest of humanity, the majority, to some nether world, some outer darkness, could be no more than temporary. The unemployed and poor of the system were, by a statistical trick, banished to 'other countries' (even that imposition of homogeneity was factually false). In the 1970s, the world returned to unity, battering down the puny defences of the 'managed economy' and inserting mass unemployment into its midst. The national village could no longer escape.

Notes to Chapter 2

1. Karl Marx and Frederick Engels, *Manifesto of the Communist Party*, February 1848, English translation 1888, in Karl Marx and Frederick Engels, *Collected Works*, Vol. 6, 1845–8, London, 1979, p. 489.

2. At 1963 prices. See Table 6 in *Expenditure Trends in the O.E.C.D. Countries, 1960–1980*, O.E.C.D., Paris, 1980, p. 31.

3. World Health Organization, *Health Trends and Prospects in Relationship to Population and Development*, W.H.O. paper for United Nations World Population Conference, Bucharest, August 1974 (E/Conf/60.CBP/26).

4. In David Morawetz, *Twenty Five Years of Economic Development, 1950 to 1975*, World Bank, 1977, p. 48.

5. This is discussed relative to opinion in the British Conservative Party in my *Competition and the Corporate Society; British Conservatives, the State and Industry, 1945–1964*, London, 1972, p. 77 *passim*.

6. Simon Kuznets, *Postwar Economic Growth: Four Lectures*, Cambridge, Mass., 1964, pp. 91–5.

7. On the changing factional disputes in the U.S. State Department, see Chapters 3 and 4 in Fred L. Blok, *The Origins of International Economic Disorder, A Study of United States International Monetary Policy from World War II to the Present*, London, 1977, pp. 32–108.

8. Organization of European Economic Cooperation (O.E.E.C.), *Ninth Report*, 1958, p. 33.

9. The notion of a 'permanent arms economy' is explored by Tony Cliff in 'A Permanent War Economy', in *A Socialist Review*, London, 1965, pp. 34–40; in relationship to the Soviet Union, in *Stalinist Russia, A Marxist Analysis*, London, 1955 (and *Russia: A Marxist Analysis*, London, 1975); on Western arms economies, see Michael Kidron, Introduction and 'International Capitalism', published in *Capitalism and Theory*, London, 1974, pp. 11–31 and pp. 143–67, and *Western Capitalism Since the War*, London, 1968; and debate with Chris Harman, *International Socialism* 100 (old series), July 1977, pp. 4–13.

10. J.S. Flemming describes this general phenomenon thus: the 'fear and reluctance [of "minor countries" to demand conversion of a major country's currency earnings: N.H.] present the dominant country with an opportunity to enrich itself at the expense of its neighbours. If it expands its money supply, it will run a trade deficit, i.e. it will be able to consume more than it produces, which implies that other countries produce more than they consume. They can avoid the payment of this tribute only by revaluing their currencies or demanding conversion of their reserves [to gold or some other "hard" medium of exchange: N.H.], either of which would precipitate a capital loss' – in 'The economic explanation of inflation', in Fred Hirsch and John H. Goldthorpe (eds.), *The Political Economy of Inflation*, London, 1978, p. 18.

11. Long period shifts in the patterns of manufacturing output in Western Europe (Paretti-Block estimates, 1938 prices; recalculated, per cent value added at 1963 prices), in United Nations, *Structure and Changes in European Industry*, Economic Commission for Europe, Geneva; New York, 1977.

12. Table III.1, in United Nations Industrial Development Organization (U.N.I.D.O.), *World Industry since 1960: Progress and Prospects* (Special Issue of the Industrial Development Survey for the Third General Conference of U.N.I.D.O.), United Nations, New York, 1979, p. 66.

13. Cited in footnote 20 of Richard Blackhurst, Nicholas Marian and Jan Tumlir, *Trade Liberalization, Protectionism and Interdependence*, G.A.T.T. Studies in International Trade No. 5, Geneva, November 1977, p. 64. A more

detailed breakdown of manufacturing exports (covering fourteen *industrialized* countries) has been constructed by John Cornwall (see table).

Commodity composition of world manufacturing exports, 1955–70 (ratios of current prices)

	1955	1960	1965	1970
Chemicals	10.8	11.1	11.6	11.2
Textiles	9.9	8.1	6.8	5.6
Iron and steel	10.2	10.8	9.1	8.6
Non-ferrous metals	5.0	4.7	4.2	4.0
Metal manufactures	5.3	3.5	3.7	3.4
Non-electrical machinery	16.0	18.5	20.0	20.3
Electrical machinery	6.8	7.5	8.8	9.5
Transport equipment	15.6	16.7	16.1	18.4
Other	19.5	19.1	19.7	19.0

(Table 10.1 in John Cornwall, *Modern Capitalism: Its Growth and Transformation*, London, 1977, p. 86)

14. For manufacturing exports, see Table 2.6 in R. L. Major, 'Recent Trends in World Trade in Manufactures', in R. A. Batchelor, R. L. Major and A. D. Morgan, *Industrialization and the Basis for Trade*, National Institute of Economic and Social Research, Cambridge, 1980, p. 29.

15. These issues are discussed in my 'Deindustrialization', in *International Socialism* 7 (new series), Winter, 1980, pp. 72–81; on the British case, see Frank Blackaby (ed.), *Deindustrialization*, National Institute of Economic and Social Research, London, 1978.

16. Table 2.6, 'Per cent composition of total employment between agriculture, industry and services', in Cornwall, op. cit.

17. The figures are attributed to a market research report of the Yankee Group, Cambridge, Mass., cited in 'Death Sentence for Paper Shufflers', *The Economist*, London, 27 December 1980, p. 56.

18. These issues are discussed in more detail in my 'The New Untouchables – The International Migration of Labour', *International Socialism* 8 (new series), Spring 1980, pp. 37–63.

19. See Table 1-5-5 in United Nations, *Survey of Economic and Social Conditions in Africa 1974*, Economic Commission for Africa, 10 December 1974, New York, 1975 (E/CN.14/632/PART 1).

20. See Annex 3, World Bank, *Health*, Sector Policy Paper, World Bank, Washington, March 1975, p. 83.

21. These issues are discussed in more detail in my *Economic Growth and the Problem of World Settlements*, Working Paper No. 4, Development Planning Unit, London, 1976.

22. Nor was the problem simply one restricted to the 'capitalist' countries; compare the problems of the People's Republic of China, as presented by C. R. Roll Jr and Kung-chiao Yeh, 'Balance in Coastal and Inland Industrial Development', in *China: A Reassessment of the Economy*, A Compendium of

Papers submitted to the Joint Economic Committee of the Congress of the United States, 10 July 1975, U.S. Congress, Government Printing Office, Washington D.C., 1975, pp. 81–93.

23. As Marx noted: 'Constant revolutionizing of production, uninterrupted disturbance of all social conditions, everlasting uncertainty and agitation distinguish the bourgeois epoch from all earlier ones. All fixed, fast-frozen relations, with their train of ancient and venerable prejudices and opinions, are swept away; all new-formed ones become antiquated before they can ossify. All that is solid melts into air, all that is holy is profaned, and man is at last compelled to face with sober senses, his real conditions of life, and his relations with his kind' (Marx and Engels, *Manifesto*, op. cit., p. 487).

24. Fred Hirsch, in Hirsch and Goldthorpe, op. cit., p. 273.

25. *Daily Telegraph*, editorial, 5 March 1956.

26. Table 2.7 in Cornwall, op. cit.

27. The catch-phrases are culled from the literature popular in the 1950s among social scientists – 'euthanasia of the rentier' is from J. M. Keynes's famous *General Theory of Employment, Interest and Money*, London, 1936, pp. 375–6; the 'managerial revolution' appeared in James Burnham's *The Managerial Revolution*, London, 1945; the 'end of ideology' features in Daniel Bell's *The End of Ideology, On the Exhaustion of Political Ideas in the Fifties*, New York, 1961; discussions of 'People's Capitalism' occur in A. A. Berle, *The Twentieth Century Capitalist Revolution*, London, 1955, and in *Power without Property*, London, 1960; the issues are discussed in my *Competition and the Corporate Society*, op. cit., Chapter 4, pp. 62–74.

28. *First Plan of India*, Government of India, New Delhi, 1952, p. 8.

29. Figures from D. B. Keesing, *World Trade and Output in Manufactures: Structure, Trends and Developing Countries Exports*, World Bank staff working paper No. 316 (mimeo), World Bank, Washington D.C., 1979.

30. Extracted from Table 3.3, 'Import content of "supplies" of manufactured goods, 1899–1971 (1955 prices)', in R. L. Major, 'Consumption and Imports of Manufactures', in R. A. Batchelor *et al.*, *Industrialization*, op. cit., p. 38.

31. Blackhurst, Marian and Tumlir, op. cit. (citing I. B. Kravis and R. E. Lipsey, *Price Competitiveness in World Trade*, New York, 1971), p. 63.

32. Extracted from Tables 7 and 8 in C. J. F. Brown and T. D. Sheriff, *Deindustrialization in the U.K.: Background Statistics*, Discussion Paper No. 23 (mimeo), National Institute of Economic and Social Research, London, 1978.

33. The book, *Le défi américain*, was published in Paris in 1967, shortly after the Arab–Israeli 'Six Day War'.

34. The figures are cited in *Over Here, A Survey of American Companies in Europe*, a supplement by *The Economist*, 10 September 1977. See also American fears in United States Senate, Committee on Finance, *Implications of Multinational firms for World Trade and Investment and for U.S. Trade and Labor*, Washington, 1973, and Committee on Foreign Relations, *Direct Investment Abroad and the Multinational Companies' Effect on the U.S. Economy*, Washington, 1975.

35. Robert MacNamara, *Address to the Annual Meeting of the Governor of the World Bank and the International Monetary Fund*, 29 September 1969, Washington, 1969.

36. See D. M. Leipziger, 'Productivity in the United States and its International Implications', in *World Economy* 3/1, London, June 1980.

37. Michael Kidron, *Pearson on Foreign Investment* (unpublished comment on *Partners in Development*, Report of the Commission on International Development to the World Bank (I.B.R.D.), 1969), London, 1969, p. 13.

38. Paul McCracken *et al., Towards Full Employment and Price Stability*, O.E.C.D., Paris, June 1977, p. 130.

39. The phrase is that of Fred Hirsch, in Hirsch and Goldthorpe, op. cit., p. 267.

THREE   SLUMP AND STAGNATION

> What is society, whatever its form may be? The production of men's reciprocal activity. Are men free to choose this or that form of society for themselves? By no means. Assume a particular state of development in the productive forces and you will get a particular form of commerce and consumption. Assume particular stages of development in production, commerce and consumption and you will have a corresponding social order, a corresponding order of the family and of the ranks and classes, in a word, a corresponding civil society. Presuppose a particular civil society and you will get particular political conditions which are only the official expression of civil society.[1]

From 1974, the world system entered a new phase. Not all the world was affected equally. Nor was it clear at the time that it was a new phase. The O.E.C.D. Secretariat envisaged in 1974 that there would be difficulties through much of the decade, but that full employment and sustained growth in the industrial core of the system would be resumed by 1980. In the event, the decade turned out to be one of stagnation, initiated and closed by slumps; and at the time of the second slump in the early eighties, there were still few prospects for a resumption of growth and full employment.

It was a remarkable change from what had happened in the preceding quarter of a century. Because the changes were spread over a number of years, people did not often perceive how dramatic a change it was. The shock took time – is still taking time – to register, to unwind the structures and preoccupations which dominated the preceding decades. People still assumed the return of prosperity, even if not of quite the same order as in the full-blown optimism of the boom's heyday, epitomized in the 1956 observation of C. A. R. Crosland:

> . . . it will really not much matter in a decade from now whether we plant to produce rather more of this or less of that . . . the level of material welfare will soon be such that marginal changes in the allocation of resources will make little difference to anyone's contentment.[2]

How did the change of direction occur? We try here to reconstruct what happened in more detail, before considering some of the developing features of the system in subsequent chapters.

The first slump

The trends which culminated in the first crisis of 1973–4 began, as described in the last chapter, in the mid sixties. Resources were being reallocated between sectors and geographical areas through the last half of the sixties, in search of improved profit rates but with, apparently, decreasing effects in terms of heavy industry. The heavy industrial sector of Europe and the United States seemed to have experienced an increasing degree of depreciation, and a declining tendency to upgrade capacity at the same tempo as was occurring in, for example, a country with already more modernized heavy industrial capacity, Japan. Investment also tended to become redirected from expanding capacity to minimizing costs. Businessmen, whether of the State or private companies, began to be more worried about having too much capacity at the peak of the boom than too little. Perhaps the symbol of the process occurred in the seventies with the introduction of robot production on car assembly lines; the Unimate robot, costing 40,000 U.S. dollars in 1978, would work two shifts daily for about eight years at a rough rate of under 5 dollars per hour, in comparison to U.S. assembly workers costing 15 dollars per hour; General Motors proposed to install 1,000 such robots per year up to 1982, 14,000 by the end of the eighties.

The processes were noted during the sixties, but not their general significance. On the surface, all was boom. The Vietnam War expanded international liquidity and began those sudden wild fluctuations in currency and price stability which ultimately overturned the international monetary order. But during the main war period, growth still seemed the dominant mode of operation.

Monetary instability undermined the precondition for the 'managed economy', a stable international environment, just as increasing rates of inflation undermined the precondition for the central pillar of the managed economy, stable high employment and income stability. In the late sixties, the class struggle swept away the mists of 'the end of ideology' – in the black struggle of the United States, in the May events in France in 1968, in a rash of wildcat strikes in West Germany and major strikes in Italy. They were new factors to discipline the perceptions of politicians contesting elections in 1972 (in the United States, West Germany, Japan and Canada).

The preceding integration of the system – in production, in the behaviour of capital and in terms of the international financial system – produced also in the core zones an unusual degree of synchronization in economic fluctuations. The three most important components of the O.E.C.D. group – the United States, West Germany and Japan, producing some two-thirds of the combined income of the group – began to move in step. The West German government endeavoured to expand out of a mild recession in 1966–7 (mild though the recession seemed in retrospect, it was the most severe one since 1948), pulling the Common Market group into the boom generated in the United States. Japan was in any case already being lifted by the economic impact of the Vietnam War in the east Asian area. Up to mid 1970, world output grew rapidly, inflation rates accelerating at the same time. Governments combated 'overheating' in the orthodox manner, and perhaps this influenced the mild downturn in 1970–71. The change produced or coincided with serious disorders in south Asia, and the first important financial collapse – that of Penn Central in the United States, the largest financial collapse in America to that time.

Expansion was resumed in 1971, and a substantial increase in international liquidity fuelled an unprecedented boom through 1972 and 1973. In eighteen months, the rate of increase in output was the fastest for any similar period since the 1950s (when the productive base of the system was far smaller). The quarter-century of economic growth ended with a bang, not a whimper.

Between mid 1972 and mid 1973, the combined product of the O.E.C.D. group increased in real terms by 7.5 per cent, and industrial production by fully 10 per cent. But the underlying profit rate in the investment industries did not change commensurately. Capacity increases were limited, so that supply constraints rapidly lifted prices: output in the basic system resisted the expansion in demand. Inflation and currency instability produced a flight of funds, not into industrial investment where returns were still relatively poor, but into property and commodity speculation. Gold prices increased two and a half times between 1972 and 1973. Raw material prices soared – on the index of 1963 as 100, the primary commodity price index, running at 125 in mid 1971, was over 300 three years later (in the same time, the price index for manufactured goods rose from 127 to just under 220). Food prices, and in particular the price of wheat, increased nearly 14 per cent in a year, shutting out from the market parts of famine-stricken Africa and south Asia. Oil prices followed the same course in real terms, even though the change seemed in the politically charged atmosphere to have been caused by a Middle Eastern war, an Arab boycott and the manipulation of a cartel, O.P.E.C. Overall, the O.E.C.D. price index moved from a rate of annual increase of 5.5 per cent in mid 1972, to 7.5 per cent a year later, and 15 per cent in the spring of 1974 (the comparable rates in Britain and Japan peaked at 30 per cent).

In 1973, the bubble burst. Real gross product in the O.E.C.D. group, increasing at an annual rate of 8 per cent in the first half of 1973, dropped to 3 per cent in the second half. In the following three years, world output increased by about 4 per cent, an increase that would have taken nine months in the previous decade.

The slump dragged industrial production in the core zones down by some 13 per cent. But the effects were not uniform. Take, first, the leading States of the industrial core (Table 8).

The most extreme range was crossed by Japan, but all experienced negative growth rates in 1974 or 1975; only the United States had negative growth in both years. It is also interesting to note that, with high rates of unemployment, nearly all were capable of quite high rates of output growth in particular years; 'stagnation' was still consistent with 1976 growth rates of 5 or 6 per cent, historically a high level. The picture for the backward countries is shown in Table 9.

On this measure, the mass of Less Developed Countries escaped the worst effects of the first slump; none moved into negative growth rates, although all experienced low growth in 1974 or 1975: the lowest rate was registered in the major oil-exporting countries in 1975. Africa apparently did not participate in the boom of 1973, and of the three regions, made the poorest recovery up to 1977. Only 'Asia' (the inverted commas indicate the extreme heterogeneity of the group, and the fact that the regional figures are overwhelmingly dominated by a small group of countries) was able to exceed the preceding trend rate (1967–72) in three successive years after the worst of the slump in 1974.

The boom in commodity prices which had fuelled part of the inflation in 1972–3 ended. Industrial raw material prices fell some 40 per cent between April 1974 and January 1975, and food prices by 30 per cent (November to June 1975). This sharp reduction in the incomes of raw material exporting countries did not cut the imports of the Less Developed Countries commensurately, as we shall see later: the effects of downturn in the industrialized regions of the world was thus reduced. Other factors also impeded the full effects of slump. The managed economy – and the political fears attached to any dismantling of it – offset in Europe the full effects of unemployment. O.E.C.D. unemployment – an obstinate 8 million at the peak of the boom, reached a postwar record of 15 million – but this was still only a rate of 5.5 per cent,

8. Real rates of growth of gross national product (percentage)

	1967–72	1973	1974	1975	1976	1977	1978	1979	1980	1981	1982[E]
O.E.C.D. Group	4.8	6.2	0.4	−0.8	5.2	3.7	4.0	3.6	1.3	1.2	0.8
United States	3.1	5.5	−1.4	−1.3	6.0	4.9	4.8	3.2	−0.2	2.0	−1.0
West Germany	5.5	5.1	0.7	−2.5	5.7	2.4	3.6	4.4	1.8	−0.3	1.0
Japan	10.2	9.8	−1.1	2.4	6.3	6.0	5.1	5.2	4.2	2.9	3.5
Britain	2.4	6.0	0.3	−1.6	2.1	0.3	3.6	2.0	−1.6	−2.1	0.8
France	6.0	5.3	2.9	−1.0	5.2	3.0	3.7	3.5	1.2	0.8	2.1

E: Estimate

9. Real rates of growth of gross domestic product (percentage)[3]

	1967–72	1973	1974	1975	1976	1977	1978	1979	1980	1981	1982[E]
Major oil exporting countries	9.0	10.7	8.7	0.3	12.4	6.7	1.8	2.9	−2.8	−4.5	−1.0
Non-oil exporting countries	6.1	7.3	5.3	3.9	4.8	4.7	6.2	7.2	7.3	6.6	5.1
Africa	5.1	3.0	6.0	2.4	4.7	2.9	2.4	2.6	4.6	2.6	2.0
Asia	4.9	7.8	2.7	6.2	5.8	6.0	8.1	3.1	3.4	5.7	5.6
Latin America	6.8	8.1	7.7	2.6	4.5	4.3	4.4	6.7	6.0	−0.1	3.5

E: Estimate

high only for short memories. Governments expected the downturn to be short, so that it was worth assuming employment would be stable. In any case, in some countries, a margin of flexibility had been preserved through the employment of immigrants. Expelling immigrant workers kept down unemployment rates in West Germany and France – the German stock of foreign workers was cut by 25 per cent between the end of 1973 and the end of 1975. The same 'rigidities', political need and the resistance of labour, also reduced the fall in real incomes in the first phase of the downturn (Table 10).

10. _Earned disposable real income (rate of change annually, per head)_[4]

	1960–69	1969–73	1973–5
United States	2.8	2.5	−3.8
West Germany	3.5	3.4	−0.8
Japan	8.1	8.1	1.2
Britain	0.9	3.8	−1.3
France	3.6	4.8	0.9
Italy	3.8	5.0	−2.2

There were numerous political results of the change of gear which, at times, seemed to threaten more than the statistics suggested. The United States government was paralysed by a succession of sordid scandals, one of which cut down the American President, and another – associated with bribes offered by Lockheed to sell its aircraft – Prime Minister Tanaka of Japan and sundry lesser fry round the world. The German Chancellor discovered his secretary was spying for East Germany. The British Prime Minister was turned out of office by a strike of miners. In Chile a military coup decimated the political class, and there were rumours of similar events to come in Italy and Britain. The Yom Kippur War in the Middle East complicated all strategic meditations. The possible future victories of the Communist party in Italy and France cast gloom in Washington and frightened investors. The Club of Rome sentenced the world to a raw material death, and famines in south Asia and Africa prompted a scientific account of the arrival of a second Ice Age. A wave of bank closures (the most notable were the closures of the Herstatt and Franklyn National Bank), as property and commodity speculators were caught by price collapses, all added to a tone of hysteria in public life. Many important people meditated in public that 'civilization as we know it' was under extreme attack and might not survive. The fever of slump, as gripping as that of boom, muddled all causes and effects.

Recovery and slump again

O.E.C.D. governments began efforts to stimulate some revival in late 1974. All were constrained in raising public expenditure to accomplish domestic stimulation, however, because public sector deficits were already high and further increases were thought certain to accelerate the already high levels of inflation. The United States made the most determined efforts to lift the level of activity. For a time it had some success. Between June 1975 and March 1976, industrial production increased by 10 per cent; and gross product for 1976 stood a remarkable 6 per cent higher than the preceding year. But the growth did not lift the world system as it had been hoped it might. Nor did it set off a domestic investment boom. The growth merely led to the replacement of depleted stocks. By the second half of 1976, the growth rate began to flatten out, leaving in its wake the wreckage of a large and growing deficit on the United States balance of payments and, closely related to it, an apparently inexorably declining value of the dollar.

Nonetheless, public spending did tend to increase in other O.E.C.D. countries, and in the case of France and Japan, produced increases in public investment (for a time, nearly a 70 per cent increase in Japan, and 50 per cent in France, between 1974 and 1980). Perhaps the Japanese increase contributed to the general growth of investment in Japan, but this was not the same pressing problem as in Europe. In the French case, public investment proved quite insufficient to stimulate a private investment boom; French businessmen did not respond. In the case of Britain and Italy, as public spending increased (by nearly 20 per cent in Italy, and under 10 per cent in Britain between the same years), public investment actually fell – by about 15 per cent in Italy, and over 30 per cent in Britain. The central problem – the profit rate in the investment industries – was only exacerbated.

Governments also took defensive action to protect what they saw as the national economy. There were schemes to assist threatened sectors, to fund steel, shipbuilding and others, to create cartels in order to regulate prices and output, and sporadic efforts to limit selected imports without causing too much offence to the letter of the rules of G.A.T.T.; whatever those efforts might do for the spirit of free trade. The quantitative effects of these measures are difficult to assess, but certainly the *formal* changes seemed significant. For example, on external trade, the constraints shown in Table 11 have been recorded:

*11. Percentage of total imports
'managed', 1974 and 1979 (22 O.E.C.D.
countries)*[5]

	All trade		Manufactures	
	1974	1979	1974	1979
United States	36	44	6	18
West Germany	37	46	–	16
Japan	51	55	–	4
Britain	38	45	–	13
France	33	42	–	14
Italy	44	52	–	15
Total (22 O.E.C.D. countries)	36	42	4	15

'Bilateralism' spread – that is, negotiated trade between two countries, rather than open multilateral trade between many countries. There were specific restrictions imposed upon particular sectors – textiles, clothing, footwear, steel, shipbuilding, consumer electronic goods, cars. By 1981, restrictions on trade in cars, covering about 6 per cent of world trade, affected virtually all the markets of the industrialized countries for Japanese exports; the December 1981 revision of the Multi Fibre Arrangement covering textile and garments affected about 12 per cent of the exports of the Non-Oil Exporting Developing Countries. Agricultural trade remained heavily protected. And finally, there was an increasing flow of complaints and interruptions in multilateral trade.

The degree of devotion to a somewhat outdated notion of 'national interest' – defence of external trade – varied considerably. For the degree of internationalization varied, as also did the perception that protection of the 'national economy' might destroy it. In so far as governments subsidized threatened sectors or companies, they held down general profit rates. For the subsidies had to be paid for – from increased taxes on profitable companies or on consumption, both of which, directly and indirectly, reduced the net return to unsubsidized sectors; or from increased public borrowing, which in turn ultimately increased the burden of debt servicing and the need for increased taxation. In the short term, and with inflation reducing the real burden, subsidies were possible, but only as temporary supports.

By limiting imports, governments reduced world trade to the loss of all, including themselves; in so far as their exports re-entered the country as imports, they limited the possibility of exports; and by limiting imports, they prevented buyers of their exports earning sufficient to keep up their purchases. Separate national economies in the industrialized regions of the world were required if the instinctive reactions of governments were to make any sense; but they existed only in severely attenuated form, so that traditional government responses became inevitably self-destructive.

The resumption of what growth there was in the last half of the decade cannot be attributed to governments, nor, indeed, to deliberate and conscious action at all. The States of the industrialized regions were far too preoccupied with their inter-rivalries to undertake sustained and coordinated action. The saviour appeared in a quite unexpected form – the most advanced section of the Less Developed Countries and some of the Eastern Bloc (the Centrally Planned Economies or C.P.E.s). The decade of integration in the system now made it possible for this group not merely to withstand slump in the world as a whole, but to accelerate the growth of their output. Lending by Western banks – both on their own account or by means of re-lending funds deposited with them by the oil-producing powers – to a small group of countries permitted continued expansion. Furthermore, some capital moved from the industrialized countries to the backward, a certain redistribution of productive capacity between First and Third Worlds (this is discussed in a later chapter). In addition, the group – some of the Eastern Bloc and Less Developed – used their domestic reserves to sustain imports (declining reserves in due course reduced the creditworthiness of the countries concerned, and thus their capacity to borrow further loans to service existing debts). In sum, those affected in the two groups of countries were able to increase their imports in order to sustain high growth rates; the beneficiaries were the industrialized group, for they both loaned the finance and provided the imports. One result of this was a rapid increase in manufacturing capacity in some Less Developed Countries – and a rapid increase in their exports of manufactures; by 1980 for the first time fully half the value of Third World exports was provided by manufactured goods (as opposed to raw materials). Thus, the impact of slump was – contrary to past experience – to increase the degree of integration in the world production system, to incorporate the most industrialized of the backward.

The expansion of exports to the Less Developed and the Eastern Bloc helped stabilize the industrialized countries. So also did the expansion of the oil-producing countries. The O.P.E.C. group (covering some 60 per cent of world oil supplies) increased its combined imports by some 60 per cent in the last half of the seventies. If we add the oil-producing and oil-importing backward countries together, between 1970 and 1976, the share of the trade between More and Less Developed countries in world trade increased from 26 to 31 per cent (at an annual rate of average increase of 9 per cent); the share of machinery and transport in this trade increased from 29 to 36 per cent (or a 10 per cent rate of annual increase). The 'New World' came to save the 'Old'. Of course, in so far as the industrialized countries endeavoured to limit imports from the Less Developed, they limited the L.D.C. capacity to import, to purchase the exports of the More Developed.

Underlying this change in trade and so in different rates of industrial expansion was a major change in financial relations. A vast expansion in debt took place, covering the globe both within and between countries. The process expanded even further the domination of the world system by the private international financial market. By 1979, the gross value of assets in the Eurocurrency market was larger than the combined reserves of gold and currencies of the O.E.C.D. group. One index illustrates the change: in 1978, 100 billion dollars was borrowed internationally (a sum equivalent to the value of one month's exports for the world); in 1970, the total borrowing was 9.3 billion dollars (equal to eleven days' exports). Cumulative debt drifted upwards – from 267 billion dollars at the end of 1978, to 437 billion in late 1981 and over 500 billion at the end of 1982.

The borrowings of the 'middle income' Less Developed Countries from private international banks were estimated as shown in Table 12.

12. (U.S. dollars, billions)[6]

	1970	1971	1972	1973	1974	1975	1976	1977	1978	1979
Claims of private banks	30	37	44	53	72	92	110	151	204	251
Percentage annual increase	–	7	7	9	19	20	18	41	53	47

Net borrowing (that is, gross borrowing minus deposits made by borrowing governments in banks abroad) by oil-importing Less Developed Countries increased from 5 billion to 44 billion dollars between 1973 and 1978, and then to 102 billion dollars in 1980. Over the same period, the new debts of the European Centrally Planned Economies increased from 4 billion to 44 billion dollars. The cumulative debt tended to reproduce itself as further borrowings were needed to cover annual interest and repayment sums. However, given high rates of inflation, the increase in the real debt was less rapid. The debts would not be a problem if export earnings of the Less Developed increased more rapidly, but that possibility depended upon the markets of the More

Developed remaining open. Without that, a much sharper cutback was likely, with ramifying effects on both Less and More Developed.

Whatever the statistics might say in terms of growth of gross products, there was little perception of tangible improvements. Unemployment remained obstinately immovable when growth rates improved, and over time, slowly drifted upwards so that the highest rates – during slump – grew higher. In the Common Market, the rate increased in every year after 1973 except in 1978 (when it was constant), edging up towards the number of 17½ million unemployed by 1983. The second slump took the rates up to within striking distance of the records of the 1930s; in absolute numbers, they were already greater; similarly, the rates of 1982 were comparable to those of 1975, but since the labour force had grown, the absolute numbers involved were nearly twice as large. They hit hardest the decaying segments of the industrialized countries – Britain and North America. But by the second slump, the problem was afflicting even the expansive countries, West Germany and Japan; Japanese unemployment was a record for twenty-six years, nearly 1½ million, with most severe effects in construction (see Table 13).

13. *Unemployment rates (percentages, separate national bases)*[7]

	Average 1963–72	1973	1974	1975	1976	1977	1978	1979	1980	1981	1982[E]
United States	4.7	4.9	5.6	8.5	7.7	7.0	6.1	5.8	7.2	7.6	9.1
Canada	4.7	5.5	5.3	6.9	7.1	8.1	8.4	7.5	7.5	7.6	9.2
Japan	1.2	1.3	1.4	1.9	2.0	2.0	2.2	2.1	2.1	2.2	2.5
West Germany	0.9	1.0	2.2	4.1	4.1	4.0	3.8	3.3	3.4	4.8	6.4
France	1.9	2.6	2.8	4.1	4.4	4.7	5.2	5.9	6.3	8.1	8.8
Britain	2.4	2.6	2.6	3.9	5.3	5.8	5.7	5.4	6.9	10.6	12.0
Italy	6.4	6.5	5.9	6.3	6.7	7.2	7.2	7.7	7.6	8.4	9.0

E: Estimate

However, despite the trend of the figures, there were many economists who argued that it was the resistance of the managed economy to laying off labour which perpetuated stagnation; 'rigidity' within the system now stabilized poor growth rather than maintained high growth. There were others who argued that it was rigidity in pay, on the other hand, that produced increasing unemployment; if only labour would accept downwardly 'flexible' wages, then there would be work for all at some level of pay. Certainly, in comparison to, for example, the slump of 1929 to 1933 or the downturn of 1938, wages were much more stable; hourly money wage rates in Germany and the United States were said to have fallen 20 per cent between 1929 and 1933 (a fall which did not, however, prevent very rapid increases in unemployment at the same time). Real earnings did show greater stability, but what was remarkable was not the comparison with the interwar years so much as with the official rhetoric of the years of growth when annual real increases were supposed to be the norm (Table 14).

14. Real earnings in industry (percentage increases, December of each year)[8]

	1965–72 (annual average)	1973	1974	1975	1976	1977	1978	1979	1980 (latest month)
United States	1.8	2.0	−3.2	−0.8	2.8	0.7	0.2	−4.6	−5.8
Canada	3.6	0.4	3.6	3.6	6.5	0.1	−1.7	−0.4	0.3
Japan	7.3	9.5	1.2	0.7	2.4	2.0	1.6	0.7	−0.6
West Germany	5.7	2.3	6.5	0.3	5.6	4.5	1.5	0.8	0.3
France	4.6	6.8	4.4	4.7	4.7	2.8	2.6	1.8	–
Britain	2.8	3.7	7.0	−3.4	−2.4	−0.8	5.9	1.6	0.3
Italy	7.2	11.7	−1.0	8.2	5.8	7.0	3.8	2.3	1.1

France and West Germany, it seemed, treated their industrial workers most favourably, although Italy and Japan were close behind. At the other extreme, there were four years – out of eight – in which American workers experienced a decline in real incomes, a quite substantial fall cumulatively in the last two years. Britain was only slightly better. There seemed little evidence to support the proposition that lower income increases would promote employment – the United States and Britain were both marked out not merely by the poor performance in terms of income growth, but by the relatively high levels of unemployment.

To the misery of growing unemployment and stagnating real incomes for those in work were added many other sources of anxiety and occasional panic. The international market place was filled with the din of squabbles between the major powers, interest rate wars and rows over exports and imports. Indeed, the imagery of trade disappeared before that of warfare in international economic matters. The dignified Europeans descended on all fours to insult the government of Japan, administering, they said, 'a nation of workaholics living in what Westerners regard as little better than rabbit hutches'.[9] As if, in capitalism, such eminent virtues were to be deplored.

Currency instability added a dimension to these surface phenomena which increased the unpredictability of policy. Inflation, despite the declines of 1978, came to symbolize the unmanageability of the managed economies. Each minor upturn in activity increasingly seemed to produce rapid price increases, so that the only method of effective price control was permanent slump. Furthermore, the inflation was establishing new relationships between different components of the world system, for the highest rates were now felt in the backward countries. The sparks lit in the core zones had become raging fires elsewhere (Table 15).

15. World inflation rates[10]

	1971–8 average p.a.	1977	1978	1979
More Developed Countries				
(M.D.C.s)	8.1	8.4	7.5	9.9
(primary producing M.D.C.s	13.5	18.1	17.3	20.0)
Less Developed Countries (L.D.C.s)	15.0	21.5	20.7	32.6
(non-oil-producing L.D.C.s	15.9	23.3	23.4	36.5)

The figures conceal the high performers, the tendency for the weaker Western manufacturing powers, Britain and the United States, to attain much higher rates than the stronger (Japan and West Germany). But even here, their rates were modest beside those of Brazil – from a rate of 42 per cent in 1976 to one of 83 per cent in 1980, and over 100 per cent in 1981.

Poor investment rates produced a cumulative decay in the capital stock which exaggerated the problem of inflation. Supply bottlenecks developed much earlier in any upturn, and the shortages pushed up domestic prices and sucked in imports to the weaker manufacturing powers, producing further ramifications in the external trade balance and the relative strength of currencies. The same sort of problem – poor investment – made raw materials especially subject to rapid price increases when world demand increased.

Inflation exaggerated other phenomena. In affecting currency values, high rates tended to push people out of holding cash into purchasing tangible assets, which in turn exaggerated the demand for goods and so produced further price increases. One effect was the increase in commodity prices as activity increased. The short-lived 1978 upturn produced rising commodity prices very quickly in the following year, the sharpest increase for five years. Food prices increased by nearly a fifth in 1979. The gold price – fixed at 35 U.S. dollars per ounce in 1970 – rose from 225 dollars in early 1979 to a peak of 835 dollars a year later. Investment in land and property tended also to be the outlet from the risks of holding currencies. One index of this was the uniform increase in house-buying (as a proportion of gross product) in most O.E.C.D. countries, followed by disproportionate increases in house prices. In the index of 1970:100, British house prices reached 400 in 1979 (when the Consumer Price Index was 300); the United States 240 (Price Index 180); and Japan about 300 (Price Index 215). An increased proportion of spending on houses and increased housing prices did not rule out a steady decline in new house-building – that is, houses changed hands with increasing speed to realize higher prices. British new housing starts in 1979 were 17 per cent below 1978, and the lowest level of starts for nearly thirty years.

The second slump, beginning in 1980, arrived in circumstances which seemed much less propitious than the first. Investment had stagnated for seven years. The brief upturns of 1976 and 1978 had gone no way to reviving heavy industry. Among the leading powers, the Japanese had performed the best, continuously upgrading and expanding their investment industries, so that, given the stagnation elsewhere, any expansion in the world system tended to be reflected disproportionately in increased imports from Japan more rapidly than elsewhere. The tendency was exaggerated by the increased appreciation of the value of the dollar – by March 1982, the effective exchange rate of the dollar was 22 per cent higher than at the end of 1980. This was partly a result of high interest rates in the United States (which were in turn the result of the U.S. government's high demand for funds – its deficit was equal in both 1981 and 1982 to about 40 per cent of American private savings – as the result of a rapid increase in defence spending while trying to hold down or reduce taxation), which sucked in funds from the rest of the world, drawing capital out of Japan, and so depressing the value of the yen and cheapening Japanese exports.

The burden of domestic and international debt, exacerbated by exceptionally high interest rates, dampened the capacity to buy and increased the proportion of national export revenues being returned to lenders to service and amortize loans (this took about a fifth of export receipts in 1981). The contraction of export revenue for the Less Developed Countries was vastly exaggerated by a collapse of commodity prices. The I.M.F. commodity price index fell 15 per cent between 1980 and 1981, the steepest fall in thirty years excluding 1975 (that is, in money terms; in real terms, the decline, about 10 per cent, took the index down to 6 per cent below the 1975 level, 'probably the lowest for any year during the postwar period' as the I.M.F. commented). This shrinkage of income – now no longer safeguarded by expanded international loans as the result of the declining creditworthiness of already heavily indebted borrowers – paralysed any expansion in world trade. For the Non-Oil Exporting Developing Countries which had saved the world economy after the first slump, the effects were severe; their imports had increased by about 8 per cent per year between 1977 and 1979; by 2 per cent in 1980, and 0.5 per cent in 1981, a figure which, given inflation, represented a sharp contraction (and the effect was maximized for the lowest income countries). The same problems afflicted the Centrally Planned Economies. For the Oil Exporting Countries, revenue shrank alarmingly (and debt burdens soared under the impact of high interest rates) as oil consumption in the industrialized countries contracted under the impact of slump. Thus, the More Developed Countries were no longer partially protected as they had been after the first slump by the buoyancy in demand for their exports from the rest of the world.

Furthermore, policy in the industrialized countries was now no longer directed at offsetting the impact of slump; indeed, policy exaggerated the downturn. From 1977, the O.E.C.D. governments in general abandoned efforts to use public expenditure as a means of stabilizing employment and incomes in the expectation that sustained growth would be resumed quickly. Now the central problems became, not unemployment, but inflation and the 'central rigidities' of the economic structure (the social expenditure budget and wages) which, it was said, prevented the reduction of labour costs to compensate for the fall in profits. Governments 'adjusted their expectations' from recovery to rationalization, and did so when mass electorates appeared for the first time since the 1950s thoroughly cowed by the scale of threatened disasters. The intimidation of actual or threatened unemployment, at least for the moment, curbed resistance. Governments moved at different speeds towards cutting the social wage (that is, the welfare, health and education components of public expenditure – while increasing the military and police components) and cutting real wages (by curbing money wages in conditions of rapid price increases, increasing taxes and other charges on wages, and by permitting unemployment to rise while output continued or expanded): in sum, cutting the real cost of the labour force of the industrialized countries closer to the average cost of the world labour force.

With excellent timing, Professor Milton Friedman was available to provide a proper rationale for these changes, and an elaborate justification for rejecting the thinker who, by accident, had become the prophet of the great boom, Lord Keynes. However, despite the messianic tone of the new ideology of governments, controlling national money supplies was as utopian as controlling systems of national production in an internationally integrated world. As the second slump progressed, governments increasingly chose to forget the wilder ambitions of Professor Friedman – and some even resorted to old-fashioned wage controls to batter the 'rigidities' (not only did New Zealand, Portugal and France reintroduce wage controls in 1982 – with Canada expected to follow suit – two pillars of financial orthodoxy, the Bank of International Settlements and the International Monetary Fund, declared themselves in favour of wage policies).

However, governments, perforce, had to learn to live with their inability to revive investment. In France, considerable concessions were offered to capital to expand, and the public sector was used deliberately to encourage this process; without success, for investment in real terms in 1979 was still below that of 1973. It might have been seen as a lesson that already the degree of international integration was so great that no individual national unit could revive investment domestically without restoring the world system as a whole. For the O.E.C.D. group, investment remained poor. Capacity was contracting, particularly in heavy industry, but even then, what there was could not be fully utilized. None of the major economies reached 95 per cent use of capacity in the years after 1973; the peak uses were usually around 85 to 88 per cent. As the second slump bit into the system, capacity use in the United States sank – in 1982 – to around 70 per cent (with 63 per cent in cars, 73 per cent in primary metals). Investment was flat or declining for four continuous years. By 1981, the steel industry – reaching an output of 100 million tonnes in 1979 – was producing about 78 million tonnes. And as capacity use declined, imports took an increasing share of the domestic market – 60 per cent in radio and television sets, 34 per cent in footwear, 44 per cent in textile machinery, 26 per cent in machine tools, 20 per cent in cars. American manufacturing seemed set for perpetual decline, driven on by the high dollar and so, cheaper imports.

The stagnation in investment entailed for many sectors and countries a depreciating capital stock. As a result, labour productivity necessarily also deteriorated. Capital per worker figures showed the losses (Table 16).

In the case of the United States and Britain, heirs in 1945 to an industrial structure still intact, and together with France military providers to the global political system of the 1950s and 60s, the picture was bleakest. In the British case, cumulative poor investment rates over a long period exaggerated the effects of world slump. Between peak and trough of changes in gross domestic product in the first slump (1973–5) there was a 4 per cent gap, and in industrial output, 9 per cent; in the second slump (or rather, between mid 1979 and mid 1981) the two

16. *Average annual rates of increase in capital per worker*

	(1) *1964–73*	(2) *1974–8*	(3) *Average per annum change between periods (1) and (2)*
United States	1.8	0.1	−1.7
West Germany	4.7	3.2	−1.5
Japan	8.9	3.5	−5.5
Britain	3.2	0.8	−2.4 (excluding oil)
France	4.5	3.0	−1.5
Italy	5.4	1.1	−4.3

equivalent figures were 6 per cent and a staggering 19 per cent (between 1929 and 1931, the decline in British industrial output was of the order of 11 per cent). In 1981, real pre-tax rates of return on capital (industry and commerce) reached their lowest recorded level, at 2.7 per cent. And if there were differences between countries, the differences within countries were even more extreme; between Northern Ireland or the Ruhr or Alsace-Lorraine and the prosperous zones. In Georgia, in March 1982, average weekly earnings were just under 257 dollars; in Michigan, 444 dollars; Georgian unemployment was, however, 7.7 per cent when Michigan's was 17 per cent.

The change of economic gear from boom to stagnation took time to affect the political climate. But by the end of the seventies, there seemed to have been a general move to the Right. This did not necessarily mean a change in governing political party, for frequently the old Leftish centre parties proved adept at moving the centre rightwards. In many countries, the old lynch-pin of the postwar *status quo*, an alliance between State and trade unions, was publicly abandoned in the face of lower real wages and increased unemployment.

Further out from the narrow circle of power, there were more quixotic manifestations of crisis. For a time, the extreme Right had a surprising revival. The Klansmen rode once again in middle America, exchanging compliments and insults with their European fellows, the Nazis and fascists. Anti-semitic outrages increased, as did violence upon black people and immigrants. In Japan the nationalist novelist, Mishima, whose suicide ten years earlier had embarrassed people, became a hero. In Germany the old nationalist student duelling fraternities, which had disappeared in the sixties, revived. The world had become a much more anxious place, and people reached for old gods with which to comfort themselves. In time some of the old gods emerged as public figures, leaders of the United States and Britain.

They were straws in the wind, accompanying a general counter-attack on the myths of 'the permissive society'. Apparently, education had been ruined by a collapse of standards and discipline; the world had become inhabited by 'scroungers' refusing to work and living off the State. Law and order now became the slogan for a retreat on many fronts, part of an attempt to reconstruct the tattered 'national identity' for troubled times. Questioning was not for a period of economic stagnation; slump required the symbols of an ugly chauvinism. The issues of immigration and import control summed up part of the economic destruction the State required to survive politically.

The central element in the stagnation of the period

The first slump fell upon an unsuspecting world. It is as if many factors had been accumulating unnoticed, until all combined to produce the abrupt change of direction. It has been suggested here that rates of investment in heavy industry had stagnated from the last half of the preceding decade in some of what were then the most important segments of world production – for example, European and American steel. The profit rate was already too low to induce an adequate flow of new investment; cumulative depreciation only compounded the problem, and finally gave new producers – pre-eminently Japan – such a lead that it was difficult to see how the gap could ever be closed. From the crisis in heavy industry, the problems spread to textiles, to consumer durables, to vehicles, to residential construction, from whence it returned to heavy industry with redoubled effect. By 1981 even electronics were floundering.

However, slump could only have the effect of restoring the profit rate if labour costs were radically cut and capital values could be collapsed – through bankruptcies, the writing-off of capital. There was some of both, but each competing national State endeavoured to protect its capacity for as long as possible, lest an upturn find it without the means to exploit a boom. No doubt there were also fears in government that their electorates would not accept, so soon after the rosy aspirations of the great boom and the myths of the managed economy, the required degree of pruning and unemployment. Thus the interests of the State collided with the interests of capital as an economic entity. Stagnation was the resulting compromise; investment stayed obstinately low.[11]

Slump affected most severely segments of old heavy industry – particularly steel and shipbuilding in the first instance, but later on, heavy engineering and machine tools. Problems were particularly acute where the industry was old – that is, where investment had not replaced equipment which by world standards was obsolete or obsolescent. In some cases, companies were caught at the same time with both old industries and spectacular debts, the result of ill-timed borrowing to upgrade equipment. At the other extreme, the Japanese, whose basic steel-making capacity had been created or upgraded in the sixties, increased their considerable lead on the rest. Japan's steel industry contracted, but profits and investment remained relatively buoyant. Gross investment figures for steel show, for example, that Japan's annual investment rose from 598 million dollars in 1960 to 3.6 billion in 1975, while Britain's moved from 409 million to 706 million and West Germany's from 270 to 682 million. What was a tolerable level of investment when world demand expanded rapidly – there was room for the output of both the most and the least efficient producers – became insupportable in slump.

By 1977 and 1978, contraction was at its most severe in the steel industry, and little alleviated by the upturn in activity as a whole. In Britain, the Steel Corporation made losses of £520 million in 1977 at a time when a full-scale rationalization programme was under way (54,000 jobs had been lost over the preceding decade). The Government had underpinned a major investment programme, promising £4.5 billion between 1973 and 1983. The 1973 Ten Year Plan was caught at precisely the wrong moment by declining demand and rising interest payments. The Plan entailed the concentration of production in five plants and the shedding of 85,000 workers. The Plan was further wrecked by the calculation of the Corporation that in 1976 it would be able to expand its share of an expanding market. In 1977, the Corporation could employ only 60 per cent of its capacity, even though, it was rumoured, it was dumping steel in the United States at below the costs of production. The brave targets – 30–35 million tonnes of steel by the early eighties – crumbled, to 20 and then 15 million tonnes; in 1980, the Corporation and its private rivals managed to make 11.3 million tonnes. By 1982, the talk was of 7.3 million tonnes, all that was needed to supply a car industry producing only half its 1972 output, a construction industry producing 60 per cent and a mechanical engineering industry, 75 per cent of the 1975 output. All this, with 120,000 fewer steelworkers.

British Steel was only one point on the map. Europe as a whole suffered elements of the same problems. By 1977, capacity was 198 million tonnes, and output 126 million. The combined losses – £2.5 billion – ranged from £10 to £40 per tonne of steel produced. Yet the industry had dropped 80,000 workers in four years, and had a stated target of shedding a further 150,000 by the eighties. Debts swamped some of the largest companies. In France, the cumulative debts just prior to the Government taking the industry over were 10 billion U.S. dollars-worth; in 1976, cumulative debts were 104 per cent of turnover. Again, capacity was slashed – from 34 to 28 million tonnes, and in 1982, to 24 million – with the loss of 60,000 jobs. In Belgium and Sweden, the governments also felt obliged to assume control of the industry. In West Germany, the cumulative losses were lower (roughly 625 million dollars), but there were more redundancies (30,000).

The Common Market endeavoured to curb the competition within Europe in order to raise prices, and so profits and, it was hoped, investment. To this end, a cartel, Eurofer, was organized to administer minimum steel prices, shared markets and discrimination against imports. It was still-born, for the unwillingness of the rivals and of governments to allow any possibility of a disproportionate decline of their share of the market, destroyed any chance of stable collaboration. No wonder there were doubts about the viability of any steel industry surviving. The future, some said, lay with the Less Developed Countries, where modern steel capacity still might make production profitable. West German Finance Minister Hans Matthöfer epitomized the pessimism of 1978: 'We are a high wage and high social security cost country. We will never be a mass steel-producing country again, nor a big textile or major shipbuilding country again either.'

Within Europe, each national producer endeavoured to dump steel abroad in order to keep up its use of capacity, thereby lowering the costs per tonne produced. High prices at home (provided imports were controlled) would subsidize low prices for exports. This was difficult within the Common Market because of the reduction in internal controls. Even where it was to some degree possible, it affected many other industries: vehicle-making companies, for example, demanded the right to import cheaper steel, in order to compete with cheaper vehicles made abroad (even the steel imported was sometimes exported from their own country of operation).

Outside the Common Market it was much easier, and the largest steel market in the world, in the United States, provided ideal opportunities for dumping. The American industry was in an even more threatened position than the European, particularly in periods when the value of the dollar rendered European steel relatively cheaper still. With a capacity of 159 million tonnes, the U.S. industry's output in 1977 was 102 million, and down to 78 million in 1981 (and an estimated 63 million for 1982, or 50 per cent capacity utilization). Since the middle of the preceding decade, roughly 120,000 workers had been laid off, yet still the major companies made heavy losses. Cumulative debts and poor returns curbed their capacity to borrow in order to finance new investment, on top of the problem of high interest rates. Thus, each upturn in the economy seemed only to produce an increase in the imports of steel, especially when the dollar was relatively high valued. Increasing controls on steel imports were the Government's response to threatened profits. The steelmen argued, as they do the world over, that restrictions should be introduced to 'save our jobs'.

The Japanese industry was the least affected. But in 1977–8, it was still operating at only 80 per cent of capacity (13 of its 66 blast furnaces were idle). The modernity of its basic equipment as well as sustained investment upgraded its means to produce, and lowered its unit costs. Although the figures used to identify this lead are frequently suspect, one report estimated that the steel output per worker in Japan was 400 tonnes per year, compared to an American figure of 250, a German of 225, and a British of 131. The saviour of the Japanese industry in the seventies was exports, which, because of the nature of the capacity employed, were less underpriced than those of its nearest rivals. By 1980, the Japanese industry was for the first time producing more steel than the United States. Nonetheless, the signs of other competitors approaching Japan were not lost on the Japanese steelmen: steel exports were emerging from Brazil and India, South Africa and Spain, Mexico and Taiwan, Poland and Romania.

The second slump broke upon a steel industry which had been unable to adjust to the first. Indeed, capacity had been increased, despite the much-proclaimed intention to reduce it. In the Common Market, crude steel capacity was increased 12 per cent between 1974 and 1980, to 200 million tonnes, when 1980 demand was about 130 million. Those pillars of European free trade, the West German steel companies, were reduced in 1981 to pleading for government subsidies. World steel output in 1980 fell by 4 per cent, but by 18.2 per cent in the United States. The temporary upward revaluation of the yen cut Japanese steel exports, rapidly increased stocks and then produced sharp cuts in output (in 1980, 70 per cent of Japanese capacity was utilized). The downturn occurred despite the race through 1980 to lay off workers. Over 100,000 steelworkers found themselves without work in 1980 in the O.E.C.D. countries, more than half of them in the United States.

The steel industry in the industrialized core zones of the system was an anvil on which to forge revival. But the ageing anvil crumbled under the blows. Steel companies responded in ways other than trying to improve the domestic industry. The larger ones became instruments for the redistribution of world steel capacity by setting up new plants in Less Developed Countries. No doubt they consoled themselves with the hope that, when the new capacity came on stream, perhaps the world would have resumed growth and there would be need for both old and new capacity. They needed consolation for the apparent irrationalities implicit in the organization of the world industry. The European States had robbed their population to keep open steel mills and to sack a large part of the steel workforce. Between 1960 and 1978, they spent 50 billion dollars in the endeavour to expand steel capacity from 111 million to 253 million tonnes, only to be defeated by world stagnation. Yet round the globe, the need for steel continued. The World Bank endlessly identified the problems of the rural poor; one of those problems was the shortage of steel for ploughs, agricultural implements, basic household goods. The steelmen saw only a 'glut' of steel, instead of the real underlying scarcity of steel.

At the other end of the relationship lay the problems of the economic devastation of former steel-making localities – in France's Alsace-Lorraine, Nord and Pas de Calais (half of those sacked were immigrant workers, so frequently the effect of lay-off was compounded by expulsion from France); in Germany's Saar and Ruhr; in Charleroi and Liège in Belgium; in Indiana and South Wales. The helots who had laboured loyally for generations amid the noise and grime of steel-making became, at the end, the sacrificial victims.

Steel was a symbol of the dying of one economic order. Coal, shipbuilding and heavy engineering were not far behind, and each dragged down the centres of the great boom, the vehicle industry. Textiles, in decline in employment terms in the industrialized countries through much of the long boom, accelerated its descent. The industry in the sixties was still Europe's largest employer (by industry), with nearly 3 million workers in 1978. In the seventies, West Germany shed over 100,000 textile jobs, and the attrition continued, compounding the decline of areas already qualifying as 'depressed'.

The explanations

The scientific cadre of Western society is large, well-funded and specialized. For such major changes in the life experience of thousands of people, one would expect there to be ready explanations. But economics is fascinating, not for its explanations, but for its lack of authoritative accounts of why major events take place. Wherever there are vital issues, the 'black holes' of non-explanation appear, and accounts disintegrate into guesses – more or less primitive – of this and that.

There were suggested explanations, but none that commanded universal support, and many that defied the evidence. What form did these explanations take? Some saw the sudden increase in oil prices as inflicting sustained deflation upon the industrial countries. Others maintained that public expenditure had grown to the point where the State drew out of the civil economy a volume of resources too large to make possible private profits: 'production' was sacrificed to 'unproductive' services. A longer-term view was presented – that a group of Less Developed Countries, the 'middle income' or 'newly industrializing' countries, were at last able to draw to themselves an increased share of some segments of the old industries of the core. For some, the slump was an accidental conjuncture, a coincidence of forces unlikely to be repeated. Theorists of 'long waves in economic life' identified disjunctures in technology; one phase of technological development had become exhausted, another had yet to develop on a scale sufficient to generate sustained world growth. And there were, further out, more moralistic accounts of the penalties that inevitably scourge greed; raw materials had been consumed with profligacy, and now were becoming exhausted; it was not, of course, necessarily a moral case, because there were others who genuinely believed that a finite end to 'resources' could be seen, and the world was approaching that point at just the time when its population had been expanded, new needs created, so that all demands could no longer be met.

The explanations do not exclude each other, and some may well have elements of truth. But most presupposed the propensity they sought to explain, the propensity to slump. Take, for example, the case on raw material scarcities. If there were a genuine supply limit, then raw material prices should increase persistently, instead of fluctuating; furthermore, the scarcities ought to generate an investment boom in the finding of new sources of old materials, and new substitutes for old materials. Such things have certainly happened in the history of the system. A 'resource' is what is identified as usable within the system, so the world has never had a finite 'resource base', only a *known* supply of resources at a given technology.

The same argument applies to the favourite explanation of the slump – that increasing oil prices have inflicted deflation on the world system. Furthermore, it is suggested that a cartel, O.P.E.C., 'held the world to ransom'. However, O.P.E.C. by the 1980s no longer provided the majority of the world's oil; indeed, between 1978 and 1982, three countries produced over half of the world's crude – the Soviet Union, the United States and Saudi Arabia. In any case, the increase in price ought to have spurred a boom in the search for new sources of oil and substitutes for oil. In fact the downturn in the world system began before the increase in oil prices. The specific weight of oil within the system is not self-evident, nor was the price increase, on some readings, of fundamental significance. If we take the long-term position, the real retail price of oil to buyers in the industrialized countries did not increase very much, and in some cases actually decreased (Table 17).

17. *Real retail price of oil (1973:100)*[12]

	1960	1970	1974	1975	1977	1978	1979
United States	115	102	121	119	117	113	137
Canada	112	104	105	108	113	110	111
Japan	–	99	120	120	112	95	107
West Germany	125	96	113	105	101	101	107
France	152	110	123	115	122	122	128
Britain	116	112	123	135	114	100	116
Italy	129	106	135	128	154	137	128

How did it arise that an oil price of one level in 1960 could be absorbed in boom, but could not be absorbed in the 1970s? Of course, there could be short-term shocks from an increase in the money price that occurred in 1974 and 1979, and there were severe problems in terms of the international payments of States. But it was difficult to see how this explained stagnation, except if we assume that there were other basic causes producing a condition in which increased oil prices had disproportionate effects. The problem was not to explain the straw that broke the camel's back – even if oil prices could be cast in that dramatic role – but the peculiar propensity of the camel's back to break.

Arguments about increases in public expenditure raised other sorts of difficulties. Public spending as a whole does not have any self-evident economic implication; indeed, a major part of it may be positive in its effects on profit rates of many sectors. Much of it, transfers, may be neutral in effect. The major increases in public spending came after slump, were the result of slump rather than a cause. And if we take as the cause the vast increase in the size of the State sector during the Second World War and immediately afterwards, we have the difficulty of explaining why this was supportable during the great boom, and insupportable towards its end. This is so unless we assume that there is some structural condition, some finite limit, to the shares of 'public' and 'private'. However, the mere existence of States which encompass all economic activity within the public domain would suggest this was not so. The distinction between public and private is unclear, and even if it could be clarified, its economic significance remains obscure. Juridical criteria have been substituted for economic ones.

The expansion of Less Developed countries' manufacturing output, dramatic though it was in the seventies, was still far too small as a proportion of the imports of the More Developed Countries, let alone final consumption, to explain slump or sustained stagnation. It might be *part* of an explanation of the difficulties of particular sectors – pre-eminently textiles, electronic goods, etc. – but not of the difficulties of the industrial core as a whole. The Third World manufacturing sector remained for the future, even at the end of the seventies, a trend rather than accomplished fact (this is discussed in a later chapter).

The thesis of a conjuncture of 'accidents' has a certain plausibility, but only if attention is restricted to the 1972–4 slump and the years immediately preceding it. Subsequent events have illustrated that when the coincidental features ceased to be effective, sustained growth has not been resumed. In any case, a vulnerability to accidents itself needs explanation. In earlier phases, the 'accidents' went unnoticed, thrown off by the robustness of economic expansion. The problem remains to explain the camel's back, rather than the straw that broke it.

Breaks in the development of technology are most difficult to assess simply because we cannot realistically measure technology. Innovations cannot be ordered by their quantitative significance, nor be attached to particular years of occurrence. The time when innovations are made technically is also quite often different from the time when they are employed economically, and it is the utilization of innovations which requires explanation rather than the technical breakthrough. Expenditure on research and development has, as we noted earlier, flagged, but that is as a result of poor profit prospects rather than the cause. The evidence on the bunching of innovations is too slight and too unquantitative to be an explanatory variable. In contrast to nineteenth-century industry, it could be argued that innovations have become institutionalized, thus smoothing out any breaks in development. The real problem is to explain why, in one period, innovations are utilized; in another, they are neglected. It concerns the 'propensity to invest': the willingness of investors to back an innovation, which is not simply a function of the technical quality of the innovation but of the profit prospects.

Explanations in society are not simply scientific responses to a problem.[13] They are weapons in a fight, the basis for praise and blame. It is for this reason that social science can contribute least where the social and political significance of the problem is greatest. The study of economies has its 'black holes', but they are not the blindness of economists so much as the blindness of the social order. For blindness serves its function too, protecting and defending a status quo.

Notes to Chapter 3

1. Karl Marx, letter to P. V. Annenkov, December 1846, in *Selected Correspondence of Karl Marx and Frederick Engels*, London, 1936, p. 9.

2. C. A. R. Crosland, *The Future of Socialism*, London, 1956.

3. Table 9 excludes South Africa and the Centrally Planned Economies. Table 8 is from U.S. Dept. of State, *Special Report* No. 41, March 1978 and I.M.F., *World Economic Outlook*, Washington, 1982, p. 143 (see note below); Table 9 from International Monetary Fund, *I.M.F. Survey*, 8 May 1978; selected from Table 1 in Economic Commission for Latin America, *Economic Survey of Latin America 1977*, United Nations, Santiago, Chile, 1978, and I.M.F., op. cit., p. 144. Note: I.M.F. figures (1978–82) are not strictly comparable to the earlier ones.

4. From Table 8 in Paul McCracken *et al.*, *Towards Full Employment and Price Stability*, O.E.C.D., Paris, June 1977, p. 175.

5. 'Managed imports' covers market-sharing agreements, quotas, anti-dumping duties, licences, certificates of origin or other administrative controls, price controls, but excludes tariffs, subsidies, patent rules, safety, health and other technical standards which may discriminate against imports. From Table 4A, in Sheila Page, 'The Management of International Trade,' in Robin Major, *Britain's Trade and Exchange-Rate Policy*, London, 1979.

6. Table V, in Robert A. MacNamara, *Address to the Board of Governors of the World Bank*, 30 September 1980, World Bank, Washington, 1980, p. 15.

7. I.M.F., op. cit., Table 6, p. 147.

8. Bank for International Settlements, *Fiftieth Annual Report* (1 April 1979 to 21 March 1980), B.I.S., Basle, 9 June 1980, p. 21.

9. Quoted from an official document of the European Economic Community, prepared as a background statement for talks between the European Commission and the Japanese Government, March 1979, report *Financial Times*, London, 9 April 1979, p. 29.

10. United Nations, *World Economic Survey, 1979–80*, United Nations, New York, 1980, p. 28.

11. .

Private non-residential fixed investment, rates of change

	1960–73	1973–9
United States	5.4	2.1
Japan	14.0	2.2
West Germany	4.6	2.7
France	7.5	1.1
Britain	4.3	1.6
Italy	4.9	−1.6
Canada	5.8	4.5

(Bank for International Settlements, *Fiftieth Annual Report*, op. cit., p. 55)

12. ibid., p. 51.

13. For a more comprehensive and systematic critique of theories of the crisis on the Left, cf. Chris Harman, 'Theories of the Crisis', *International Socialism* 9, Summer 1980, pp. 45–80, and 'Marx's Theory of Crisis and its Critics', ibid., 11, Winter 1981, pp. 30–71.

FOUR THE STATE AND CAPITAL

> One of the main themes that international economics has to teach
> about international relations is that most beliefs that motivate
> national policies are irrational, most of the alleged facts are not
> facts, and most of the alleged lessons of experience are the result
> of ignorance or falsification of the actual facts of experience.[1]

The slump of 1974–5 and the years that followed precipitated a number
of contradictory features in the world economy. The process of integration in terms of production was accelerated. For example, if we calculate
the proportion of imports and exports to total domestic production of
goods for Britain, the 1970 figures were 54 and 48 per cent respectively;
for 1979, the equivalent figures are 80 and 72 per cent. For the last year,
the figures for the major powers were: for Canada, 81 and 86 per cent;
for France, 52 and 51 per cent: for West Germany, 46 and 53 per cent;
and for the giant United States economy, 30 and under 25 per cent. The
ratios had nearly doubled in the 1970s.[2]

The figures revealed the degree of interdependence, yet simultaneously the States controlling the industrial core of the world system
endeavoured to increase their national economic independence to offset
the impact of downturn. This had been the reaction of States after the
crisis of the years 1929 to 1931. But the production system now – as
opposed to then – was far less susceptible to being reshaped in national
enclaves. Furthermore, the financial centralization of the system contradicted – indeed, nullified – many of the efforts of States to protect or
even administer their economies. Within the system, also, the centralization of finance and the redistribution of production covered not only the
industrial core; slump accelerated tendencies to redistribute part of
productive capacity well beyond the core.

Within the national village, beneath the umbrella of a State, the
villagers, by and large, sympathized with the efforts of the local State to
hold and expand the share of the world's industry which was located
within its borders, even though that effort – as mentioned in the last
chapter – tended to generalize lower profit rates to all. Now a properly
entrepreneurial State might have taken steps to rejig the relationship of
labour costs to capital values, by cutting the first and bankrupting part of
the second. It could, for example, seek to substitute cheap imported
labour for expensive native workers; or substitute cheap imported
manufactured inputs for expensive domestic supplies, so rendering

cheaper its own exports. But the State could do so only in certain limited areas, for its own political credibility was at stake. The need for political stability collided with the economic needs of both national and international capitalism.

Meanwhile, rates of investment remained immovably low. Debts accumulated to daunting levels, producing a periodic frisson of terror that default might begin a process of pulling down the temple of finance capital. Rates of technical innovation declined, so improvements in productivity also fell away. Stocks were held at very low levels to minimize costs when interest rates were high – but, as a result, there were no cushions to offset fluctuations, and increases in demand only more swiftly reached the limits of supply. Equipment users moved away from purchasing new machines to leasing old – equipment hiring firms boomed, equipment sellers stagnated.

Many of these features were shared by all States. In so far as they were equally shared, all could have tolerated slump. But implicit in the stresses was a redistribution of power between States. No one was quite sure what the correct symbols of this redistribution were, the correct measures of relative power, but such a tiresome methodological quibble consoled no one who felt they were being robbed. Figures were tossed on the wind of panic. At the Halewood plant of British Ford, the management said, it took forty-seven hours to build an Escort car in 1977; at the Cologne plant, eighteen hours. The yen capital per worker in vehicle manufacture in Japan was said to be 4.7 million; for General Motors, 2.1 million, and for British Leyland, 0.7 million. British Leyland was said to operate at a quarter of the productivity of Japanese plants, which were being re-equipped to double productivity in the following five years; thus, Leyland workers would have to increase output per worker eight times over to equal their Japanese brothers. Who knew how truthful the figures were? The facts were part of the din, the noise of intimidation launched at respective workforces to persuade them to continue or to increase their efforts: no other world was possible except one where the majority must be devoted to destroying each other's livelihood.

The year 1980 seemed to epitomize the increasing differentiation between what States saw as their respective performances. In that year, the manufacturing exports of the Less Developed Countries – running at 14 per cent of their total exports in 1960, and 26 per cent in 1975 – equalled their non-manufacturing exports. In that year Japan, which had produced 32,000 cars in 1956, overtook the United States in size of output – its 11 million vehicle production was 40 per cent more than the American. It produced more steel than the United States, and took fully half the new shipbuilding orders in the world. For a time, given the wobbling exchange rates between dollar and yen, Japanese income per head roughly equalled the American.

One year's swallow did not make it the spring of the epoch. But from the tunnel vision perspective of States, it could have seemed as if a momentous year was passing, equal to that time in the 1890s when German and American steel output overtook the British and began the process of conquering the British Empire. But the share of world manufacturing located within the borders of the United States was only one criterion of status. There were others of possibly greater significance for the power of Washington, if not necessarily for the welfare of that portion of the world's people subject to its direct rule. After all, U.S.-registered companies spanned the globe; they were even a part, albeit a small one, of that very 'Japanese threat'. American banks controlled the largest single 'national' chunk of world finance. The American State commanded overwhelmingly the largest part of the world's means to kill, as well as the largest part of the tradeable means to live, agricultural production.

Nonetheless, a balanced assessment of strengths and weaknesses was not politically useful in sustaining popular panic that foreigners were eating away at the national patrimony. The connection between vehicles put together in Japan and the massive losses of U.S. motor companies was one of those 'self-evident' matters that usually conceal falsehoods. In 1980, General Motors lost 763 million dollars, the first loss of that size since the twenties; Ford broke all records for corporate losses in the United States with a 1.5 billion dollar loss, only to be overtaken a week later by Chrysler with 1.7 billion dollars (American Motors, the fourth, was more modest at 197.5 million dollars). By contrast, Toyota – which with Nissan overtook Ford in total output in 1980, becoming second and third largest world producers – declared a profit of 1.25 billion dollars. Toyota expanded its output from 1979's 2.9 million vehicles to 1980's 3.3 million, as General Motors contracted by more than a quarter to 4.7 million; the Japanese company was approaching the point of overtaking G.M. as the world's largest vehicle-maker. No doubt the Americans would have made even larger losses if they had not dispensed with the services of possibly half a million of their workers.

The competition of States dominated the stage. But behind the noise, there were other features which tended to become obscured in the gut reactions. First, the shaping of the competition between States, the ways in which each imposed upon the other the same responses, and in combination, ensured that stagnation and slump continued. Second, the effect of the growth of debt, and third, the integration of capital. We take each in turn.

The States

In the golden age of capitalism, the distinction between the activities associated with the State, 'public', and those of capital, 'private', seemed clear-cut. Ownership seemed unequivocal, as did the incumbent rights and duties which flowed from it. By the 1970s – and indeed, much earlier – while the old protagonists in the political arena, Right and Left, still argued as if the distinction were clear, it had ceased to be so. The State funded large parts of what was supposed to be 'private' business, and private business accepted the obligation to perform a vast array of supposedly public tasks (not least, where taxes were deducted 'at source', that of tax collector). Nationalization might be deplored, but everywhere conservatives and social democrats alike appropriated industries. Activities where the State had a majority interest were most often indistinguishable in behaviour from private corporations; some State corporations were indeed 'multinationals'. It was central banks who were major speculators on the Eurocurrency market, producing part of the fluctuations in exchange rates which they then, in their official guises, deplored; the O.E.C.D. central banks solemnly agreed not to speculate in 1971, and reaffirmed their decision in 1979; but it was the British and Italian central banks which placed their large Eurodollar lendings back in the Euromarket in order to maximize their revenues. On all sides, the market massaged all institutions into a common form.

States reacted to crises they saw as 'external' by efforts to hold capital and to bribe capital abroad to locate activities within their territory. Governments usually claimed that these efforts were devoted to protecting or increasing local employment levels; but the sums involved were so great and the employment impact frequently so trivial, it could not be so – unless we assume that the officials making the decisions were utterly foolish. The drive was to retain or capture part of the world's productive system regardless of whether employment rose or fell.

The elements of warfare between States followed no coherent pattern – frequently the activities of one hand contradicted those of the other. Furthermore, each action tended to set in train courses of events with unpredictable consequences which might indeed be negative for the State that began the sequence. Competition in domestic interest rates to offset exchange rate fluctuations conjured flows of finance from Riyadh to Frankfurt, to New York and back again, leaving a trail of wrecked exchange rates which in turn transformed the relative prices of traded commodities. The manic-depressive cycle of vehicle exports from Japan frequently had more to do with the arbitrary changes in the dollar–yen exchange rate than any intrinsic virtues of the goods. The index of yen values (December 1971:100) varied from over 150 in mid 1978 to 115 at the end of 1979, sucking cars out of Japan at very varying rates. On the other ocean, a decline of the dollar imposed a 'threat' of cheap American textiles on the Europeans.

The areas of competition were not stable. Of course, exports and imports remained a continuing preoccupation. But each time a conclave of governments agreed to measures designed to order their affairs, to reduce ambiguity and room to manoeuvre, a new area of contest appeared. In the late seventies, for example, the arena of subsidized export credit suddenly became an issue of economic warfare. In 1978, an international agreement between twenty-two of the O.E.C.D. powers sought to lay down binding rules to prevent States competing in the degree of subsidy contributed to exports directly – covering insurance guarantees, subsidized loans, insurances against inflation, exchange risks, country risks, etc. But it scarcely affected the growing volume of export credit – by 1980, 39 per cent of Japanese, 35 per cent of British, 34 per cent of French, and 18 per cent of United States exports depended upon State funding; the State financial institutions concerned had become major elements in the trading network, with an increasing number of bad debts to cover (the U.S. Ex-Im Bank made its first losses in 1980, and the French Banque Française du Commerce Extérieur and the associated insurance agency doubled their pay-outs). Nor did the agreement govern aid budgets, so virtually all governments began to use official aid programmes as a substitute for export credit – from late 1980, all major powers were competing to offer soft loans to Less Developed Countries with which they could purchase exports from the donor power. For example, the British and West German Governments offered loans and export credits to the Indian Government to construct a new steel plant, half of the output of which was to be exported under the terms of the agreement (at the same time as the two donor powers were bitterly complaining of 'excess capacity' in the world steel industry). The French used a lavishly extravagant aid budget to persuade Delhi to drop its contract to import over 100 Jaguar fighter aircraft from Britain (a deal also secured through the use of the aid budget) and take up one for the French Mirage instead. The aid budget permitted many different variations in terms not of the interest rate charged, but of the period of repayment – and on large projects, it was frequently the repayment period which was a key element in the auction between different donor

States. Perforce, governments returned to negotiation, and in June 1982 produced another agreement, to last one year. The United States, the main force seeking to control the competitive greed of its rivals, forced an increase in rates of interest on preferential credit, making the Eastern Bloc countries subject to rates governing the Western industrialized countries, and stiffened the terms for Middle Income Developing Countries. But few nourished the hope that this agreement would prove more effective than its predecessors in combating the ingenuity of governments defeating the spirit of an open trading system.

Domestically, States endeavoured to use public funds to increase profit rates. One area for this activity was taxation – either reducing taxation, rendering official taxation merely nominal, or tolerating the legal activities of companies in evading taxation. U.S. Congressman Charles Vanick, in his annual review of U.S.-registered companies paying little or no taxes, noted in 1978 that seventeen of America's largest corporations paid no tax at all (the list included the five largest steel companies, General Dynamics, American and Eastern Airlines, Chase Manhattan Bank, Singer and Phelps Dodge); forty-one others paid in tax under 10 per cent of their world income (Mobil paid 4.5 per cent; Exxon, the world's largest industrial corporation, paid 8 per cent; Gulf 7 per cent; and A.T. and T. 9.5 per cent). A British study produced similar results – the largest companies either paid no tax (and this included Allied Breweries, Bowater, British Leyland, British Petroleum, Courtaulds, Dunlop, Esso, Ford, Grand Metropolitan, G.K.N., P. and O., Reed International, and Rio Tinto Zinc) or very little. The U.S. study showed a steady decline in tax payments over the preceding five years; the British study suggested that the 'mainstream tax' yield on all industrial and commercial companies declined from £1.5 billion in 1969 (about a fifth of all tax revenue collected by the Board of Inland Revenue) to some £101 million in 1975 (or 0.5 per cent of tax revenue).[8] Households made up the difference.

This decline in tax payments was not simply the result of the generosity of the State. Companies became more adept at escaping taxation as a result of the relative internationalization of activities. In particular, international companies employed overseas tax havens to avoid payments. The United States Commerce Department calculated that the value of U.S. company operations in tax havens overseas grew disproportionately faster than all U.S. company activities abroad in the seventies. On an index of 1968:100, tax haven operations by U.S.-registered companies reached 500 a decade later, compared to all other overseas activities at 270 (and an earnings index for the same period reached 900 and 350 respectively). Governments endeavoured to prevent what they saw as the transfer of profits, but without notable success. The same problem arose within the United States, where Vermont and Wisconsin, for example, sued a clutch of international companies before the Supreme Court on the grounds of tax evasion.

The network of State funding to business reached a level of complexity which made it impossible to assess as a whole. Nor was it possible to identify any agreed 'national interest' that guided decisions. The British Government funded a supposedly 'American' corporation in 1975 to the tune of £162 million, only to have Chrysler's European assets purchased by a supposedly 'French' corporation, Peugeot. Volvo, a supposedly Swedish company, negotiated for a large part of its assets to be purchased by Norway. Renault, a company owned by the French Government, reappeared across the Atlantic as heir to a private corporation, American Motors. Nor was it only in the earlier period or Social Democratic governments; despite protestations of reformed virtue, the British Conservative Government in mid 1982 was considering public funding for a Finnish paper mill in Shotton, North Wales, equivalent to £159,000 per job created.

The criteria were constantly ambiguous – States reacted in one way or its opposite on quite obscure grounds. For example, the French Government was supposedly opposed to 'foreign' acquisition of assets located in France, even when this was within the Common Market. The French State dragooned two locally registered companies, Thomson and C.G.E., to counter a takeover bid by the British registered company, Thorn, for Locatel (just as the French Government was spurring, and no doubt funding, Thomson to purchase electronic companies outside France). But the French Government wooed Ford to build a new engine plant in Alsace-Lorraine; it was Renault and Peugeot who were active in attempting to foil the proposal. They were similarly energetic in protesting at the deal between British Leyland and Honda which permitted manufacture in Britain of a 'Japanese' car; the Italians were sufficiently incensed to seize the first shipment of Leyland's Triumph Acclaim car to Italy in the spring of 1982 on the grounds that only 60 per cent of the vehicle's value was contributed by European-based manufacture; British Leyland countered by saying 70 per cent of the 'ex-factory price' was European produced; others in Britain said that the car was only 20 per cent European produced. Whatever the figures, it did not stop British car manufacturers protesting vigorously when Mitsubishi Australia announced the export to Britain of the first 12,000 of its cars, each one of them 85 per cent locally manufactured.

Others joined the fray, each company infinitely careless of the employment implications of their efforts to defend privileged markets.

Fiat in Italy protested against Nissan's purchase of the Spanish truck manufacturing company, Motor Iberica (Spain then being a candidate for membership of the Common Market); to a deal between Nissan and Alfa Romeo for joint car production; and to an Innocenti proposal to import engines from Japan. There were no doubt 'American' companies on both sides of the Atlantic opposing imports, which would include their own products as exports. In Britain, local television companies (most of them, in fact, assembling imported components from the Far East) successfully blocked a proposed Hitachi factory in the north-east of the country. I.C.I. endeavoured to prevent Dow Chemicals of the United States building capacity in Scotland. The conceptual confusions were symbolized in a proposal that the British Government should fund roughly half the cost of building car manufacturing capacity for Nissan–Datsun in Britain, just after it had agreed to a renewal grant of £1 billion to the State-owned British Leyland; *The Times* editorial (30 January 1981) was headed 'Datsun within the Walls'. In the event, Nissan called off, and the British motor industry was blamed for pressing the Government to set the terms for the investment too high; Ford of Britain, ever patriotic in the defence of its profits, maintained that a Japanese car maker in Britain would force British car companies to buy their components from cheaper sources in Japan, and 30,000 jobs would be lost in the British component industry.

In world shipbuilding – like the picture in steel examined in the last chapter – State intervention was extreme. All governments offered subsidies, and sacked massively. The British nationalized the industry; the Swedes took over some three-quarters of capacity to shoulder the private debts. The British subsidized ship prices by some 25 per cent, and engaged in special deals which were an endless source of losses; some £68 million was said to have been lost on the building of twenty-four ships for Poland in 1977. The Swedish Government introduced a complex scheme whereby the 'domestic buyer' (as if this were a clearly identifiable creature) had to meet initially no more than 5 per cent of the purchase price. The French Government set up a fund to subsidize selling prices by between 15 and 20 per cent (with an additional grant of 15 per cent for 'domestic' buyers). The Bundesrepublik permitted 'domestic' buyers to reclaim 17.5 per cent of the purchase price. The Japanese Government offered to shipbuilding companies cheap government credit – the volume of funds rose from 75 million dollars in 1971 to 700 million in 1976 – and, like the British, intervened to arrange special deals; for example, it loaned the Pakistan Government 45 million dollars over thirty years (at a rate of interest of 3 per cent per year, not payable for the first ten years) to purchase six cargo vessels; it also initiated the merger of companies in order to 'reallocate overhead costs' to cut ship selling prices. By 1980, despite major cuts in capacity, there was still no end in sight – European shipyards had built only 23 per cent of the world's output, a drop of 10 per cent on 1979 (world demand for ships dropped 8.3 per cent). The European shipbuilding employers followed the current fashion and blamed the Japanese for increasing their share of the world market – from 33 to 47 per cent in 1980 (and thus, they said, breaking the market sharing agreement of 1976 which had aimed to cut the capacity of the industrialized countries – O.E.C.D., including Japan – to some 39 per cent in that year). But the Europeans measured the world market in volume not values; the Japanese countered by saying the Europeans had a much higher share of the high-value ship market, that it was Japanese shipowners who were the largest buyers in the world, and that what expansion there had been had come from Japan's traditional markets in the Far East (particularly, Hong Kong). Furthermore, as Japan had cut its capacity in line with the European recommendation, new shipbuilding powers in the Less Developed Countries had expanded their share from 16 to 34 per cent – O.E.C.D. 'restraint' had not at all solved the problem of excess capacity, it had merely opened the way for others to replace the O.E.C.D.

The rights and wrongs of world shipbuilding were not of great substance. For all were equally self-righteous in deploring the compromise of principle – whether the principle was that of free trade or of cartel organization – and equally dishonest in cheating each other. Even if they might be more virtuous in the field of shipbuilding, they were less so in other fields – in steel, for example. Or in coal: the West German Government in 1978 introduced a four-year investment programme worth DM582 million annually, to finance an enormous increase in coal stocks – with measures of tax concession, limits on imports, giving mines priority in power supply, increases in taxes on heating oil, and preferential finance for coking coal. There was no logic in restricting attention to one industry – 'fairness' could not operate within that narrow compass. But there was hardly any way of putting together all the bits of apparently unrelated concession and subsidy to assess who was the freest trader of all.

There was equal obscurity over the competitive auction between States to attract new capital from abroad. The formal rituals of the 'managed economy' – whether limitations on the speed and safety of work, or on the principle that profit ought to be the net return earned on the capitalist's capital (as opposed to his political skill in milking the State) – were all subject to negotiation. Capital itself quickly appreciated the returns available from organizing an auction for its favours. For example, Ford Europe deliberately trailed its coat before successive European governments in order to stimulate their rivalries in offering concessions for a new car plant. Indeed, it laid down a minimum 'asking price' – a subsidy of 35 per cent of the proposed investment of 450 million dollars, exemption from duties due on imported equipment, subsidies for training the workforce, cuts in local taxes, guaranteed infrastructural provision, and loans at preferential interest rates from State banks. 'This is how one big company's careful gamesmanship', *The Economist* commented, 'shows up the structure of grants, loans, tax holidays, interest subsidies and other promises and caresses that underlie so much of Western Europe's big investment schemes these days' (29 January 1979, p. 73). For Ford's Bridgend engine plant – costing £180 million – the company was originally said to have recouped some £100 million from the British Government, or roughly £35,000 per job created in terms of public assistance; subsequently, it emerged that the British Government had contributed £140 million to the final costs of the plant, or 78 per cent of the total investment.

Ford's was only one case among many. In Britain, the De Lorean motor plant in Northern Ireland had by 1980 cost the Exchequer some £30,000 per job, only to collapse in due course. A Courtaulds textile mill at Campsie, Londonderry, received a contribution from the Government of £21.9 million (the total investment was £38.3 million) – or, as the House of Commons Public Accounts Committee noted, £28,000 per job. For a Hoffman–La Roche vitamin C manufacturing plant built in Scotland, the Government continued to increase its bid to offset the attractions of other locations in Europe until it reached an estimated £100,000 per job in public support. Nissan set an auction going with its proposal to build a vehicle plant in Britain. An unseemly scramble ensued between the authorities of twelve potential sites; the State in one form or another was due to meet about half of the proposed £300 million total outlay. There was no way of telling whether the deal – a net transfer from consumption to business investment – made any long-term economic sense; as the *Financial Times* observed on the Hoffman–La Roche project: 'Whether they [the Government] raised their selective bid more than they needed to may never be known. In Whitehall yesterday they seemed sure they had achieved a considerable coup' (17 October 1978).

Governments felt constrained by the competition with each other to bid as high as possible. The British publicly bemoaned the level of Irish grants. Britain was said to have lost a £40 million microchip plant to the Irish Republic by not exceeding Eire's offer of development grants – 'up to 50 per cent on capital spending and to guarantee that profits on exports will be exempted from all taxes until 1990' (ibid., 5 April 1979). Although it was international investment which received the most attention, in principle domestic investment operated in much the same way. For example, in the United States, individual States set up a comparable market to attract investment from each other. Delaware passed a special Financial Centre Development Act in 1980 to lure banks away from New York. It is said that two New York banks, Chase Manhattan and Morgan Guaranty, drafted the bill in a form especially favourable to banks – taxes were to start at 8.7 per cent and fall to 2.7 per cent when profits exceeded 30 million dollars; there was to be no ceiling on interest rates (as existed in many other States), and the rules of operation heavily favoured the banks as opposed to users (that is, which party covers banking costs, whether the banks have rights to foreclose on outstanding loans, etc.). The two banks saw the bill as a method of forcing New York State to cut the 12 per cent State tax and 13.8 per cent city tax. The move in part imposed on all States the need to go as far as they could to match Delaware's terms if they wished to hold what they had or increase their share. Nor was this simply domestic competition. A U.S. Chamber of Commerce study listed European incentives to business, 500 in all, which then became part of the standard within the United States, all being bound into a single system by the market.

The gifts people offered capital were not expected to induce gratitude. On the contrary, people were expected to feel grateful if their gifts were accepted, and by and large, they were. When the Chairman of the Irish Development Authority spoke at the ceremony of laying the stone of a spinning mill, established in Wexford by the West German Nino A.G. of Nordhorn, he epitomized this spirit:

> The plans for this expansion here in Wexford not only depend on the state of the economy, but also on how much you people here in Wexford are willing to cooperate with this undertaking. You should regard yourself as fortunate in having a company like this here ... you should also bear in mind that we are competing with many other countries in the world to obtain new industries ... we have to convince the investor that he is going to find himself in surroundings which will let him succeed.

The Chairman also noted that the company 'had no difficulty in convincing the influential Church that Nino ought to work twenty-four hours a day, seven days a week; this means a four-shift operation, with a total of 168 hours per week. By contrast, the plant could only be worked with three shifts in Nordhorn, giving 120 hours a week, or 126 at most without overtime.'[4]

Direct funding to new capital was only one instrument. Old capital endlessly pressured States to protect them against imports. Agriculture had always been tightly controlled in Europe, the United States and Japan. Textiles and garments were added in Europe in the 1960s through the Multi Fibre Arrangement. Thereafter, whether explicit or not, endless petty restrictions were introduced at different times to impede trade, particularly on steel, fertilizers, shoes, soya oil, cars and so on. A favourite means to evade the G.A.T.T. rules on free trade was 'voluntary restraint'. A government would threaten to suspend imports from a particular exporting country unless it accepted a 'voluntary' quota. Thus, the British forced South Korea and Singapore to limit the export of electronic products to Britain. The United States endlessly resorted to the same tactic – on chemical and farm products, special steels, television sets and, in 1981, Japanese cars. If only foreigners would raise their prices or lower the quality of their goods, all would be well and there would be 'orderly marketing'. Of course, it was not a matter of substance for the American Government, a pillar of competitive enterprise, that each negotiation with other governments forced local companies to collaborate in meeting the American demand, forced cartelization and the restraint of competition.

In the late seventies, the cases under study at the European Commission rose steadily. The Italians shut two-thirds of their customs posts to block steel imports from their European partners. The French were suddenly afflicted by amazing delays in processing the import applications for Japanese cars (as the Japanese replied: they were not the source of increasing car imports into France, but rather Volkswagen and Fiat). The din of complaints increased with the restrictions – the British complained that their vehicle exports were impeded, that Italy blocked British television imports (because they were alleged to be from a 'Japanese' factory in Britain); the West Germans, that the French restricted drug, textile and electrical equipment imports; the Italians, that the French prevented furniture and wood imports; the British, that the West Germans restricted beer and spirit imports; the West Germans, that the Italians blocked vinegar imports. And so on, a bedlam of claims and counter-claims.

It was the politics of import controls that were important, the constant emphasis that the State protected its citizens – by forcing prices up. Endlessly, the popular wisdom was inundated with the argument that, if local industry weakened, this was not the result of the failures of local capital, but of 'unfair' competition. The foreigners had low wages, it was said, as if punishing the poor for their poverty and trying to ensure they could do nothing to ameliorate that condition was a valid answer. There was enough evidence available to show that unemployment could rarely be attributed to increased imports. A West German study suggested that three times as many jobs were lost as a result of modernization of the textile industry as from increased imports (garment imports from the Less Developed Countries took only 8 per cent of the German market in the period of study, 1962–75); for West German manufacturing as a whole the ratio was one job lost through increased imports for every forty-eight lost through rationalization.[5]

In any case, import controls did no more than shift the problem from one sector to another. The British coal industry might secure a ban on the import of Australian or American coal, but its major customer, the British Steel Corporation, would then argue that, with resulting prices of British coal so high, it could not compete in steel production. In mid 1980, British Steel argued that the National Coal Board coal price added £30 million to its (then) £400 million loss each year. British Steel also complained that imported steel in 1980 took 25 per cent of the market in Britain – British prices of, for example, hot rolled steel coil were said to be £190 per tonne in comparison to West Germany's £150 and Bulgaria's £135. But in reply, yet a third State-owned corporation, British Leyland, argued that unless it were permitted to buy steel wherever it was cheapest, it would be unable to compete in vehicle prices with imports, nor to export. Whatever the deficit, it seemed bound to appear in one or other corporation; import controls would merely shift it from one to the other. And if it were not car manufacturers complaining at high steel prices, then it was shipbuilding, machine tools or construction. Staunching one wound only opened dozens more.

Nor were import controls practical in another sense. Take, by way of illustration, the clash between the governments of Britain and Indonesia. In mid 1980, the Indonesian Government requested an increase in its quota for textile exports to Britain under the terms of the Multi Fibre Arrangement. Indonesian exports to Britain the year before had been worth some £60 million (of which textiles were £10 million); British exports to Indonesia, £90 million. The British Government countered with a demand for a reduction of Indonesia's textile quota on the grounds that Djakarta had exceeded it and required restraining. In retaliation, the Indonesian Government took steps to cancel contracts for imports from Britain valued at £150 million, covering chemical plant, oil equipment, Hawker-Siddeley passenger aircraft, radar equipment, British Leyland buses, steel bridges and so on. Thus, protection in textile imports, denying Indonesia the capacity to earn export revenue with which to buy British exports, now threatened sundry other sectors, some of which would entail increased State funding of its own loss-making corporations. In the event, the British Government was persuaded that to lose £150 million in order to save a couple of million pounds on textile imports was unwise; it permitted an increase in the Indonesian textile quota.

Import controls had another function, as was demonstrated in the heyday of protectionism in the 1930s. The largest companies endeavoured to organize domestic and world markets by cartel arrangements with their nearest rivals. There was no possibility of organizing the international market without the dominant local company controlling its domestic market. Import controls were a precondition for effective international cartels as well as domestic monopoly.

In like fashion, trade restraints had another – unintended – result, for they forced cartelization on other trading powers. Japan could not 'restrain' its exports fo, say, the United States, without constructing an organizational mechanism to control Japanese exporters. Thus, in crisis, 'managed national capitalism' endeavoured to reproduce segments of managed international capitalism. To no avail, for the international market was not to be mastered by simple organizational tricks; there were now too many competitors to control. Cartels could at best operate only on a regional basis, and therefore, were intrinsically unstable.

Nonetheless, there was a fashion for cartels. O.P.E.C. was only the most famous, and even there, was fissured by the rivalries of its members and by the fact that it initially controlled only 60 per cent of oil supplies (and under 50 per cent from 1981). But it did produce an attempted cartelization of its richer customers, the International Energy Authority; again, however, this could not curb the rivalries of its members. The Europeans tried to manage chemicals, man-made fibres, reinforced steel bars, and steel itself. Japanese petrochemical companies pleaded for a cartel in 1982. The United States endeavoured to corral all grain exporters in one organization, but succeeded only with the U.S.–Canada Wheat Board. No one trusted anyone else sufficiently; no organization could encompass enough of capacity, and no world authority could exercise sanctions over rebels. Even within Europe, the European Commission might decree that no more public finance should go to new oil refinery facilities in order to reduce capacity, but the British Government refused to lose the opportunity of capturing an increased share of the future European refined oil market by ending its 40 per cent funding of the new Nigg Bay refinery. And who could blame it when Spain, in the same spirit, refused to limit the expansion of its steel capacity?

In the middle of 1982, all the issues threatened to explode simultaneously in what the press identified as a 'trade war'. The Europeans bitterly complained that American interest rates had wiped out the possibility of the revival of profits and investment; that the high valued dollar nullified part of their efforts to stem inflation; that the wilful American defence policy was forcing increased defence spending on the Europeans and jeopardizing valuable markets and outlets for loans in Eastern Europe (on which the Europeans depended much more heavily than the Americans). The Americans endeavoured to block steel imports from Europe (imposing a 40 per cent countervailing duty on the exports of the ailing British Steel Corporation to the States), protested to G.A.T.T. at Europe's subsidized agricultural exports, and imposed an embargo on the use of American manufactured or licensed parts in the contracts signed by European firms with the Soviet Union for a giant Siberian pipeline. The Europeans protested at the inconsistency of Washington's approach to Moscow when the Americans were simultaneously seeking massive grain export contracts to Russia; and in their turn, formally complained to G.A.T.T. that the United States subsidized exports through its Disc system (claiming 2 billion dollars compensation for 'excess' American imports to Europe). There were many more complaints, slights real and imagined, as each participant scrabbled to grab what could be grabbed. But all were united in turning upon the hapless Japanese. The Americans demanded access to the Japanese market for agricultural exports; the Europeans demanded – and then tried to block, by means fair and foul – Japanese investment in Europe to replace Japanese exports to Europe. The cacophony became deafening, reflecting a severe stretching of the seams of a global economy as States struggled against the web capital had woven around them.

Whatever the efforts made, whatever the increased subsidization of capital or reduction of real labour costs, it did not restore the boom. Despite all the lavish funding, controlled contraction of capacity in the core industrial zones, fixed prices and market sharing, the massive job losses in heavy industry and textiles, at best the fluctuations of the process of stagnation were smoothed. What continually robbed the best laid plans of serious effect – whether at the level of prestigious Summit conferences of the leading industrial powers, the repetitive meetings of the International Monetary Fund, the Bank of International Settlements, or the sundry agencies of the United Nations, or at the level of a cartel – was the market, a genuinely independent international master of all. The market was not a controlling mind, but the accidental and unpredictable outcome of tens of thousands of decisions. The world market massaged the plasticine of world activity into infinitely varied forms, and that it should continue to do so was the precondition of the survival of the economic power of States, even if that fact contradicted the pretensions of national political power.

The debt world

We noted in the last chapter how the rise of the Eurocurrency market – a private market outside the control of either any individual State or the collective of States – broke the Bretton Woods monetary system. It was one aspect of the re-establishment of private power over the pretensions of the territorial State. The competition of banks inevitably led them to try to minimize costs. One of the costs was the local charges levied by governments. Governments could be persuaded to give 'their' banks an advantage over those abroad by relieving them of charges; this was part of the process whereby the City of London captured such a large share of the Eurocurrency market. However, the moment the privilege was secure for external transactions, it tended to roll back into domestic banking, blurring the distinction between external and internal. If banks had an incentive to go 'offshore' to escape charges, governments were then under pressure to decontrol domestic deposits or, as the New York authorities conceded, to create domestic 'free banking zones' in the existing bank area so that the current share of world banking transactions could be preserved.

By the end of 1979, the Euromarket gross assets were valued at 1,600 billion U.S. dollars,[6] a sum larger than the combined reserves of the O.E.C.D. group. The interpenetration of domestic and international finance meant that the interacting pool of liquidity was even greater than this. Furthermore, there was evidence that many markets had become fused in that of international finance in the 1970s – commodities, silver, soya-beans, equities and currencies tended increasingly to interact, with funds flowing rapidly between all activities.

If markets became fused, financial companies lost their specific role in a particular market. Financial survival required operation in all markets. Thus, if company ownership had become depersonalized (the private shareholder was a declining species), companies were tending to become unspecific. Lending companies moved between all segments of activity, from banking to retailing merchandise, to manufacturing or running an airline. The conglomerate, bound in unity by no technical need, only a common direction and loyalty, was becoming much more characteristic of capital.

Eurocurrency activity was only one phase of 'offshore' finance. Like Delaware's bid within the United States, many localities tried to capture a larger share of offshore banking by offering special privileges to finance – some of the Caribbean islands (the Bahamas, the Cayman Islands, Barbados, Bermuda, Netherlands Antilles and New Hebrides), Bahrain, Panama, Singapore and Hong Kong. The liabilities and claims of these activities were estimated at about 140–150 billion U.S. dollars in December 1979, some 12 to 14 per cent of the financial activities reported officially.[7]

We should note in passing – the topic will be discussed more fully later – that offshore banking was only part of offshore activities. There was a growing sector of 'offshore' production – export processing zones, free trade zones, 'In Bond Plants', and even at least two 'free cities', Hong Kong and Singapore. There were 'flags of convenience' and a whole array of other 'anomalies' in terms of national power. The world had produced a sector operating outside national boundaries or in areas where States had volunteered to suspend the operation of their normal prerogatives. To service such zones, there was 'offshore' capital, permanently suspended in limbo as it were between territorial units. And there was even 'offshore labour', international migrants, some of them perhaps travelling on 'passports of convenience'.

The growth of international finance was also the growth of international debt. And parallel with that growth was the increase in domestic debt. The system purchased an extension of its existence, an additional lease on life, by borrowing. It was not simply a matter of the growing burden of debt on States, public authorities and corporations, on companies, but also what the I.M.F. called the 'dangerously rising trend of household indebtedness'[8] in the United States. Between 1975 and 1978, consumer credit in the U.S. increased 49 per cent, mortgage debt by 54 per cent, corporate debt by 36 per cent, and government debt by one third. In the longer-term picture, total net borrowing (by businesses, farms, banks, consumers and government) increased from 38.5 billion dollars (or 8 per cent of the gross national product) in 1960 to 378.3 billion dollars (or 18 per cent) in 1977. With the new government of President Reagan, defence spending increased public borrowing dramatically – some 4,300 dollars per second of 1982. At that time, it was estimated that the American public deficit would rise to 200 billion dollars by the mid 1980s.

High American interest rates compounded the problems, both by increasing the charges on companies and farms, and in international terms, contracting markets by reducing world liquidity (non-bank capital was sucked into the United States in search of high interest, without a matching outflow; a process reflected in declining official reserves elsewhere in the world). International rates – the London Interbank Lending Rate (L.I.B.O.R., the benchmark for international lending), with the preferential rate for sovereign borrowers (that is governments) moved as follows:

	L.I.B.O.R.	Preferential rate
1972	5.46	5.23
1978	8.73	9.25
1981	16.38	18.92
(3rd quarter of 1981:	18.44	20.17)

At the highest levels, cumulative debt totals expanded very rapidly as borrowers tried to increase their borrowing to cover inflated interest payments as well as amortize their debts. Thus, the debt of Mexico escalated with great speed – from 60 billion dollars in mid 1981 to an estimated 83 billion dollars at the end of 1982.

The bankers became increasingly alarmed at the possibility of default, even though interest rates began to fall somewhat in mid 1982. There were rumours that the banks considered up to 200 billion dollars of the cumulative 4–500 billion dollars L.D.C. debt outstanding in 1982 to be 'doubtful', and particular fears attached to East European borrowing (some 80 billion dollars in 1981) and those of Latin America (220 billion dollars). The fears discouraged new lending, producing fierce 'liquidity crises' both for governments and companies. The increase in international lending – running at 101 billion dollars in the last quarter of 1981 – dropped to 38.6 billion in the first three months of 1982. European banks swiftly curtailed lending to Eastern Europe following the military coup in Poland, hitting the Comecon sharply. They were obliged to impose sharp cuts in imports (so importing slump to their domestic economies), run down official reserves and deposits overseas, and increase their exports – the Soviet Union pushed down prices in the gas and gold markets by offloading supplies at cut prices when the markets were glutted.

The effect of debt was to centralize an increasing part of the system – from household to State – on financial markets, to impose on all borrowers a common discipline which was ultimately a function of the competitive outcome of the world market. Thus, in principle, the cumulative debts of, say, New York City in the mid seventies, of British Leyland in the late seventies, of those of Zaire or Brazil, were no different. The borrower was painfully aware of the discipline forcing a reduction in 'consumption'. But the lender was also disciplined by the need not to bankrupt his client lest thereby he lose all; lenders were obliged, at least for a time, to continue lending lest the borrower default, and where a default was large enough, not only threaten the financial survival of the lender but administer a shock which would cause a general collapse of the financial system. President Ford was firm and self-righteous in refusing further Federal loans to New York City until it was discovered that New York, like Brazil, had acquired through its borrowings an extraordinarily dangerous potential to wreck the banks; 546 American banks, it was found, had holdings of New York City bonds equal to 20 per cent of their assets. In an analogous manner the British Prime Minister, Mrs Thatcher, discovered it cheaper to extend further funding to British Leyland since that cost was much lower than that of bankrupting the corporation.

Companies, faced with declining profit rates and therefore declining real equity values, were also pushed in the doors of the bank. Between the mid sixties and mid seventies, for companies the ratio of equity to debt changed in most industrialized countries – from 1 to 1.5 to 1 to 2.2 in France; from 2.5 to over 3 in West Germany; from 4 to 5.5 in Japan; 0.9 to 1.2 in Britain, and 0.6 to 0.9 in the United States.[9] Much of the debt was borrowed for short periods – the nervous bankers tried to guard the security of their loans by extending them only temporarily; but the result was much higher costs of borrowing. When interest rates simultaneously rose rapidly, company finance was doubly burdened.

The sharp increases in interest rates – part of the 'interest rate war' between States – caught a number of companies and corporations in the rapid increase in cumulative debt servicing. The payment of interest replaced oil as the biggest worry of managers and, as they saw it, the heaviest burden of profits. The American corporate net interest bill climbed from 45 billion dollars in 1979 to 56 billion in 1980 and possibly 65 billion in 1981. In a contracting market, companies were hammered between rising interest payments and declining sales revenue, a problem made worse by a relative decline in inflation (in contrast to the seventies when rising inflation lowered the real burden of past borrowing). In the first half of 1982, the number of American bankruptcies exceeded the whole of 1980, a rise of 44 per cent in comparison to the first half of 1981 (in Britain, there was a 32 per cent increase, in West Germany 22 per cent). The failures particularly hit construction, some services, farm machinery and tractors (the indebted farmers refrained from buying), airlines and vehicles. Chrysler, at least for the moment, survived. Braniff International Airlines and Laker succumbed. Sea Containers were obliged to sell off a third of their fleet. Massey Ferguson and International Harvesters teetered on the brink, as did West Germany's giant A.E.G.-Telefunken. Mexico's Alfa Group, the largest in Latin America, defaulted on its 2.5 billion dollar borrowings.

Banks and governments were urged to save the lame ducks, and often they did. But the lessons of the seventies were partly that help for the one failing increased the problems for those left – assistance to Massey Ferguson and International Harvesters jeopardized John Deere; help to Chrysler increased the possibility of failure in Ford or General Motors. But the lessons were not always convincing when there seemed a chance that foreigners might have to take the rap. The Europeans tended to try to continue, as they had before, to secure the survival of 'their' companies. In the seventies, the Italian Government had been the most energetic in pursuing this course. The problems of ailing public corporations, in particular, dominated economic discussion; public corporation debt forced on the Government servicing burdens that pushed up the scale of public borrowing to unprecedented heights – the 1979 public sector borrowing requirement reached some 18 per cent of the Italian gross domestic product, an estimated 65 per cent of the credit officially available in the country. Governments could and did escape some of these problems by diverting borrowers to the international market; something like a third of international lending in the late seventies was to public corporations. But what was saved in terms of the Government's accounts was lost by yet further integration of domestic and international finance.

In 1982, some of the financial institutions themselves came in for hammering, vindicating the fears of the bankers that underlay the contraction in lending. Penn Square of Oklahoma went under, and Banco Ambrosiano of Milan likewise (its chairman, Roberto Calvi, was found hanging from Blackfriars Bridge in London in June). Drysdale Government Securities on Wall Street wiped out the quarterly profits of Chase Manhattan. The failure of Abdullah Saleh al Rajhi's in Saudi Arabia afflicted a flock of foreign banks that had loaned it cash – Midland Kredietbank of Belgium, National Westminster, Lloyds, the Bangkok Bank. There were fears for the Bank of Nova Scotia (the fiftieth largest in the world), for the West German trade union owned Bank für Gemeinwirtschaft (seventy-third) in the world), caught in the decline of A.E.G.-Telefunken, and for Continental Illinois (sixth largest bank in the United States). The miracle was that the failures did not spread more widely to pull down the international financial system (the fears also attached to the possible default of a sovereign borrower), for some 40 per cent of the big banks' international deposits were redeposited with other international banks: the failure of one could easily pull down all.

The competition between banks increasingly spread their activities into each other's base areas. This was part of the explanation for the unprecedented extension of European banking activities in the United States. The reverse process was equally important, particularly for

Britain, where, in the early eighties, banking was the most profitable in the world. Just under half of the total bank assets in Britain in 1979 were those of banks registered abroad. For Belgium the equivalent figure was 43 per cent; for Switzerland, 37 per cent, and for Canada, 34 per cent. By contrast, the figures for France, the United States, West Germany and Japan were respectively 18, 18, 10 and 3 per cent.[10]

Another way to approach the same question is to note the sustained increases in overseas activities by banks, and in particular the growth of third party activity – that is, banks handling not 'domestic to international' activities but 'international to international', or those between other countries and the international market. The U.S.-registered banks led the way in the early seventies, fuelled by the recycled dollars of the O.P.E.C. powers which tended to flow through dollar-based agencies. In the second half of the seventies, U.S. bank loans to the leading twelve Less Developed Countries (1976–9) increased by about 17 per cent per year (to a total of 40 billion dollars), but non-U.S. bank loans to the same countries increased by about 42 per cent per year (to 48 billion dollars). At its peak, the largest U.S. banks came to earn a disproportionate share of their income abroad – for example, in 1976 and 1977, Citibank had some 63 per cent of its current loans abroad, earning 72 per cent of its current profits in 1976 and 82 per cent in 1977. U.S. bank lending became increasingly constrained by the growing risks entailed in its earlier extension. The Europeans then had an opportunity to move in. Britain's Barclays and Lloyds launched themselves as multinational banks, and became for a time the first and second largest commercial banks operating in the world. West German banks – beginning with the first overseas branch in 1967 (that of Dresdner in Luxemburg) – had by 1979 reached the stage where, for seven of the top ten banks, between 25 and 40 per cent of their profits derived from activities abroad (five deriving a third or more of their earnings internationally).

Part of the other side of the coin was the growth of cumulative indebtedness. The Less Developed Countries and the Eastern Bloc attracted most attention in this respect. For the oil-importing Less Developed Countries, the deficit on current account tended to continue rising throughout the decade, with sharp increases towards the end as the second round of oil price increases arrived – from 8.3 billion dollars in 1970, 39.6 billion in 1975 and 61–68 billion in 1980. The gap in external trade was covered increasingly by commercial borrowing. In fact, borrowing capacity is contingent on the commercial viability of a country, its 'creditworthiness', a combined assessment of national reserves, existing debt, capacity to export and propensity to import, etc. Thus, the debt burden could never be a problem of the Less Developed

Countries as a whole – for the majority, their creditworthiness does not permit extensive borrowing. Since 1971, three-quarters of all Eurocurrency lending to the Less Developed oil-importing countries has been to six countries – Argentina, Brazil, Mexico, South Korea, Peru, and the Philippines. Turkey and Poland joined this select group later in the decade. The cumulative debts of the largest borrower, Mexico, were put in the early 1980s at over 80 billion dollars.

It is the burden of servicing cumulative debts which causes most alarm to the financiers. 'Servicing' means the annual payment of interest and repayment of those loans falling due in that year. That burden tends to shift radically with interest rate changes, but overall it is expected to become of greatest difficulty in the first half of the eighties. For interest payments alone, the leading twelve Less Developed Countries were paying some 10 per cent of their export earnings in 1979, and an estimated 16 per cent in 1981. It is at this point that the danger of default arises – the State concerned cannot meet the payments, and as a result, its creditworthiness ends, it is no longer able to secure imports nor can it obtain credit for exports. Default occurred at various times in Zaire, Peru, Argentina, North Korea, Indonesia, Turkey, Poland and Sudan. To maximize the receipt of foreign exchange in order to service loans, governments are driven to try to cut domestic consumption and imports as much as possible in favour of exports. This may precipitate domestic resistance to cuts in consumption, particularly where part of the population is scarcely much above subsistence. In 1980, battles in Poland, South Korea, Bolivia, Brazil, Jamaica and Senegal were all interwoven in the attempts of the governments concerned to escape the implications of high external debts.

Credit is available in one special form – loans from the International Monetary Fund. But for those close to default, that usually entails conditions in terms of domestic policy; unless the conditions are fulfilled, the loans are withheld. Most governments seek to avoid recourse to the I.M.F., since it involves relinquishing a major and strategic element in their power over their population.

The real value of the cumulative debt is lightened by continuing high rates of inflation. Even if the burden increases in absolute terms, it can be lightened relatively if revenue increases from exports, other external transactions, or official aid from overseas. Nonetheless, cumulative debt as a proportion of the combined gross national products of the oil-importing Less Developed Countries increased between 1974 and 1980 from 13 to 17 per cent. The burden became heaviest at just the time of the onset of the second slump, just the time when Western governments were seeking to deflate their domestic economies together – so cutting the demand for the exports of the Less Developed Countries – and seeking, by fair and foul means, to cut their imports. In sum, this offloaded the burden of increasing balance of payments deficits – derived in part from the increase in oil prices – from the industrialized countries to the oil-importing Less Developed.[11]

Increasing debt in the system entails increasing financial centralization of all activities and increasing vulnerability of all sectors to a failure in one. A strike of car workers in São Paulo which looks as if it might set off a general rebellion against Brazil's military rulers, a general strike in New York (as some bankers predicted in 1975), the assassination of South Korea's dictator and riots in Gwang-ju, that unpredictable conjuncture between personal biography, clique politics, local class interest, and the vulnerable networks of a world system, can set off panics which oblige a major bank to 'close its doors', a misleadingly homely phrase for the financial nightmare when everybody calls in their loans. All the fine words of statesmen then are lost on the wind of panic.

The movement of capital

The period of slump and stagnation was marked by a remarkable increase in the movement of capital. The proposition must be treated with care, for the statistical support is less than adequate. A United States House of Representatives subcommittee, discussing the Federal Government's research on the foreign ownership of American assets, might complain that it was 'so inadequate, so disjointed and poorly implemented that federal estimates of the total amount of foreign direct investment constitute little more than guesswork', but it was a most unfair comment. The nationality of capital was not at all a clear notion. Asset and equity ownership, local borrowing and capital movements, sales dependence and profit source, even personnel, were too complex a matter from which to derive the simplicity of a loyalty to a particular State. Did the Shah of Iran's purchase of 25 per cent of the share capital of Friedrich Krupp Huethenwerke, 25 per cent of Friedrich Krupp Gmbh, or 40 per cent of the two giant Krupp subsidiaries in Brazil, make Krupp an 'Iranian' company? Did the 34 per cent holding of General Motors in the Japanese vehicle building company, Isuzu, make Isuzu's exports to the United States 'American'? Did the link between Honda and British Leyland and with South Africa's United Car and Diesel Distributors (itself owned 25 per cent by Daimler-Benz) to manufacture the same car (the 'Ballade' in South Africa, the 'Triumph-Acclaim' in Britain) give the output a new nationality? Companies registered in three separate countries could own 25 per cent of the assets in a company in a fourth, and each could claim, on some of the statistics, ownership of the entire company for their capital abroad.

Perception from the national village was a betrayal of the truth. Ownership might seem a tangible criterion, linking the identity of the villager and abstractions in the world. Persons, in general, did 'belong' to countries. But companies increasingly did not. They did not belong to the mass of shareholders any more than to particular countries. They were guided by the imperatives of corporate survival – just like States – in a world market, not by residual sentiments of loyalty to particular patches of territory.

The reality did not affect the conditioned reflexes within the national village. Italy refused to admit 'British' television imports because they were manufactured in Britain by a 'Japanese' company; for its part, the British Government made the Queen's Award for contributions to British exports to a 'Japanese' company manufacturing in Britain. In the Common Market there were learned disputes about what proportion of components in a finished product should have been manufactured in Europe in order for the final article to be counted as 'European': disputes not dissimilar perhaps to those in the legal departments of the Nazi Government of Germany in the thirties, when it was required to frame a legislative distinction between 'Jew' and 'Aryan'. Meanwhile, the complexity proliferated endlessly. A Swiss holding company with a majority share of a West German manufacturing company turned out to be controlled from New York by agents who, in turn, were acting for companies in Saudi Arabia and Brazil, which were part subsidiaries of intermediaries registered in the Cayman Islands, the largest owners of which were insurance companies and pension funds in Sweden and Britain, and so on and so on – as if the world system were one single garment, and to pull one thread unwove the whole of the world capital.

Periodically, the complexities would emerge to startle those accustomed to unequivocal nationality. The British Department of Trade was asked to make an inquiry in order to identify who was secretly purchasing shares in the British tyre company, Dunlop Holdings (Dunlop estimated that some 28 to 30 per cent of its equity had been purchased). The trail led to a Mr Ghafer Baba, a Malaysian, holding nominally 17.5 per cent of Dunlop equity. But Mr Baba was no more than a nominee for others, and there was no way of penetrating the darkness beyond him. As the Department commented, 'It is ... both usual and inevitable for these nominee companies to have no knowledge of whom the beneficial owners for the time being are.'[12] In fact, the piece of paper constituting 'ownership' was no more than a medium of exchange, swapping hands like banknotes. Who held what shares was, for much of the time, of no importance; it was a claim on future earnings, not a right to management, nor an indication of nationality.

The same problems concerned the 'multinational corporation'. The concept was clear – a company with integrated production processes spanning more than one country – but there was no way in practice of identifying the totality of such companies, nor of deducing the likely behaviour of such businesses according to where their head office was registered. The statistics covered only – in a confusing variety of definitions – 'foreign ownership' (the definitions ranged from 100 to 10 per cent of the assets owned by a 'foreign' company, which might turn out to be the subsidiary of a native company). There was no economic logic in separating companies with foreign subsidiaries from companies integrated in production with independent companies abroad. Only the need for loyalty by the State demanded that the diversity of reality be pressed through the eye of the national needle.

However, if we suspend disbelief in the invalidity of the concept, and look at the figures produced, there does seem to have been increased movement of capital, an increased internationalization coincident with or precipitated by the stagnation of the seventies. The annual direct investment overseas by 'U.S.-registered' companies gently increased from around 3 billion dollars in the early sixties to 5 billion at the end of the decade and 7 billion in the early seventies; from there it rose to between 11 and 16 billion dollars after 1973, producing a cumulative total (recorded book values) of about 214 billion dollars, compared to the 66 billion foreigners invested in the United States. The high value of the dollar encouraged an outflow, but high interest rates sucked funds into the country – 1981 was the first year for thirty years when foreign investment in the U.S. exceeded American investment overseas (18.6 billion dollars compared to 7 billion). British investment overseas, cumulatively the second largest, followed a comparable pattern – drifting upwards to between £600 and £700 million in the early seventies, before 'taking off' to around £2 billion in the late seventies (see the chart opposite). The abolition of exchange controls and the disastrous profit levels in Britain accelerated the growth – by 1981, £10.7 billion left the country, three-quarters of it for the United States (the inflow dropped from £2.6 billion in 1980 to £1 billion). French and Dutch overseas investment conformed to the same pattern. West German investment abroad – running at between DM 1.5 and 3.5 billion in the second half of the sixties, rose in the second half of the seventies to around DM6–7 billion (in dollar terms, an increase from 650 million to 3 billion dollars).

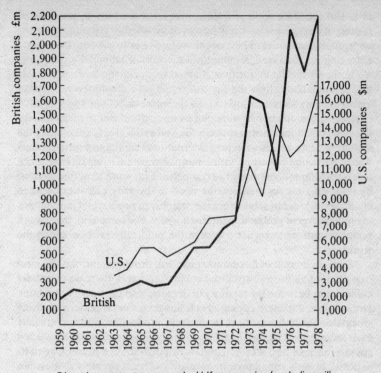

*Direct investment overseas by U.K. companies (excluding oil),
and U.S. companies (including oil)
Current values, £m and $m*

Sources: Department of Trade Overseas Transactions (*Business Monitor* M4, Overseas Transactions); U.S. Department of Commerce, *Survey of Current Business*, various issues.

It was not clear how much of this movement was the purchase of existing assets as opposed to the creation of new ones. Nor how much of it was directed at expanding world productive capacity rather than merely the profits of a particular company. For car buyers, there is no reason in principle why plants in Japan should not manufacture all the world's cars if they can be produced there more cheaply (and for those addicted to competition, the rivalry between Japanese car manufacturing companies is at least as great as that between them and car-making companies abroad). Indeed, the world's non-Japanese assembly workers might well be tempted to rejoice if Japanese workers volunteered to assume responsibility for the frenetic tedium of this particular task. But the State seeks to hold a diversified structure of activities, to protect its economic self-reliance even when this entails supporting unprofitable activities. The State therefore tries to prevent the market enforcing a specialized geographical division of labour. Furthermore, while the lot of the majority is chained to work, and work is the sole means available to live, the fight to retain jobs of whatever character seems to many – wrongly – to conjoin the interests of State and workers.

Restrictions on imports were one factor in the dispersal of capital, the dispersal of manufacturing capacity, as well as the great expansion in the system of State bribes to induce international capital to locate production in particular countries. Other motives were changing relative profit levels in different countries, the competitive pressure to minimize costs by relocating nearer markets, the need to diversify activities between countries in order to achieve greater stability of profits, and the continuing integration of production internationally. For some also, there was a political motive: to secure assets in the politically safest areas of the world.

Japan, by reason of its peculiar historical development, was the most 'national' of all the industrialized countries; that is, there was a greater coincidence between the territory of the State and the activity of capital. Nonetheless, Japanese capital also followed a similar pattern of diversification. Direct investment in overseas production did not officially exist in the sixties (it was illegal up to the early seventies), after which it rose to reach some 3.4 billion dollars in 1975–6. As a percentage of its exports, Japan's cumulative investment overseas (in all activities, not simply production facilities) was roughly 27 per cent of the value of its external trade, as compared to, say, Britain's, which was 88 per cent. Furthermore, most of the investment overseas was in trading and banking which, at least initially, was intimately associated with servicing Japanese exports. About a third of Japan's overseas investment in the second half of the seventies was in manufacturing facilities (as compared to three-quarters for West Germany). In the seventies also, Japan's overseas investment was strongly affected by its much greater relative dependence upon imported raw materials and the need to secure safe supplies. Nonetheless, the scale of overseas investment began to rise rapidly (Table 18).

Within the 1979 total, 17.5 per cent represented direct investment in manufacturing facilities abroad. The figure considerably underestimated the acquisition of assets in many fields, for the investment was heavily concentrated in certain sectors. For example, in the production of electronic goods, the movement has been considerable. By 1980, the six largest 'Japanese' television manufacturing companies produced 3 million sets in the United States, an output total larger than the number of sets exported from Japan in the peak year for such exports, 1976 (when the U.S. Government imposed restrictions on television imports from Japan). About a quarter of U.S. television manufacturing capacity is now owned by subsidiaries of companies registered in Japan. The same phenomenon is becoming true for amplifiers and other 'audio equipment', microwave ovens, semi-conductors, video cassettes, etc.

18. *Japan: Long-term capital exports*[13]
average annual value, U.S. dollars

1965–70	:	1.243 billion
1971–5	:	4.635 billion
1976–8	:	8.218 billion
1978	:	14.837 billion
1979	:	16.605 billion

By 1982, the cumulative total of Japanese overseas investment was in the second rank of industrialized countries – about 25–30 billion dollars, on a par with West Germany and Switzerland. About a quarter each of this investment was in the United States and Asia, 17 per cent in Latin America and 12 per cent in Europe (and in terms of countries, the United States was the most important with 8.9 billion dollars, followed by Indonesia, 4.4 billion; Brazil, 2.9 billion; just over 2 billion each in Australia and Britain; and then around 1 billion each in South Korea, Hong Kong, Saudi Arabia, Ireland, Singapore, Canada and Mexico). There was a rapid increase in 1981–2, reaching a record outflow of 8.9 billion dollars. Import controls in the main markets for Japanese exports as well as attempts to safeguard exclusive raw material supplies were factors forcing the pace. In the first case, there was some measure of international diversification of Japanese car-making facilities taking place; Nissan was undertaking important investments in 1982 in Mexico, Australia, United States, India, the Philippines and Taiwan.

The picture was complicated further by joint ventures between Japanese and foreign registered companies – for example, as between Rediffusion and Sharp, G.E.C. and Hitachi, Thorn and Victor of Matsushita. There are also a large number of 'Original Equipment Manufacturer' contracts whereby foreign companies sell goods produced in Japan (or imported to Japan from other sites in the Far East) under their own brand labels. Thus, one of the leading West German audio-television manufacturing companies takes more than 50 per cent of its components from Japanese sources, selling the output as West German made. The leading U.S. manufacturers in the field of audio equipment (amplifiers, tape decks, stereos) actually manufacture only a few per cent of the 20 million items produced each year. The flow is not simply in one direction, as we shall see – foreign investment in Japan is rising, and Japanese imports of components are becoming increasingly important. Nonetheless, the dispersal of manufacturing facilities is proceeding, now affecting motor car manufacture – with Honda building a plant in Ohio, Nissan setting up a truck building base in the United States (shortly after the Federal Government announced an increase in the tariff on imported pick-up trucks – from 4 to 25 per cent) and in Europe.

It was the giant United States market which provided the most important destination for capital movement in the late seventies. And if the American 'raiding' of European assets in the sixties produced a nationalist protest by Servan-Schreiber, the same thing happened in the United States when European capital began 'raiding' twelve years later[14]. The movement reflected rising American restrictions on imports, but also the fact that European and Japanese companies had for the first time attained a size capable of competing with their giant American rivals. Between 1959 and 1976, European companies secured representation in terms of the top twelve companies in the world in nine of the thirteen major industrial groups, and Japan in eight of the thirteen.[15]

The decline in the relative value of the dollar in the seventies considerably cheapened American assets – a 50 million dollar U.S. company would have cost DM 183 million to buy in 1970, but DM 123 million in 1980. American wages declined in relative terms; between 1970 and 1979, the increase in U.S. labour costs was a fifth of the increase in Japanese labour costs, a quarter of West Germany's and half that of Britain. Furthermore, American States learned to bribe like their formerly weaker European brethren, with the signal advantage that they could not only match the gifts but could also give access to overwhelmingly the largest single market in the world, to the maximum economies of scale, and to those sectors of technology where the United States was ahead of its rivals. In the States of the South, there was the additional advantage that trade unions were weak, much weaker certainly than anywhere in Europe; there were weaker controls over safety at work and over hours worked, fewer restrictions on the time for which machinery could be operated. Finally, the United States offered locations at furthest remove from the Soviet Union, bounded by the largest and best equipped armed forces in the world.

It is hardly surprising, therefore, that two-thirds of the world's largest 500 companies should choose to compete in the American market. Indeed, for international capital, whether its owners were by origin

British or Italian or Indian or Brazilian or Iranian, the United States remained home.

Some 69 per cent of foreign investment in the United States was by companies registered in Europe. The shares changed over time – the British share, a third in 1950, fell to 18 per cent; the Canadian, from 29 to 13 per cent; the Dutch rose from 10 to 24 per cent; the West Germans increased rapidly, to reach nearly 10 per cent, the Swiss 6 per cent and the French 4 per cent (by 1979). The flows did not reflect the cumulative shares. Of all foreign investment in the United States, the British remained the leading – with a 1979 value of 16.9 billion dollars; they were followed by Hong Kong interests at 15.9 billion; France at 5 billion; a 'European Consortium' at 4.7 billion; and Brazil at 4.5 billion.

A survey of the assets of foreign companies in the United States put their total value at 131.5 billion dollars, or some 2–3 per cent of U.S. corporate assets. The gross sales of these subsidiaries was put at 182 billion, and their U.S. employment at some 2 per cent of the American labour force (they also owned 0.5 per cent of U.S. farmland). A third of this 1979 total was involved in manufacturing – particularly chemicals (including oil), and engineering (metals and general machinery); another important share was involved in services, hotels and restaurants. In the late seventies, it was the growth in foreign ownership of banking assets that evoked most public excitement – with the largest takeover in U.S. financial history, the Hong Kong and Shanghai Bank's bid for the thirteenth largest bank in the country, Marine Midland of New York, followed by an even larger one, the British Midland Bank's bid for Crocker National Bank. The 'foreign' share of U.S. commercial banking assets was about 6 per cent in 1979, covering 20 per cent of corporate lending (but 35 per cent in California, 42 per cent in New York).

The process of the acquisition of assets or activities overseas was not simply restricted to companies in the industrialized core of the world. In the late seventies, a series of companies in Less Developed Countries began the same development. Korean companies built giant projects in Kuwait, Ecuador, Portugal and the Philippines. Taiwan-registered companies built steel capacity in Nigeria and the Philippines. Tatas of India successfully bid against international companies for contracts to build soda ash plants in Argentina and Malaysia. Hong Kong's Stelux took over the American Bulova Watch Company. In Fortune's listing of the top 500 companies in the world, there were thirty-three registered in Less Developed Countries. They still had a small share, but nonetheless the process of international diversification had begun.

The same was true, on a much smaller scale, of companies whose original home lay in the Eastern Bloc. There were some 500 of these operating within the OECD group in the 1970s, most of them servicing the exports and external financial activities of Eastern Bloc countries. Of the 500, only twenty-two are reported as engaged in manufacturing and assembly abroad.[16] One of them, however, achieved some notoriety as a multinational bank, the Moscow Narodny, when it was caught like so many of its rivals involved in property and company speculation in Singapore.[17] In manufacturing, in so far as restrictions on imports developed in O.E.C.D. countries, there would be no alternative for such companies but to locate manufacturing facilities abroad to sustain hard currency earnings (from repatriated profits rather than export sales). But that was for the future.

There were different stages and rhythms of the process of integration. Britain, as a result of its imperial past one of the most 'international' of the leading powers, was integrated most thoroughly. Japan – and also France – less so, and the respective States varied in their reactions to the process. Nonetheless, the pressures were severe to render integration uniform. Japanese capital was obliged to diversify abroad in order to escape controls on its exports. It was further obliged to open its domestic patch to foreign entry as the condition for its capital securing entry to countries abroad. The restrictions on foreign acquisition were slowly unwound, assisted in the late seventies by the Government's search for O.P.E.C. funds to stabilize the value of the yen and cover external deficits. In electronics, the foreigners endeavoured to locate in Japan precisely to secure access to Japanese technology and management. Texas Instruments – starting production in Japan in the sixties – had four manufacturing plants there by the early eighties. It was then that five American companies – Motorola, Intel, Fairchild, Advanced Micro Devices, and I.B.M. Japan – and one European, Siemens, set about the task of developing production in Japan. The same trend was beginning in chemicals and other fields.

Direct investment was only the most visible form of the internationalization of the world's capital. Insurance companies, pension funds and sundry other financial entities also diversified their holdings to stabilize returns. In the British case, the export of funds under this heading increased two and a half times over in the late seventies; financial companies set as their aim the increase in the share of foreign stock in their assets from 20 to 50 per cent.

In sum, the seventies brought to fruition a long process of the integration of capitals. Among other things, it made impossible or certainly very difficult a repetition of the reaction of States to the crisis of 1929–33. Then, the State in the industrialized countries assumed it held a separate section of world capital that could be deterred from movement beyond its boundaries or, at least, movement only on terms which preserved the pre-eminence of the State. Even then the system survived not on the basis of the territory of a national State, but on much larger blocs – the sterling, dollar, Reichsmark areas.

The process of integration had greater antiquity – from Europe's eighteenth-century commercial invasion of Asia and the Caribbean in search of marketable commodities, through the world-wide pursuit of raw materials and markets, to the overwhelming U.S. domination of world manufacturing in the 1950s. In the postwar world, American manufacturing exports were replaced by American capital exports, the two going to assist the recreation of European and Japanese capacity on a scale to equal the American. The counter-attack of European and Japanese exports to the United States followed with a much smaller interval of time, followed in turn by capital exports. Within the multiple exchanges, the dim outlines of a new 'division of labour' began to emerge. The United States commanded the most important single segment of world finance, internationally marketed agricultural and raw material output, armaments and aircraft (assisted by Britain, specializing in finance and services); West Germany and Japan were increasingly dominant in the most expansive segments of manufacturing.

It had little stability, for it was not a smooth transition but the result of increasingly fierce competitive battles. Beneath the division between the industrial core zones, another kind of division was beginning to appear. For the seventies saw capital spreading its wings much further. A selection of Less Developed Countries and parts of the Eastern Bloc were being pulled into the world order. There, the capital–labour ratio, the intensity of use of equipment, the State-supplied services, could be on qualitatively different lines. Indeed, some saw the Third World as the only home for capitalism – 'for an investor such as Mannesmann,' one such representative of capital commented, 'Brazil is one of the last oases of early capitalism.'[18] Here, the elaborate and costly restraints of the managed economy in the core industrial zones could be evaded. But this qualitative 'rejigging of the relationship between capital and labour' assumed that the managed economy was effective, the market mastered. It was not so, and if Brazil was early capitalism, in part early capitalism was returning to the core industrial zones as well.

Extending capital internationally on this scale meant also extending the labour market, bringing the poorly-paid workers in the poor countries into direct competition with the higher-paid ones in the rich countries. The long promise of the market, of capitalism, was beginning to emerge – the competition of capitals for profits without the diversion of national identity. The system was being homogenized. It had always been a myth that poverty had been eliminated in the core zones, just as it was absurd to suggest that the rich did not inhabit the periphery. Now the geographical segments were being rendered more uniform – 'third world' production appeared in the More Developed, just as 'first world' production accelerated in the Less Developed.

Notes to Chapter 4

1. Harry G. Johnson; 'The Role of International Economics Teaching in the Analysis of International Relations', in *Les relations internationales dans un monde en mutation*, Sijthoff (for the Graduate Institute of International Studies, University of Geneva), Leiden, 1977, p. 102.

2. External trade in goods relative to total production of goods (resources, food and industrial production), from *International Economic Indicators*, U.S. Dept. of Commerce, Washington, June 1980.

3. See J. Kaye and Mervyn King, *The British Tax System*, Oxford, 1978.

4. Cited from *Frankfurter Allgemeine Zeitung/Blick durch die Wirtschaft*, 6 March 1975, by Folker Fröbel, Jürgen Heinrichs and Otto Kreye, *The New International Division of Labour, Structural unemployment in the industrialized countries and industrialization in developing countries*, trans. Pete Burgess, London, 1980, pp. 122–3.

5. World Bank, *World Development Report 1978*, World Bank, Washington, 1978, p. 17.

6. J. F. Sterling, 'How Big is the International Lending Market?', *The Banker*, London, January 1980.

7. See 'External Positions in Domestic and Foreign Currencies of Banks in Reporting Area of Certain Offshore Branches of U.S. Banks', Bank for International Settlements, *Fiftieth Annual Report* (1 April 1979 to 21 March 1980), B.I.S., Basle, 9 June 1980, p. 119.

8. International Monetary Fund, *International Trade, 1979–1980*, I.M.F., Washington, 1980; see G.A.T.T. press communiqué 1271, Geneva, 9 September 1980.

9. Cited by Paul McCracken *et al.*, *Towards Full Employment and Price Stability*, O.E.C.D., Paris, June 1977, para. 244, p. 166; on the British growth of liabilities of selected financial institutions, 1960–78, see Mervyn Lewis, *Lloyds Bank Review 137*, July 1980, table 1.

10. Cited *The Economist*, London, 18 December 1980.

11. Deflation in the More Developed Countries, reported the Bank of International Settlements, would produce recession which would 'shift the burden of the current account deficits from the stronger industrial countries to the weaker ones, and in particular to the non-oil [exporting: N.H.] Less Developed Countries' – cf. *Fiftieth Annual Report*, op. cit., p. 175.

12. Department of Trade, *Interim Report into Dunlop Holdings*, Her Majesty's Stationery Office, London, 1981.

13. Toshiko Yoshino, in *World Economy*, Nijmegen. 2/4, February 1980. p. 441.

14. See Kenneth C. Crowe's *America for Sale*, New York, 1979.

15. Lloyd Franko, 'Multinationals: The End of U.S. Dominance', *Harvard Business Review*, November–December 1978.

16. See H. McMillan, in *World Economy*, Nijmegen, 2/3, September 1979.

17. See 'Charting the Asian Trail of Moscow Narodny', *Far Eastern Economic Review*, Hong Kong, 28 July 1978, pp. 80–88.

18. *Frankfurter Allgemeine Zeitung*, 30 March 1977, cited by Fröbel *et al.*, *The New International ...* , op. cit., p. 231.

FIVE

**THE SWEATED TRADES
AND THE THIRD WORLD**

> All theory, dear friend, is grey, but the golden tree of life
> springs ever green.[1]

Competition is continually pressing capitalists to reorganize and relo-
cate production. In slump and stagnation these pressures upon particular sectors and companies become severe, and the sanction exercised
over those too tardy in readjusting, bankruptcy, becomes more than
merely hypothetical.

Let us divide these readjustment processes into two types, although in
practice the two are imperfectly distinguishable. First, the 'distillation of
production', that is its reorganization at the place where it originally
operates. For example, it has long been familiar that large employers of
labour in central business districts of big cities are frequently driven by
the high costs of transporting and maintaining large staffs in high-cost
areas to divide their staff between headquarters and the rest of the staff,
the first remaining in the city centre, the second being relocated to the
cheaper periphery or a relatively remote area. Second, the 'relocation of
production'. An example of this is the movement of New York textiles
production; cost increases in New York in the 1930s impelled a movement of the mills from the city, first to upstate New York, and finally to
the southern States where the labour supply was far cheaper and the
local authorities much more eager to please (in fact, some of the mills
may not have 'moved' – some were bankrupted, and new units
developed in the new location). Let us look at these two types of
readjustment in turn, noting again that the two are not mutually
exclusive.

(a) Distillation

There is a wide variety of methods whereby the relationship of capital
and labour can be 'rejigged' without large changes in location. A
company might shut down the labour intensive sections of its operation
and subcontract this work to other companies. It might become merely a
purchasing agency for many formally independent manufacturers, producing to its specifications and putting its brand name on the product.

These 'manufacturers' might escape tax and social security obligations by operating in the 'black economy'; they might be self-employed; they might be households (where all members of the household, including the children, work in the trade).

The garment trades have always provided some of the most striking examples of this complex structure of production and selling. Where fashion is volatile or demand highly specialized, production can depend less on simple standardized parts and the machines that make them; it becomes dependent upon nimble fingers. The extraordinarily expensive dress in the fashionable boutique may thus be linked to children running sewing machines in damp basements and draughty garrets. The 'sweated trades' are not at all producers of inferior goods. The workers here perform the most arduous and ill-paid tasks involved in the creation of superior goods. Nor are the tasks restricted to the highly specialized sectors. Even in vehicle production, the prototype of modern manufacture, the threads can be traced 'upstream' through the component makers to the tiny workshops, the Nissen huts, which are supposedly the mark of nineteenth-century capitalism.

Reorganization may thus involve several dimensions – changes in the scale of production, of relationships between different segments of production, of the legal and illegal. The division of production between several 'independent' producers is not necessarily inconsistent with increased concentration of production in terms of ownership or control.

In particular, subcontracting activities seem to have become more important in the industrialized countries in recent years. The 'lump' labourer, the self-employed subcontractor worker, long familiar on building sites, may not at all be peculiar to the construction industry. The 1981 wage settlement in British agriculture prompted discussions by farmers of the need to increase the employment of temporary and seasonal subcontracted labour, the 'lump farm labourer'. This would allow the farmer to avoid paying the cost of full-time employees all year. Furthermore, he would not need to purchase machinery outright, but rather hire it simply for the period when labour was hired. Small companies were already developing which offered both machinery and labour on a subcontractor and seasonal basis. Already common as a system in continental Europe, it was strong in Britain only in dairy farming (the 'self-employed cow-man' handling several farms).[2]

Employers were not simply preoccupied with achieving the lowest wages; indeed, low wages were of no importance unless they contributed to high returns. But even in relationship to wages alone, the issue was not simply the price of labour power, but its price relative to the intensity and conditions of work (which includes the danger, physical hardship, cleanliness, noise, tedium of work, the provision of paid holidays, the hours and shifts worked, the health and safety conditions, and so on). Wages might be low, but the cost of meeting legally required minimum standards prohibitive. Forms of production that could escape such costs were thus important when profit margins were under pressure, even when they contradicted the mythology of the managed economy, that all were decently paid and protected.

Japan provided an extreme example of the complexity that had always existed in an advanced economy, even in the heyday of affluence. The well-known great companies, the former *zaibatsu*, might offer levels of pay and conditions of work comparable to the best in the world; it was these which received most public attention. But the performance of the great companies rested upon a fluctuating mass of small enterprises, subcontractors to large firms. Here productivity was relatively low, as were the pay, conditions of work and security of employment. Other things being equal, we might expect stagnation to produce an increase in this 'submerged' sector, even where this coincided with a decline in the share of profits accruing to small-scale subcontractors (and indeed, with a high rate of bankruptcies among them). But the overall information is not available.

American agriculture offers a different method of adjustment. There farmers depend upon a mass of seasonal labour, frequently illegal immigrants, working at illegal pay levels (that is, below the minimum wage level) in illegal conditions. In the hotel and restaurant trades, pay rates are frequently well below what is thought to be socially tolerable; and in order to recruit sufficient workers, it is common to recruit labour abroad or illegal immigrant labour at home. Because of their illegality, such workers cannot refuse to accept pay and conditions which are below the legal minimum. In the United States, the first slump and stagnation of heavy industry and other sectors – producing relatively high rates of national unemployment – coincided with a weakening dollar and a booming tourist trade, drawing in, it is said, very large numbers of illegal immigrants to work in the services provided for tourists; the pay rates on offer in hotels and catering are, in general, below what would be acceptable to unemployed American car or steel workers.

Perhaps there has been an expansion in the employment of subcontractors by well-known sellers of branded goods as a result of stagnation and slump. In the garment, glove and shoe trades this appears to be true, with both local subcontracting and subcontractors abroad providing bulk production. Much of the activity within the core industrial zones remains publicly unrecognized, except for a rare public exposure by investigative journalists or the continuing but little-read work of voluntary agencies. The 1978 strikes in Paris of some 60,000 – mainly illegal immigrant – workers in the garment trades was one such revelation, or a short press campaign concerning the employment of children in garment manufacture in East London. Another press study indicated that in a Lancashire town, Nelson, some 6,000 women – many of them of Asian origin – were engaged in home production, sewing ribbons and bows; the pay rate was equivalent to roughly 10p per hour (when the then-current national rate for manual workers was something over £2.00 per hour). Other garment workers in home-based work in 1979 were said to receive between 9p and 35p per garment processed, a rate that might achieve for them – in a fifty-hour week – some £20 to £25 per week.

Parts of 'manufacturing' industry may also depend upon imported components from sectors of even cheaper labour abroad. Some of the great manufacturing names are now no more than companies selling goods under their own brand name, but which in fact are manufactured by others. Most Swiss watches are now manufactured in Taiwan, or, if finally assembled in Switzerland, made from components imported from the Far East. We have noted, in the last chapter, the complex pattern in which Japanese companies import components from other Far Eastern sources, and sell them to manufacturing companies in the United States and Europe who then sell them as locally branded and manufactured goods. In fact, one of the few remaining 'British' television manufacturing companies, Thorn Electric, now in the main assembles only components imported from overseas.

The complex of activities involved here is not measurable; it merely indicates the imperfections of our perceptions about activity in the industrialized countries. Nor do these activities exactly coincide with a well-known concept in each of the industrialized countries – the 'black economy' (Britain), the 'underground economy' (United States), 'le travail noir' (France) and 'schwarzarbeit' (West Germany). Here the criminal, the clandestine and the merely unrecorded jostle, illustrated only by anecdote. The concepts conjoin the working 'unemployed' and 'inactive', the illegal earnings of legal activity (including theft), moonlighting, those who reduce their taxes by means legal and illegal, the perks of business managers and so on. It is an unsystematic category with little in common between the elements other than that they are unrecorded. The estimates of size vary accordingly – in Britain, from 2 to 3 per cent of the national income (or £300 per household) to 7.5 per cent (between 11 and 12 billion pounds, estimated by Sir William Pile, former head of the Inland Revenue); in the United States, the estimates range from 200 billion to 500 billion dollars, with the Internal Revenue Service estimate at 184 billion dollars (perhaps small by American standards, but still nearly equivalent to the – then (1978) – value of output of Canada). Edgar Feige in *Challenge Magazine* (November 1979) made the highest estimates, claiming that 1 in 4 dollars in the American economy was not recorded, and that if they had been recorded, then the rate of growth of the U.S. economy between 1976 and 1978 would have been raised from 4 to 9 per cent per year. In the building trades, the British employers estimated the black economy was worth some £2 to 3.5 billion per year. Finally, in Japan, the strictly criminal activity was reported by the police to be worth some 5 to 5.2 billion U.S. dollars (or about half the value of sales of a giant company, for example Nippon Steel or Toyota). The size of the element cannot, of its nature, be accurately assessed, let alone its fluctuations plotted. The sole function of the exercise is to suggest something of the unseen sector that lies behind the surface statistics.

The growth – or the discovery – of the sweated trades in Italy has been most documented within the industrial core zones. The Social Research Institute, Censis, estimated that in 1979 what it calls the 'parallel economy' provided between 4 and 7 million jobs (including second jobs and part-time home work as well as full-time employment). Sr Agnelli of Fiat publicly suggested that this form of activity added some 30 per cent to Italy's national income, others perhaps an additional fifth; Censis finally agreed, revising its estimates of the 1978 net output figures upwards by some 15 to 20 per cent. The massive debts of Italy's large-scale sector – particularly, public corporations – seemed to imply that Italy was in growing slump in the late seventies. But the sweated trades – half of the output of which was exported – transformed the picture to the highest rate of growth in the Common Market in 1979 (5 per cent) and 1980 (3.8 per cent). They helped to bring Italy in 1980 the fourth highest official reserves in the world (valued in 1980 at 40 billion dollars, compared to the 1977 Italian reserves of 9 billion dollars, or Japan's of 20 billion dollars).

What did the trades cover? There were gloves from Naples, textiles and leather goods from the villages around Mantua and in the Tuscan Prato, jewellery from Arezzo, Vicenza and Valenza Po in Piedmont, and mechanical engineering work from the Luzezzano valley north of Brescia. The electric arc steel makers of Brescia were among the best known. Numbering about eighty, with an average employment per plant of 175, they produced in 1979 some 4 million tonnes of steel (or 15 per cent of Italy's steel output). They were accused of wrecking the Common Market cartel arrangements, Eurofer.

There were said to be some 3 million Italians engaged in home-based piece-work in the textile, clothing and footwear trades, some 800,000 of them clandestinely. They were not a new phenomenon, and they were a source of considerable resentment among other European textile manufacturing countries. As the *Financial Times* (22 September 1976) noted:

> Under this system, companies put out parts of the manufacturing process to workers at home, causing allegations of unfair competition to be levelled by other textile producers in Europe who claim Italian companies can in this way reduce costs by avoiding social and other charges accompanying full-time employment.

Take for example the woollen industry. The production of Prato (near Florence) by the eighties had emerged as the dominant force in the European woollen trades. The major part of production was originally concentrated in large vertically integrated plants, but, the managers alleged, these were difficult to administer, inflexible in fluctuating market conditions, and the frequent victim of strikes. From the late fifties, the companies began to dismantle this structure, and accelerated the process in the sixties – the looms were sold or leased to former workers. By the eighties, there were 10,000 firms and 65,000 workers. 1,200 *impannatori* (converters) secured raw materials for their subcontractors and sold the output; some of these firms also manufactured, often with relatively capital intensive methods; they employed directly about 30,000 workers, or an average of 25 per firm. The 8,000 or so other firms employed about 35,000 workers (or an average of 4 per firm); the characteristic firm was a family with three or four machines, working on piece rates to supply contracts to a larger firm, absorbing variations in market demand in their own labour time (that is, working 16 hours per day when demand was high, much less as demand slackened). The family enterprises were usually classed as 'self-employed', so were able often to escape paying pension or social security contributions; were not governed by trade union skilled labour requirements; dodged safety regulations and probably much of the V.A.T. requirements.

The existence of an unseen sector of the economy went some way to help economic commentators explain a number of anecdotal paradoxes – the powerful performance of the Italian economy despite the bankruptcy of its large-scale industry; the appearance of relatively high levels of prosperity alongside official stagnation; or, for example, the steady 6 per cent rate of increase in the demand for electricity when official industrial output was stagnating. The onset of the second slump caused some check to this process – national exports declined by over 4 per cent in 1980, and the decline seems to have included (if the figures are to be trusted) the sweated trades. The Brescia steelmen were operating at some 15 per cent below their 1979 output. However, in 1982 when much of the rest of the world was continuing downwards, the Italian economy was again performing relatively creditably – in the contest between the leading powers. Italy, despite its continuing political problems, seemed to have discovered a means to secure 'flexibility', overcoming the rigidities of managed capitalism, and rejigging the relationship between capital and labour.

Whether cause or effect, there was a general revival of praise for 'small-scale business' in the industrialized world. The fashion was a periodic one, promoted – like the return to Christianity – by the anxieties of troubled times prompting people to reach back for earlier verities when capitalism was recognizably capitalist and 'the individual' had a will and a way. Governments took some modest measures to assist small business. There were proposals for 'export processing zones' in the industrialized regions which, it was hoped by some, might provide sheltered nurseries for little businesses rather than sanctuaries for the little subsidiaries of larger ones. The British Government proposed to set up 'enterprise zones' in decaying inner city areas, areas which at one stage looked as though they might be relieved of all planning and tax obligations. The business weekly, *The Economist*, in a spirit of mischief, urged the Government to turn over the inner city areas to small Asian businessmen, the only authentic 'capitalists' still left. The Government in turn toyed with the idea of putting the unemployed to work without wages, an even more dramatic readjustment of labour costs in favour of profits from the viewpoint of the employers; no doubt that would have made many 'white' businesses competitive with the 'black economy', particularly if they had been able to lay off their existing labour force in favour of the Government's army of costless conscripts.

The black economy – the sweated trades – operated outside the controls or even the perception of the State. Its size and composition, its variation over time, were unknown. It seemed to be the creation or recreation of sectors with a factor endowment appropriate to the dominant forms of competition within the world system, not the prescriptions of the managed national economy. It was a private capitalist system, although often dependent upon filching supplies from the public sector, which operated independently of the pretensions of the State. It was not at all inappropriate that, in Italy, it should be called 'Third World production'. The label drew attention not simply to the fact that in some parts of the industrialized regions it was immigrants, legal or illegal, who manned part of the black economy, but that beyond the narrow compass of industrialized countries lay another, covering two-thirds of the world's people, where the sweated trades were not a clandestine qualification to the system but its main component. Indeed, the overwhelming majority of the world's labour force outside farming was engaged in the sweated trades.

(b) Relocation

In the seventies, many observers noted that it seemed that manufacturing capacity was on the move, not just between the industrialized countries, but for the first time on a significant scale, from industrialized to Less Developed. Often, these results were confused with the causes of stagnation in the industrial core zones of the system.[3] But there was no reason in conditions of sustained boom why redistribution geographically should not take place at the same time as employment was sustained in the core zones. After all, the great boom had seen both redistribution and a steady pruning of activities taking place without affecting employment levels. The two processes cannot take place, however, when collapsed profit rates simultaneously afflict the core zones. Then marginal redistribution is interpreted as 'theft'. The relatively high unemployment levels in the core zones cannot be the *result* of a redistribution of activity; on the contrary, any increase in redistribution of activity in terms of geography is the result of slump. If the role of the Less Developed in the world system was so great as to have been able to inflict slump and stagnation upon the More Developed, we need to explain why the growth in the output of the Less Developed – and the disproportionate growth in their imports of machinery and industrial inputs from the More Developed – did not produce a boom in the industrialized zones of the world. In fact, even in the late seventies (some time after the first slump), the Less Developed still contributed only 8 to 10 per cent of world manufacturing trade, and about 1 per cent of the O.E.C.D. final market for manufactured goods.

Nonetheless, relative to the size of the manufacturing base in the Less Developed Countries, there was movement, or rather some redistribution of world capacity. The first wave of accelerated growth of manufacturing in the Less Developed was in the sixties, well before the first slump. It affected a group of six countries – four in East Asia (South Korea, Taiwan, Hong Kong, Singapore) and two in Latin America (Mexico, Brazil). There were others, either less secure in the process (India), or more ambiguous as 'Less Developed' (Yugoslavia). Nor was the group of similar character. The four East Asians and Yugoslavia expanded on the basis of exports within a fairly narrow range of products – in particular, garments at first, and later the 'labour intensive' segments of the manufacture of electronic products and components. The two Latin Americans, with far larger national economies, had high rates of domestic growth on many fronts, without this production at that time creating dramatic increases in exports. Brazil and Mexico were also much more closely integrated in the activity of international capital compared to, say, autarchic India. The group as a whole, sometimes referred to as the Newly Industrializing Countries (N.I.C.s), in many cases not only survived the first slump intact, but actually accelerated during the period of ensuing stagnation. Furthermore, in the seventies others began to join their ranks, or at least form a further ring separating the N.I.C.s from the rest of the Less Developed – Malaysia, Thailand, Philippines, Venezuela, Colombia, Salvador (up to 1980, at least), Indonesia, Egypt, and, after some political changes, the People's Republic of China. However, the second slump in all cases afflicted growth rates.

The process was the result of a number of connecting causes, of which the slump – the drive of capital to minimize the costs of production for world output – and the 'maturation' of a number of Less Developed Countries, were the most important. 'Maturation' in this context had nothing to do with growing older and wiser; it was the result of a cumulative improvement in educational levels of the domestic labour forces,[4] a cumulative improvement in the available infrastructure (roads, airports, power, water and developed land), and the cumulative effect of a transformation in external transport costs (particularly in air freight, but also in road and sea transport, in containerized freight movement). The changes, assisted by subsidies and favourable tax terms, made some of the Less Developed competitive in certain sectors with those who had hitherto been their rivals, cheap labour – primarily women and immigrants – in the core industrial zones.

It was a leapfrogging process. Some Less Developed arrived first, only to find that their initial production base then moved on to other sectors as the tempo of activity changed. Already Hong Kong and Singapore are losing their lowest cost operations to other Less Developed Countries (in 1979, for the first time, employment in textiles in Hong Kong fell). By the mid seventies, the large Textile Alliance of Hong Kong was beginning to develop alternative production sites in Malaysia, Indonesia, Thailand, Mauritius and Nigeria. By the late seventies, half the Alliance's world employment was located outside Hong Kong, where it both escaped local tariff barriers and had access to under-utilized national quotas under the Multi Fibre Arrangement (whereas in Hong Kong, all companies had to scramble to get a share of the quota).

The most important change, however, was in external opportunities.

In much of the fifties and sixties, many States in the Third World had little option but to defend local production against the threat from the manufacturing superiority of the First World. The defensive reaction was rationalized as 'import substitution programmes' of domestic industrialization. In the late sixties, and particularly in a stagnating seventies, an increasing number of States have seen an opportunity that did not exist before – growth based upon 'export promotion'. Slump transformed an opportunity into a necessity – now the pressures to balance the external account drove countries to force the pace of export growth, and in order to do it, to introduce elements of 'liberalization' of the domestic economy. Virtually all developing countries were forced into the process to a greater or lesser extent; even those giants, powerful autarchies, China and India were sucked into the process. Of course, in accepting the opportunity and the necessity, States opted to pursue the same path as those of the industrial regions, increased integration in world production rather than pursuit of the aim of 'an independent national economy'. For the opportunity is the product of the need of international capital to find new low-cost production sites.

In the first instance, the spread of production was in the main to geographically proximate areas (as was the source of immigration to the core zones) – Yugoslavia, Spain, Greece, Tunisia, Hungary for Europe; Central America and East Asia for the United States. Japan produced a series of spin-offs along the East Asian seaboard. Imports to Japan from East Asian sources increased from about 4.5 per cent of total imports at the end of the sixties to over 20 per cent in 1976–7. There seemed to be a specialized division of labour emerging, partly, but only partly, supervised by Japanese overseas capital – Taiwan specializing in petroleum exports to Japan; Taiwan and South Korea in steel; South Korea in fertilizers, etc. A considerable degree of vertical integration between Japan and overseas producers took place in, for example, the manufacture of electronic components, watches, garments, etc. Indeed, from one point of view, it is possible to see the new East Asian growth economies as offshore production sites for Japan, or better, intermediaries in the exchanges between Japan and the United States. South Korea, for example, processed imported raw material (much of it from the United States) with Japanese machinery and exported the products back to the United States (the picture became more complicated than this in the late seventies). The surplus on these exchanges could be seen as part of the considerable U.S. deficit on its trade with Japan. However, it should not be thought that the East Asian growth was simply Japan in disguise; Korean and Taiwanese capital increasingly took over the most important roles.

The advantages of relocating production – or, what amounts to something very similar, redirecting purchases by industrialized-country buyers from local to overseas suppliers – are of considerable significance for particular sectors of capital. Productivity levels for plants of comparable technical quality are similar between More and Less Developed Countries, but total costs are frequently tiny in the second compared to the first. Take the somewhat extreme example of the average hourly cost per operator in textiles between some fifteen countries (Table 19).

19. *Average cost in U.S. dollars per operator hour (three shifts), 1978–9*[5]

	Total cost	Ratio to U.S.: 100	Planned operator hours worked per year
North Germany	10.19	168	1,776
South Germany	8.76	144	1,776
North France	7.05	116	1,848
Italy	7.00	115	1,740
United States	6.08	100	2,096
Britain	4.82	79	1,888
Japan	4.53	75	2,023
Mexico	3.13	51	2,112
North Greece	2.83	47	2,400
Hong Kong	1.72	28	2,424
Portugal	1.62	27	2,070
Taiwan	1.16	19	2,496
South Korea	0.75	12	2,400
India	0.53	8.7	2,232
Egypt	0.35	5.7	2,368

The enormous spread of labour costs is immediately apparent – the hour which costs 10.19 dollars in North Germany fetches only 35 cents in Egypt. The number of hours on offer is an indication of a different form of cost-saving, and perhaps a rough surrogate for how unregulated management may be. British labour costs may be substantially below those in the United States, but American spinners and weavers work nearly 10 per cent more hours per year – and Taiwanese workers work more than 40 per cent longer per year than those in North Germany (the figures are official, and from particular sources which do not necessarily compare with those from other sources; thus, an International Labour Organization study of hours worked in all trades in sixty countries in the mid seventies put South Korea at the top with average hours worked per week at 57.7[6]).

Nor does the table encompass all management's preoccupations. Labour costs may be low and hours worked long, but if the local State cannot guarantee adequate power, services, a long enough runway, security and 'order', the legal right and financial possibility of expatriating profits in a reasonably stable form, and so on, the cost advantages may disappear. A special arrangement may have to be negotiated to cover special needs – such as the agreement signed by the Singapore government with five U.S.-registered companies to prohibit trade unions in their plants for an initial three years (at the end of which, the workers would be given the right to vote on whether there should be a union); the condition was said to be required to induce the companies to bring a particular technology to the island.[7] Thus, in general, the possibility of starting production is intimately interwoven with the political strength of the local State; it cannot be accidental that so many of the N.I.C.s are commanded by generals, ex-generals or similar figures, and compete as well in the contest for the largest number of untried and tortured political and trade union leaders (the Amnesty ratings, we might say) as in the field of comparative export performances.

What evidence there is, suggests that the rewards to international capital are not insignificant. For U.S.-registered companies, the rates of return on overseas activities (U.S. Department of Commerce figures) in the More Developed Countries was 12 per cent (in 1977); in Less Developed Countries, 26 per cent, and in Asia, 24 per cent. By sector in the three categories (M.D.C.s, L.D.C.s, Asia), the comparable figures were: *manufacturing* – 11, 11 and 16 per cent; *finance and insurance* – 14, 18 and 50 per cent; *petroleum* – 8, 127.5 and 28 per cent.

The speed of growth in comparison to low starting points, once begun, was phenomenal. The current value of the manufacturing exports of the Less Developed increased from 4.6 billion U.S. dollars (1965) to 43.8 billion in 1976, an increase of about 1,800 per cent (but for East Asia, 14,000 per cent, and Latin America, 10,900 per cent[8]). Eighty per cent of the total, however, was provided by eight countries only. Within the total of exports, the share of engineering goods has steadily increased – from 13 to 29 per cent between 1963 and 1976 (particularly in office, telecommunications and other electrical equipment – the share of these items increasing from 9 to 19 per cent of the total). By the mid seventies, some 12.5 per cent of manufacturing exports from the Less Developed were capital goods. The potential growth in other sectors appears very high – in iron and steel, machinery, vehicles and vehicle components, durable consumer goods.[9]

Then there are special deals. The price of a contract to construct a major manufacturing plant abroad for a Western company is an agreement whereby the company takes part of its payment in the form of output from the new plant, a 'Buy Back' deal. European chemical companies found themselves the recipients of a growing torrent of chemicals from Eastern Europe as the product of such deals. Shell agreed to sell part of the new stream of petro-chemical products emerging from the gigantic developments in Saudi Arabia (where the planned target was to secure between 7 and 8 per cent of the world basic petro-chemicals market by 1985[10]). Renault–Peugeot, complaining bitterly at the 'glut' of cars in Europe, nonetheless agreed to accept as payment half the output of the new Maruthi car plant the company was to build in India (in the event, Suzuki won the contract). India planned a series of giant aluminium and steel plants with foreign companies on the same basis.

Nonetheless, despite the rate of growth of increasing output, it has not yet been of great significance for the industrialized zones of the world except in certain narrowly circumscribed fields or for particular countries. The share of O.E.C.D. domestic consumption or supply taken by L.D.C.s was very low, and of imports, still far smaller than intra-O.E.C.D. supplies. For the O.E.C.D. group, the 1977 picture in those sectors where N.I.C.s held more than a 10 per cent share of all imports was as shown in Table 20.

20. *O.E.C.D: Imports from Less Developed Countries,*[11] *percentage share of all imports in sector*

	1963	1977
Electrical machinery	8.3	10.3
Miscellaneous finished manufactures	9.0	10.2
Transport equipment	12.2	18.2
Machinery (excluding electrical)	20.1	16.6
Chemicals	12.1	12.9

Thus, the increases over a period of some fourteen years were not so remarkable, and in one case, machinery, there was an actual decline. In the garment trade, which provoked most public agitation, the N.I.C. import share increased from 3.3 to 4.9 per cent (and if all Less Developed and Eastern Bloc imports are included, from 8 to 18 per cent, a much more substantial increase).

The expansion of exports from the Newly Industrializing Countries initially depended heavily on the direct participation of foreign capital – whether in the form of production by a subsidiary in the country con-

cerned or by companies overseas purchasing goods to their specifications and, often, bearing their brand name. Often the sellers in South
Korea and the buyers in Tokyo were part of the same company; indeed,
production in a Less Developed Country could frequently only gain
entry to a More Developed Country through the sponsorship of a
company there. The figures on the proportion of Newly Industrializing
Countries' exports generated by the subsidiaries of foreign companies[12]
are gathered on different defintions, but they indicate nonetheless
some of the close involvement. However, over time there was some
tendency for local manufacturing companies to displace the subsidiaries of multinational corporations – or the multinationals found it
cheaper to terminate their own production and rely on subcontracted
work once the technical skills and quality of output had become locally
secure. Intra-firm trade (that is, trade between the subsidiaries of
multinational companies) has tended to decline as a share of the
exports of the new Far Eastern N.I.C.s, being replaced by the exports
of the local companies (particularly in Taiwan and South Korea). On
the other hand, in the countries where foreign capital is tightly
controlled – for example, India and China – it is buyers from the
industrialized countries who are important in stimulating exports.

The most rapidly growing segment of O.E.C.D. imports from Less
Developed Countries has been that derived from 'Free Trade Zones', a
large – and what seems to be growing – proportion of which appears to
be intra-industry trade, indicating not merely a trading integration of
More and Less Developed, but also an integration in production. Free
Trade Zones (F.T.Z.s) are forms of 'offshore production', permitting
duty free imports of machinery and raw materials provided the bulk of
output is exported. Usually, operations in such areas either escape
taxation entirely, or are given special tax privileges, as well as other
incentives to produce (F.T.Z.s have a variety of names, including Export
Processing Zones and, in Mexico, In Bond Plants). Between 1966 and
1972, imports from the Less Developed to the United States increased
at a rate of 12 per cent annually, but 'Offshore Assembly Products'
(O.A.P.s) by a rate of 60 per cent. Roughly comparable figures for West
Germany and Netherlands were: 11 and 36 per cent; 2 and 39 per cent.
The cumulative total increases for U.S. imports, 1970 to 1976, were 305
per cent, and 530 per cent. Or, to look at the figures in a different way,
the O.A.P. share of Less Developed Countries' exports to the United
States, 1966 to 1976, increased from 6 per cent to nearly half; and in the
category 'metals and metal products' (mainly electronic goods) to nearly
77 per cent. In the case of West Germany in the seventies, O.A.P.s
played a much more important role in textiles (particularly garments),

and an increasing proportion of O.A.P. imports came from Eastern Europe (if we include Yugoslavia, 59 per cent of West German O.A.P. imports from outside the Common Market countries came from Eastern Europe).[13]

In conditions of increasing competition, Free Trade Zones were ideal for receiving the labour intensive segments of production formerly located in the core industrial zones of the world system. Such segments had no life of their own, no identity separate from the integrated production line of which they were a part. In the field of electronic production, the rate of turnover of equipment was very high, as waves of innovation rendered machinery obsolete with great speed. So, quite often, international companies located in F.T.Z.s could be very mobile as costs varied. They were not, as it were, snared by particular governments and rendered immobile by location in a F.T.Z., any more than their original location (where they had had one) in a More Developed Country had rendered them incapable of subsequent movement. Whereas at one stage workers from Less Developed Countries were induced to emigrate to the industrialized zones of the system for work, now they could work abroad 'while at home'; F.T.Z.s made possible home-based daily emigration, receiving immigrants to the world production system.

The incentives offered for location in F.T.Z.s were frequently considerable. For example, Manaus in Brazil offered tax exemption for thirty years, low land prices; businessmen need raise only 10 per cent of the capital they needed, the rest being on offer locally at a rate of interest of 6 per cent over a ten to twenty years repayment period.[14]

However, as if this lowering of costs were still insufficient, F.T.Z. employers have generally chosen the lowest-cost worker with 'manual dexterity' (to minimize wear and tear on machines rather than determine the quality of the output). This entailed the employment, in the main, of young women of sixteen to twenty-four, who were generally laid off when they exceeded the upper age limit. For what was frequently a sixty-hour week (or possibly 2,400 or more hours per year), they received under half the low level of adult male wages.[15]

The uniformity of this section of the world labour market, the homogenization of conditions, is remarkable. The young women in the eighty or so F.T.Z.s of Asia, those of the Mexican border, of Mauritius or India, of Manaus in Brazil, frequently produced identical goods on identical machines for the same buyers. Clad in identical clothes, working at the same speed, it became impossible to tell at a glance where you might be. Just as capital had lost nationality, commodities ceased to have any national identity, the conditions spread from capital to product to worker; for labour, nationality and national culture became the indulgence of the hours of leisure.

If F.T.Z.s have proved rewarding for international capital in the Less Developed Countries, the innovation perforce must spread back to the More Developed. As States competed to attract capital, it was inevitable that if capital threatened to move, those in the industrialized zones would begin to imitate those outside. 'Subteropolis' in Kansas City, a privately owned industrial estate located in former quarry caves, is a Free Trade Zone; its owners claim to have persuaded some fifty companies to set up operations there (the oldest F.T.Z. in the United States is Staten Island, close to New York City, which has been in operation since the 1930s, without remarkable success). The Kansas City operation is one of fifty-six sites in the United States approved since the mid 1970s as export processing zones. Ford Motor Company, ever alert to innovations in cost reduction, has even applied to have a Free Trade Zone wrapped round its new agricultural equipment plant near Detroit. Thus, American workers are also obliged to become foreigners in their working lives, to emigrate daily to the world production system, just like their brothers and sisters in the Less Developed Countries.

Beneath the world system of integrated company production, of connected free trade zones, of networks of subcontracting, lies an unknown base to the iceberg. World production depends on a multitude of petty suppliers, fading into family labour working in one-room tenements. The plastic flowers on sale in Los Angeles originated in this great section of the world system, but a section unmapped by statisticians. Take the Newly Industrialized Hong Kong:

> Only 619,684 of the total labour force work in 21,386 industrial units registered with the Government – those with more than twenty employees. A total of 136,300 are self-employed; the rest run small-scale family enterprises or work in small units, usually in a single room in a high rise slum. These are a fire hazard; they are the main source of the seven fires a day that occur in Hong Kong.[16]

The creation and destruction of firms and people will be high. In Calcutta, the smallest businesses, earning less than is required to subsist,[17] die at least as frequently as people.

Part of this world is a black economy, but most of it is white – or at least that grey which means neither illegal nor publicly recognized. The black economy was not an invention of the industrialized zones of the world, a market response to the peculiar taxing system of the managed economy. Rather is its natural home at the heart of the sweated trades of the Less Developed – even when graced with the neutral name, the 'Informal

Sector' (the fashionable phrase of the seventies, as if scholars needed to make a virtue of dreadful necessity).

Black money – cash which does not flow through the tax system – in India may be equal to half all the white money; a government inquiry in the early seventies estimated that black was growing faster than white.[18] Like its international equivalent, Indian black money is fluid, flowing into commodity speculation, construction and property, as ready to finance gold smuggling as the credit required to allow richer farmers to hoard their grain in the prospect of pushing prices up (and, as an incidental by-product, create a famine).

The future prospects for the continued expansion of internationally integrated production are now affected by the entry of China into the contest. The People's Republic, like the other competitors, is endeavouring to develop subcontractual production relationships with foreign companies, to create free trade zones[19] and to lease groups of workers for temporary work abroad with international companies. The numbers of workers available as well as the prices quoted would seem to make the task of competing with China daunting indeed for the smaller Asian powers. That problem becomes even more severe as India also moves towards an export promotion strategy, part of its exports now being labour.

The States at the industrialized core of the world system did not eliminate the 'reserve army of labour'. They merely walled it out for a short time, exiled it to where it could no longer be seen. But the market continued to encompass all, even those walled out from the heartlands. The competition between States produced the continuing investment in education, infrastructure and transport which, in the tighter seventies, suddenly became relevant to the needs of international capital. The sweated trades boomed, when those with a lower rate of perspiration stagnated. As they boomed, they integrated the world's production system in a new phase. In the first instance, the process affected textiles, garments, electronic components and 'miscellaneous manufactures'. But the knowledge gained in these first forays is now susceptible to generalization. India, Brazil, Taiwan and South Korea are moving on to armaments and aircraft. On the initiative of Ford and General Motors, 'world cars' are being invented, drawing on components in countries throughout the Less Developed. Shipbuilding, general machinery, and a widening range of chemicals are no longer restricted to the core regions.

Were the process to be sustained, it would produce a striking change in the distribution of manufacturing – with the West European and North American share of output falling from about two thirds in 1960 to under a half in 1990. The President of the World Bank commented in

1981 – 'there is simply no precedent in history for the dynamic rate of change in the geographical spread of global output in our era and in the structure and character of world trade'. But there were many obstacles, not least the fearful volume of cumulative debt and the protectionist impulses of the industrialized countries. But, if they could be surmounted, world profit rates might, it seemed, be sustained. The rejigging of the relationship between world capital and labour could, at least for the moment, have been accomplished, with the incidental by-product of the industrialization of part of the rest of the world. But there were many qualifications to any such perspective, qualifications which must await later discussion.

The Third World

The gap between the world of public doings and private reality is the same in all countries, and the same in many different dimensions. Gross domestic products may seem to bound ahead, but the figures do not say how many people have work and how many have tolerable incomes. All the growth in the world has not so far produced full bellies for all. Even for those four small countries of East Asia where there has been sustained growth in jobs and incomes, the majority experience lives of extreme harshness.[20] For most, incomes are low, work long and arduous. Consider this fragment from the *Korean Times* (8 August 1976): 'More than 1,000 workers were killed and 80,000 injured in industrial accidents and occupational diseases, resulting in Won 50 billion in economic losses in 1975 alone.' Or reflect on the results of the 1971 Hong Kong Census:

> Of persons of ten years of age or more who worked 15 or more hours in the week before the Census, over half worked over 54 hours per week. The average working hours in manufacturing industry were 56 hours, with nearly a quarter working 55 to 64 hours, 14 per cent 65 to 67 hours, and 8 per cent 75 to 84 hours (and another 3 per cent, over 85 hours). Nearly 36,000 children under fourteen worked, 25,000 of them full-time.[21]

In Brazil and Mexico, the output achievements in absolute terms have been even more impressive, but what proportion of Brazilians and Mexicans have seen tangible benefits? The absolute figures of those who have seen improvements are large, but relative to those in need, small. In San Cristobal de las Casas, the Indians still walk barefoot; in the doorways of downtown Mexico City, people crouch asleep in the small hours.

Outside Recife, the world is much as it always was, and so it is for many in the cardboard shanties of São Paulo. It is not enough to say that such changes take time; it has already been an age, whole lifetimes have been swallowed up. Such reassurances would in any case be more credible if 'time' had been enough to end poverty even in the industrial heartlands of the system.

And these, the Newly Industrializing Countries, are the showpieces of economic development. For the Less Developed as a whole, nearly thirty years of sustained application to economic development in the period of the most rapid growth ever seen have still left a very large number of people – possibly 500 million or nearly an eighth of the world's inhabitants – experiencing no improvement of substance; some have seen deterioration. The miracles that so preoccupy the public world, the great surge of Brazilian growth or that of Pakistan in the fifties, scarcely nudged anything down below. India's exports of engineering goods may soar, but still one year's increase in the United States income per head would take a century to achieve in India. For the poor countries as a whole, the World Bank estimates it would take 746 years to reach the income per head of the More Developed if they did not grow at all; if the More Developed grew at the rate of the years between 1970 and 1976, then the Less Developed would never 'catch up'.

Economic development

What was the experience of 'economic development' in the period of the great boom? The concept of 'national economic development' is the invention of the fifties. It includes at least three elements: a 'self-sustaining' growth in the capital stock of a country, a sustained change in the structure of production (between low productivity activities, primarily agriculture, and high productivity sectors, pre-eminently industry), and all on the basis of a *national* economic unit. There are many ways of seeking to detect this process, but some of the most important are by measuring the cumulative growth in domestic savings and investment, the growth and changing composition of output, and changes in the structure of employment.

In general, the Less Developed have achieved high rates of capital formation – between 11 and 26 per cent of their respective gross domestic products in the late sixties.[22] The growth of output and changes in its composition have been dramatic in comparison both to their low starting point and to the nineteenth-century experience of the industrialized countries. There has been a change in the structure of production and considerable increases in labour productivity. If we limit ourselves simply to the distribution between 'agriculture' and 'industry', and accept the World Bank distinction between 'low income' (countries with a gross national product per head of 360 U.S. dollars or less in 1978) and 'middle income' countries (the other Less Developed), then the change looked like Table 21.

21. Share of Gross Domestic Product deriving from agriculture (with industrial shares in brackets)

	1960	1976
Low Income countries	52 (12)	45 (19)
Middle Income countries	26 (23)	21 (32)
More Developed countries	9 (41)	6 (41)

The Middle Income have become, in terms of output, effectively industrialized. The Low Income have swapped 7 per cent of agriculture for industry, along with a considerably absolute increase in both. The change has increased the Less Developed Countries' share of world domestic product from 17 per cent in 1950, 17.7 per cent in 1960, 18.5 per cent in 1970, to 21.4 per cent in 1978, a pattern of growth that shows the increasing speed of change. Their share of world industrial production for the same years went from 10.8, 13.3, 14.9 to 20 per cent.

These are figures for shares in the value of output, and they show a clear and sustained change in the structure of production. But is there a comparable process in the structure of society, in the distribution of employment? For if labour productivity were to rise with great speed, changes in output could be achieved without comparable changes in jobs, and so, in incomes. In 1950, 41 million people in the Less Developed Countries[23] were employed in industry (extractive, manufacturing and constructing), and in 1970, 85 million, more than double. However, the labour force in agriculture in the same period increased from 304 to 435 million, which in turn ensured that the structural change in industrial employment (as a percentage of total employment) was from 10 to 13 per cent.

The relative change, in terms of jobs, was quite small, despite the peculiarity of the period. We can see some of the implications of this if we look at the two largest countries of the world – China and India, with some 1.8 billion of the possible 4.5 billion inhabiting the globe (3.5

billion of whom live in Less Developed Countries). The contribution to China's gross domestic product by industry, on one estimate, increased from 28 per cent in 1952 to 37 per cent in 1972; agriculture's contribution fell from 45 to 21 per cent. But in both years, 75 per cent of the active population was employed in agriculture; very little had happened in terms of jobs.[24] In the case of India, we take a different set of categories – primary (including agriculture and mining), and secondary, at 1960–61 constant prices. The contribution of the primary sector to net domestic product fell from about 55 to 41 per cent, while secondary increased from 18 to 24 per cent, between the two periods 1950/51 to 1959/60 compared to 1968/9 to 1976/7. Over the same period, employment in the primary sector, as a proportion of the total workforce, increased from 69 per cent (1951) to 70 per cent (1971); and secondary employment fell from 12.6 to 11.2 per cent.[25]

The figures involve a lot of imperfections and they are not comparable between the two countries. But even with qualifications, the crude picture is impressive in terms of output, but not in terms of employment. If the promise of industrialization is the transformation of society, the structural change in employment and incomes is hardly substantial. Output can grow rapidly but without commensurate implications for work. For the period of the great boom was one of accelerating labour productivity; the same proportion of workers could produce apparently ever more. To give a vivid example of this phenomenon, Bairoch[26] estimates that the 0.02 per cent of the Third World's labour force engaged in oil production contributed 33 per cent to the total value of exports.

Furthermore, the progress that has been made gives little confidence in any perspective of 'national' economic development. Only in the initial stages did the attempt to build independent national economies seem to achieve high growth. Thereafter, the high growth rates have come from increased integration in the world system, increased specialization rather than diversification of national output. The decline in national 'self-reliance' means that, if any national growth process could ever be 'self-sustaining', it is not the growth experienced – future growth depends increasingly on a favourable international context. Indeed, in retrospect, the drive to create economic independence – the 'import substitution programme' – seems only to have prepared the Less Developed for increased incorporation in the world system. The maiden who made a bold move for women's emancipation woke to find herself merely prepared for an old-fashioned wedding.

World stagnation

The return to the ruling orders of those Less Developed Countries which have opted for 'export promotion' programmes has fully vindicated their choice. But the more successful they have been in this respect, the more closely integrated the local economy has become with the world system. Thus, although there have been a number of variations, the impact of world slump and stagnation could not be evaded. The N.I.C.s in the first instance were able to offset slump, as we have seen, by increased borrowing and exports. But the majority of Less Developed Countries began to slow down. Furthermore, just as with the More Developed, there was increased differentiation between them (Table 22).

22. Growth of Gross National Product and Gross National Product per head for oil-importing and exporting Less Developed Countries, 1960–80 (average annual percentage growth rates, 1977 prices)[27]

	Gross National Product		Gross National Product per head	
	1960–70	*1970–80*	*1960–70*	*1970–80*
1. Oil-importing countries	5.6	5.1	3.1	2.7
a) Low Income Countries	4.1	3.3	1.6	0.9
Subsaharan Africa	4.2	3.0	1.6	0.2
Asia	4.1	3.4	1.6	1.1
b) Middle Income countries	6.1	5.5	3.6	3.1
East Asia and Pacific	7.8	8.0	4.9	5.6
Latin America, Caribbean	5.4	6.0	2.7	3.5
North Africa, Middle East	2.3	3.0	−0.2	0.4
Subsaharan Africa	4.9	3.9	2.4	0.9
Southern Europe	7.0	4.6	5.4	3.2
2. Oil-exporting countries	5.5	6.1	2.8	3.5
3. All Less Developed Countries	5.6	5.3	3.1	2.9

Thus, growth rates in both 'all Less Developed', and the two sub-groups, Low and Middle Income Countries, declined between the two decades; in the case of Subsaharan Africa, the decline was to stagnation. However, the oil-exporting countries and three groups of Middle Income

Countries escaped in the seventies. In the case of East Asia, Latin America and North Africa/Middle East, there were countries which accelerated in growth terms; and the last group turned a negative rate of growth in the sixties to a slight positive one in the seventies.

The acceleration for a minority of countries was purchased, as we have seen, at the price of increasing debts. By the end of the decade of the seventies, cumulative Less Developed Countries debt stood at nearly 400 billion U.S. dollars (in comparison to 64 billion at the end of 1970), and by the end of 1982, something over 500 billion dollars. There were great difficulties in estimating the size of the debt, not least of which was government desire to conceal the total debt, private and public, for fear of injuring its own capacity to borrow. In the second half of the seventies, an increasing proportion of borrowing took the form of unpublicized short-term credits not included in the official statistics. This affected the debt-servicing ratio dramatically – on one estimate, the ratio increased from 16 to 19 per cent between 1977 and 1981; but if short-term credits were included, the ratio had increased from 32 to 50 per cent. However, even on the official figures, bankers were alarmed – the debt-servicing ratio (ratio of debt-servicing to export revenue) had everywhere risen. Thus, of the twenty-one Less Developed Countries (of those not exporting oil) which borrowed from the Eurocurrency market between 1977 and 1979, a third had a ratio well above 20 per cent in 1979, and two above 50 per cent. For all Less Developed, the current servicing burden is equal to about 3 or 4 per cent of their combined gross national products or 20 per cent of export revenue (for low-income Less Developed Countries, official government-to-government aid covers nearly three-quarters of their capacity to import).

While inflation tends to lower the real value of the debt (and obviously, declining inflation increases the burden), high interest rates tend to increase it. For example, in 1970 the twelve leading Less Developed Countries in terms of borrowing paid 1.1 billion dollars in interest, equal to 6 per cent of export revenue and an average interest rate of 3.2 per cent; in 1980, the equivalent figures were: 16 billion dollars, 16 per cent of export revenue, and 9 per cent rate of interest. For large borrowers, interest rate rises are now a heavier burden than increases in oil prices – for each one dollar per barrel oil price rise, the Less Developed must pay roughly 2 billion dollars more; on 100 billion dollars-worth of floating debt, every one point increase above Libor (the interbank lending rate for Eurocurrency markets, the bench mark for international loans) increased servicing payments by 1 billion dollars; in 1980, the Libor rate increased from below 10 to 20 per cent. For Brazil, interest rate movements have become much more decisive than oil price rises; Morgan Guaranty compares the effect of a five dollar per barrel rise on Brazil's oil imports, and a five point rise in Libor – the first would take an extra 7 per cent of Brazil's export revenues, the second 13.5 per cent.

The Less Developed Countries have increased balance of payments deficits – requiring increased borrowings abroad – not simply because of increases in oil prices. Quite often just as severe have been increases in prices of imports from More Developed Countries, matched in the early eighties by the collapse of primary commodity prices. Price inflation in the More Developed seems to have a disproportionate effect on price inflation in the Less Developed – for every 1 per cent increase in prices in the one, there appears to be a 2 per cent increase in the other.[28] Certainly, the figures for inflation were very high as the world moved into its second slump (Table 23).

23. *World Inflation Rates (changes in consumer prices, per cent)*[29]

	Average 1963–72	*1973*	*1974*	*1975*	*1976*	*1977*	*1978*	*1979*	*1980*	*1981*E	*1982*E
Industrial countries	3.9	7.7	13.1	11.0	8.2	8.4	7.2	9.0	11.8	9.9	8.1
	Average 1968–72										
Oil exporting countries	8.0	11.3	17.0	18.8	16.8	15.5	10.2	10.5	12.6	11.8	10.5
*Non-oil developing countries*b	9.1	22.1	28.7	27.0	27.6	27.0	23.6	29.0	36.9	37.2	34.5

E: Estimate
b: Excluding People's Republic of China

Such levels of inflation produce random redistributions of income, favour profits over wages, produce depreciating currencies and devaluations as the only means to sustain exports (without which imports and debt servicing cannot be maintained) – and in conditions of tight food supplies, exclude poor eaters from the grain market.

Furthermore, the terms of trade for oil-importing Less Developed Countries have been deteriorating – by 2 to 3 per cent in 1979, and an estimated 4 per cent in 1980 (and a cumulative 20 per cent on 1970). In effect, a much larger volume of exports becomes necessary to sustain the same, or even a reduced, quantum of imports. If at the same time the States in the industrialized zones of the world are cutting imports, then the Less Developed face shrinking export markets, and must cut their imports even more drastically: thus hitting the industrialized countries' exports. For the poorer Less Developed the effects are increased, since so much of their import capacity in the past has been sustained by aid, but now many Western governments are tending to cut aid as well as their contributions to multilateral aid agencies; the World Bank's 'soft loans' agency, the International Development Agency, was virtually in suspension in 1981 as a result of the new U.S. President's cuts in aid contributions.

The effects of world contraction were felt for the first time very sharply in some of the most expansive N.I.C.s, in contrast to their experience in 1974. Hong Kong's manufacturing sector was sharply checked as the result of poor exports; unemployment increased some 40 per cent between March 1980 and a year later, and many of the textile mills were working a four-day week; only the continued growth of services for China kept up incomes. Brazil experienced increasing difficulties in sustaining the pace of activity, and increasing problems in raising foreign funds to service its debts. Argentina in 1981 witnessed a wave of bankruptcies, and an industrial workforce that had shrunk since 1976 from 1.03 million to 790,000.

In South Korea, the gross national product contracted by nearly 6 per cent in 1980 (as compared to an average rate of growth of 9.2 per cent between 1962 and 1979); wholesale prices increased 44 per cent in the preceding year; the cumulative debt of some 27 billion dollars (1981) was a factor in the sudden drying-up of foreign investment in 1980 (although a more substantial one was the murder of the dictator, Park Chung Hee, and subsequent riots throughout the country before a new dictator secured power). The debt – 37 billion dollars in 1982 – was projected to reach nearly 65 billion dollars by 1986. The heavy industrial programme of the seventies was very sharply affected: car production was running at half the installed capacity in the early eighties. By dint of severe cuts in domestic consumption, measures to rationalize capacity, and a sharp devaluation (by 36 per cent), the Korean economy was stabilized. But, for a moment, the rulers looked into the abyss.

There were difficulties for some of the N.I.C.s, but they were small in comparison to the experience of others – Turkey, Peru, Zaire, Pakistan, Poland. North Korea and Egypt were driven to default on debt servicing at various stages. Bolivia was effectively bankrupted – aid ceased, trade shrank, debts mounted as the military undertook the country's 189th coup in 165 years of independence (July 1980); only cocaine smuggling increased (bringing an estimated 600 million dollars to the trade balance in 1980). Jamaica began the seventies with the second highest income per head in southern America and ended it with an income per head 25 per cent lower, one in three of the adult labour force out of work, a massive flight of capital and skilled labour, hundreds killed in street warfare, and stocks of just one month's foodstuffs and medicine. It was borrowing from the 'lender of last resort', the International Monetary Fund, which produced in the context of world stagnation shattering pressures on the island. As Minister Richard Fletcher put it, 'I don't know of any other population which would have stood it without over-throwing the government or martial law.'

Zambia offers another instructive example. Here the problems of an external political crisis – events in Zimbabwe, Angola and South Africa – are intimately interwoven with the problems of a country which is essentially a complex of copper mines. Imports depend upon the export of copper; 90 per cent of export revenue derives from copper, and in the early seventies, half the government's income (copper exports con-tributed nothing to government revenue between 1977 and 1979, and only 6 per cent in 1980). The price of copper fell from its peak – £1,400 per tonne in early 1974 – to £612 in March 1977. At that price, three-quarters of Zambia's mining operations ran at a loss. The huge Luanshya mines, for example, cost more in imported equipment and oil to keep open than they earned in export revenue. Attempts to form a cartel of copper exporters – Zambia is the fourth largest producer after the United States, the Soviet Union and Chile – foundered on the refusal of Chile to collaborate.

By 1978, the gap between revenue and expenditure was growing to a point where it could no longer be covered by private borrowing. The maintenance of a high level of defence spending could be secured only by successive cuts in expenditure, hitting public expenditure (health, education) and popular consumption. 'One has the feeling,' the Lusaka *Daily Mail* observed, 'that everything is collapsing around us.' Govern-ment policy had produced 'an austerity regime, falling standards, physi-cal shortages, shut-downs and rising unemployment – malnutrition if not starvation in places' (*The Times*, London, 15 May 1978). Only the imprimatur of the I.M.F. could reopen the possibility of commercial borrowing. In preparation for this, the price of the domestic staple, maize meal, was increased by 22 per cent. The I.M.F. reached agree-ment after tormented negotiations and after a promise to devalue the national currency, the kwacha, by 10 per cent (after a 20 per cent devaluation a year earlier) – so again cutting consumption by pushing up import prices. There was some relief in 1979 as copper prices rose again; the two main mining companies (51 per cent owned by the govern-ment) did not make losses for the first time since 1975.

Zambia, winded by the first slump, had not recovered by the time of the arrival of the second. Copper prices again fell, and coincided with two bad maize harvests (the price of imported maize meanwhile soared some 300 per cent). Again, the Government cut its expenditure (but protected defence) and pushed up consumer prices (maize prices increased between 30 and 50 per cent). Imports were, at various stages, suspended because past imports had not been paid for – shipments of oil were delayed in the Persian Gulf awaiting the settlement of debts. Foreign exchange reserves were exhausted, investment cut, strikes spreading and the Government threatened by coup (October 1980). An International Labour Organization report recorded the melancholy history of the decade – a 46 per cent decline in real gross domestic product between 1974 and 1979; public investment cut by 65 per cent; agricultural producers now being required to pay three times more in real terms for what they purchased from the cities than in 1965; schools and transport decayed – Zambia had been moved backwards. As the I.M.F. again began the torment of new negotiations, the terrible sacrifices of the past came to represent nothing; for, as the London *Financial Times* (20 February 1981) put it, 'The worst may be yet to come.'

Beneath the abstractions, people were being crucified on the relationship between one patch of territory, Zambia, and a world economic system, between one State and the market of competing States. Economic commentators, with that tone of Victorian self-righteousness which seems part of the inheritance of orthodox economics, declaimed the need for the poor 'to live within their means', as the means evaporated. Individual leaders – Mr Manley of Jamaica or President Kaunda of Zambia – were upbraided for being indulgent with their peoples. Neither were particularly indulgent, nor could the sum of individual error by government leaders explain the necessity for the war of attrition on human beings. Would that mere error or indulgence played such an important role, for then remedies would be easy. The commentators were not obliged to look behind the balance sheet to count which children did not survive because, by conscious decision, the price of maize meal had snatched nourishment from their mouths.

In time, the brute demographic measures catch up with reality. The decline in the rate of increase in the average expectation of life in the sixties may represent, when the results of the 1980–81 round of censuses are finally published, a splendid but past achievement. Protein intake seems to be declining for important sections of the population of the world. Famine has become once more an increasingly frequent punctuation mark in the long sentence of contemporary history. Malaria and cholera have become re-established as endemic disabilities in Asia, and sleeping sickness in Africa.[30] The triumphs of the great boom are being slowly reversed. For the need of stagnation is to eliminate 'excess capacity' – whether the excess be in steel or shipbuilding or labourers.

Demographic changes are only part of a process. Under the hammer blows of world crisis, social structures crumble. From the mid sixties, parts of the Third World led the way to slump. Ruling orders became demoralized. The great task they had set themselves – to create a confident and growing national power – gave way to the imperative of merely hanging on, administering drift; without glory or high purpose, they remained defended only by guns, the loyalty of which turned on the soldiers being paid on time and having goods available on which to spend their pay.

The demoralization can be seen most vividly in the nervous 'flight of capital'. A slight chill, and solid respectable patriots bend all efforts, fair and foul, to scramble their money out of the country to the world's homelands of the rich, the industrialized core countries. The balance of payments, poor to begin with, thus becomes a disaster. Demoralization can be seen also in the spread of the black economy. Whether it is the great smuggling trails – of, for example, cannabis worth between £7.5 and 12 billion, from Colombia, Ecuador, Peru, Bolivia or Morocco northwards – or more discreet transactions through Swiss bank accounts, increasing numbers of the rich indicate by behaviour their lack of faith in their own financial survival in the territory of their birth. They must launder their gains; for money is only black within a State – outside its borders, all becomes white. To an innocent observer, it might seem that there is no objective economy at all, only the simple battle of greeds.

The decline of efforts to plan is part of the process of demoralization. The end of planning is an admission that the future cannot be created by conscious and deliberate action. A plan requires a stable environment and a stable income. In the seventies, governments were increasingly persuaded, in practice if not in theory, that, as one giant Dutch company put it:

> Planning is just a waste of time nowadays, especially so-called strategic planning. In today's world, there's no point in looking further forward than a one or two year budget. Anything long term is just not worth the paper it's written on.[31]

For Zambia, being a smaller agency than the Dutch company, one or two months was probably the limit of realistic perspective. Of course, governments were more in the public eye than companies, and a minority of the tutored eyes looked still for the rituals of planning as a source of comfort for the future, even if the substance had disappeared. Plans appeared on bookshelves in serried ranks, but they expressed no commitment; they had become merely part of government's public relations. Those that continued some measure of planning moved far away from the heroic ambitions of 'national economic development', settling for 'flexibility', 'breathing spaces' or, in the charming phrase of the Government of India in the sixties, a 'plan holiday'. More still relinquished the aim of building industry and settled for expanding agriculture; home-grown food at least guaranteed that ruling orders could survive a little longer; they no longer trusted their ability to earn more by exporting and so being able to import food grown more cheaply abroad. The necessity of self-reliance was made into a virtue, and theories run up to decorate it.

The armies and police forces of the world were the beneficiaries of slump. As their numbers increase, so does lawlessness, until the two trend lines become indistinguishable, and Bihari policemen are found putting out the eyes of the accused with bicycle spokes or breaking the knees of those suspected of something. The prisons grow faster than the national economy, and the nameless throng of political prisoners grows into a legion – 140,000 held without charge or trial in Mrs Gandhi's Emergency rule. Self-flagellation follows as well – the compulsory vasectomy campaigns in India which ruined hundreds of thousands on a doctrine that, if only people could be eliminated, governments could be eminently successful; or the million Vietnamese set adrift in boats on the high seas; or the barbarisms of Chilean and Argentinian generals; or the endless hopeless streams of refugees trekking across Africa.

Whatever the cause, the effect is a neurosis of insecurity among the rulers. In the industrialized core zones, the same phenomenon produces a great increase in private arms, and public obsessions with 'law and order'. In Britain, despite the favour shown the police and the armed forces by successive governments, private security services boomed in the seventies. Some 32,000 were employed in the sixty-seven main private security forces, and 133,000 employed all told as surrogate policemen; that was somewhat more than a third of those employed in the official armed forces, and not far short of 40 per cent of those employed, for example, in coal-mining. The world had grown alarmingly fearful for those with property to lose.

As the means to violence increases, so also does violence itself, to the point of civil warfare. The thousands slaughtered – in Uganda, Cambodia, Nicaragua, Salvador, Lebanon, South Philippines, Pakistan, Ethiopia, and so on – beggar the losses from other sources. It is as if the system, unable to expel the virus of stagnation, inflicts successive haemorrhages on its silent inhabitants. And each savaging only serves to increase the power of those who can wield the bayonet; only generals or their surrogates can hold the national patch together. Representative government, a supposedly free press, decay, the casualties of slump.

The 1955 Bandung Conference created the idea of a Third World, a third alternative to the sterile confrontation of Western 'capitalism' and Eastern 'socialism'. But the lead given was actually slightly different to the one proposed. The Third World showed that the world was one, not three, and all the horrors that might befall the poor could also be visited on the rich. There was another, different, lead. Competition drove the States of the Third World to gear their societies to intensified effort. The role of their inhabitants was to work in silence, not flaunt their consumer goods. Some in the industrialized cores misunderstood this puritanism as the birth of a new society, not a repetition of primitive capitalism. They did not see the inner meaning of the austerity of China, nor read the proclamation of the *People's Daily*: 'To love manual labour is the intrinsic virtue of the proletariat and other working people.'[32] Nor did they understand that that austerity was intrinsic to the behaviour of a poor State in a world of competing States, intrinsic to that liberation of the State called 'national liberation'. Stalin understood it in Russia, when people pleaded with him to slow down the pace of industrialization:

> No, comrades ... the pace must not be slackened. On the contrary, we must quicken it as much as is within our power and possibilities. We are 50 or 100 years behind the advanced countries. We must make good this lag in ten years. Either we do it or they will crush us.[33]

The same theme is echoed in the speeches of the arch-capitalists of the Third World. Consider Kim Woo Choong, head of the Korean Daewoo Group:

> To catch up with the rich countries, we must work three times as hard ... In advanced countries people do business for profits. In Korea, we must do it for the nation ... profits are for reinvestment, not for enjoyment. Leaders must make sacrifices so that the people will follow them.[34]

The Less Developed Countries were dragged pell-mell into the stream of world economic growth during the great boom. The world market for the first time penetrated all corners of the globe. In doing so, it forced governments and businessmen to impose the disciplines required to compete. The austerity was part of the process of the accumulation of capital. But as part and parcel of the increased growth came increased integration. National economic development became increasingly impossible, increasingly utopian; growth within a specialized division of labour replaced it. But this in turn imposes an impossible conjuncture – societies are geared to sacrifice for economic growth, but growth becomes increasingly only possible as a world phenomenon. Then the drive to work turns to a drive to self-destruction – governments are snapped like dry sticks between the brute unemployment and hunger at home and an obdurate environment abroad. National ruling orders suddenly stand exposed as, not the national leadership, but parasites, unable to shape their world but still leeching off the local product.

Within the Third World, an inspiration remains: to build an economically independent foundation to independent political power. If only the links with the rest of the world could be ended or at least controlled, is it possible that accumulation can be accelerated to the point where full employment is attained? The most extreme form of this doctrine is embodied in the States of the Eastern Bloc. They remain, in principle, planned societies, governed by authorities that claim they can shape their national units in whatever ways they choose. High inflation and unemployment are, they say, features of capitalism, not of socialism. The next chapter seeks to examine some of these claims.

Notes to Chapter 5

1. Translation from the German of Johann Wolfgang von Goethe, *Faust*, I, lines 2038–9.

2. These questions are explored in more detail in my 'The New Untouchables, The International Migration of Labour', *International Socialism* 8 (new series), Spring 1980, pp. 37–63.

3. L.D.C. industrial expansion as a cause of M.D.C. stagnation is argued, from a Marxist standpoint, by Fröbel *et al.*, *The New International Division of Labour*, London, 1980; and from a neoclassical position by Michael Beenstock and Patrick Willcocks, in *The Causes of Slower Growth in the World Economy* (mimeo), London Business School (Economic Forecasting Unit), Discussion Paper No. 76, September 1980.

4.

Numbers enrolled in education as a percentage of the respective age group

	Primary Schools 1960	Primary Schools 1977	Secondary Schools 1960	Secondary Schools 1977	Higher Education 1960	Higher Education 1976
Argentina	98	110+	23	41	11	29
Bangladesh	47	81	8	23	1	2
Brazil	95	90	11	24	2	12

Numbers enrolled in education as a percentage of the
respective age group – continued

	Primary Schools		Secondary Schools		Higher Education	
	1960	1977	1960	1977	1960	1976
Egypt	66	72	16	46	5	14
India	61	80	20	28	3	6
Indonesia	71	86	6	21	1	2
Iran	41	98	12	48	1	5
Malaysia	96	93	19	43	1	3
Mexico	80	116+	11	39	3	10
Nigeria	36	–	4	–	–	1
Pakistan	30	51	11	17	1	2
Philippines	95	105+	26	56	13	24
South Korea	94	111+	19	43	6	–
Thailand	83	83	13	27	2	5
Turkey	75	98	14	43	3	8

(+ over 100 indicates primary school enrolment including those outside the age group, 6 to 11 years.) *Source*: U.N.E.S.C.O. (1960) and *World Development Report 1979*, Table 23, pp. 170–71, and *1980*, Table 2.3, pp. 154–5.

Paul Bairoch estimates that 'general, vocational and teacher training' higher level L.D.C.s students increased from 7.6 million (1950) to 18.2 million (1960) and 42.5 million (1970); in university education, from 940,000, to 2.1 million and 5.6 million – cf. Table 42, *The Economic Development of the Third World Since 1900*, trans. Lady Cynthia Postan, London, 1975, p. 141.

In terms of one country, Mexico's literate population of 1960, 17.4 million (of 35 million) was 45 million in 1980 (of 68 million); the 5.5 million students of 1960 had become 21.7 million in 1980 – cf. President Lopez Portillo, 4th State of the Nation Report, extracts in *Comercio exterior de México*, September 1980, p. 322.

5. Selected and reordered from a selection of thirty-seven countries (with other data), from *Spinning and Weaving, Labour Cost Comparisons, Winter 1978–79* (mimeo), Werner International Management Consultants, Brussels, 1979.

6. For more detailed discussion, cf. my 'The Asian Boom Economies', *International Socialism* 3, Winter 1978–9, pp. 1–16.

7. Report, *I.U.F. Bulletin*, International Union of Food and Allied Workers, Geneva, 1980, No. 6, p. 6.

8. Figures from Sanjaya Lall, 'Exports of Manufactures by N.I.C.s', *Economic and Political Weekly*, Bombay (weekly), 6 and 13 December 1980.

9. See B. Balassa, 'Export Incentives and Export Performance in Developing Countries: A Comparative Analysis', *Weltwirtschaftliches Archiv*, 1972, pp. 345–80.

10. The speed of growth of chemical exports, once begun, can be seen from the Brazilian case, 1975–9 (see table below).

Exports of selected Brazilian chemical products (tonnes)

	1975	1979		1975	1979
Ethyl acetate	51	6,470	Dimethyl terephthalate (DMT)	–	10,693
Hydrofluoric acid	–	4,000	Ethylene glycols	25	20,991
Sulphuric acid	90	15,839	Monosodium glutamate	–	8,530
Phthalic anhydride	–	9,627	Sodium hydroxite (caustic soda)	2,207	37,953
Sodium bichromate	10	6,238	Propylene oxide	–	10,163
SBR rubber and latex	1,238	14,299	Polypropylene	–	7,505
Ammonium chloride	100	1,295	Polypropylene glycol	4,017	7,753
Dichloroethane	–	8,066	Carbon tetrachloride	–	23,802

(from *Brazilian Trade and Industry*, Associacão Brasileira da Indústria Química & Produtos Derivados, São Paulo, October 1980.)

11. See 'Shares of total O.E.C.D. imports of manufactures', 1977, in O.E.C.D., *The Impact of N.I.C.s on the Pattern of World Trade and Production in Manufacturing* (mimeo), O.E.C.D., Paris, 1978.

12. The situation, exports of a country by degree of foreign ownership of exporting sector concerned, can be seen in:
Sun-Hwan Jo, *The Impact of Multinational Firms on Employment and Incomes: The Case of South Korea*, World Employment Programme (mimeo), International Labour Organization, Geneva, 1976.
Census of Industrial Production 1975, Government of Singapore, 1976.
F. Jenkins, 'The Export Performance of Multinational Corporations in Mexican Industry', *Journal of Development Studies*, 1979, pp. 89–107.
M. L. Possas, *Employment Effects of Multinational Enterprises in Brazil*, Multinational Enterprises Project (mimeo), Working Paper No. 7, International Labour Organization, 1979.

13. See Sanjaya Lall, 'Offshore Assembly in Developing Countries', *National Westminster Quarterly Review*, August 1980; see also G. K. Helleiner, *Intra-firm Trade and Developing Countries* (mimeo), University of Texas, 1977.

14. See *Projectos Industriais aprovados pela Suframa, 1968/75*, Suframa, Manaus, 1978.

15. See Fröbel *et al.*, *A New International . . .*, op. cit., p. 352 *passim*. See also R. W. Moxon, *Offshore Production in Less Developed Countries, A Case Study of Multinationality in the Electronics Industry*, New York, 1974; and Donald B. Baerresen, *The Border Industrialization Programme in Mexico*, Lexington, 1971.

17. See A. N. Bose, *Calcutta and Rural Bengal*, Calcutta, 1978.

18. The Wanchoo Committee; cf. my *India–China, Underdevelopment and Revolution*, Delhi, 1974, p. 6 *passim*.

19. Among other sources, the *Far Eastern Economic Review* (Hong Kong, weekly) has covered these issues; cf. on the Shekou industrial zone near Hong Kong, 1 February 1980, p. 56; on the sale of labour, 21 March 1980, pp. 93–4; on

Hainan developments, August 1980; see also feature in *Newsweek*, 2 June 1980.

20. See my 'The Asian Boom Economies', op. cit.

21. From Robert Porter, 'Child Labour in Hong Kong and Related Problems: A Brief Review', *International Labour Review*, III/5, 1975, p. 436.

22. Paul Bairoch, *The Economic Development* . . ., op. cit., Table 48, p. 174.

23. 'Less Developed Countries' as defined by Bairoch, ibid., p. 2, covering about 80 per cent of the population of the L.D.C.s; see also Table 47, 'Changes in the structure of the active population of the L.D.C.s, 1900–1970', p. 160.

24. See Alexander Eckstein, 'Economic Growth and Change in China: A Twenty Year Perspective', *China Quarterly*, 54, April–June 1973, pp. 221–41.

25. V. K. V. R. Rao, 'Changing Structure of the Indian Economy: As Seen from National Accounts Data', *The Economic and Political Weekly*, XIV/50, Bombay, pp. 2049–58.

26. Paul Bairoch, *The Economic Development* . . ., op. cit., p. 163.

27. World Bank estimates, reproduced in 'The Decade of the Seventies', *Report*, World Bank, Washington, September–October 1980.

28. United Nations, *World Economic Survey 1979–80*, United Nations, New York, 1980, p. 28.

29. *Source*: I.M.F., *World Economic Outlook*, op. cit., pp. 145 and 148. See this source, introduction to appendix, for definition of the countries included in each group.

30. See United Nations: (i) *Economic and Social Survey of Asia and the Pacific*, United Nations, New York, 1975; and (ii) *Survey of Economic and Social Conditions in Africa 1974*, United Nations, New York, 1975.

31. Christopher Lorenz, 'Corporate Strategy in an Age of Uncertainty', in *Planning in an Age of Uncertainty*, special articles reprinted from the *Financial Times*, London, 1979.

32. Hsiao Tung, People's Liberation Army, 'To Idle or Not to Idle', in *Jen Min Jih Pao*, 13 January 1969, and *Survey of China Mainland Press*, 1 June 1969, p. 350, discussed in my *The Mandate of Heaven: Marx and Mao in Modern China*, London, 1978, pp. 181–2.

33. Speech to managers, February 1931, reprinted in *Problems of Leninism*, p. 356, cited by Isaac Deutscher, *Stalin: A Political Biography*, London, 1966, p. 328.

34. Reported in 'Focus: Korean Economy', *Far Eastern Economic Review*, Hong Kong, 20 May 1977, p. 56.

SIX

A SOCIALIST ALTERNATIVE?

> From the moment warfare became a branch of the *grande industrie* (iron clad ships, rifled artillery, quickfiring and repeating cannons, repeating rifles, steel covered bullets, smokeless powder, etc.), *la grande industrie*, without which all these things cannot be made, became a political necessity. All these things cannot be had without a highly developed metal manufacture. And that manufacture cannot be had without a corresponding development in all other branches of manufacture, especially textiles.[1]

In the quarter of a century between 1929 and 1954, the Soviet Union was transformed – from being one of the more backward countries of Europe to a major world industrial power. In the 1930s, while much of the world was prostrate with intractable slump, Russian industrial output soared; its cities grew rapidly, and there seemed no limit to the expansion possible. In the Second World War, Russia withstood the most devastating blows of German arms and was still, in the end, able to repulse them. In the years after the coming of peace, industrial growth was resumed at a rapid pace, now in conjunction with many more States in the Eastern Bloc. The pattern of growth seemed a confirmation of the idea that, however unpopular or undemocratic the People's Democracies might be, they had an amazing capacity to secure industrial growth; only in the fifties and after, did Japan, Korea and others demonstrate that even higher industrial growth rates were possible without a Communist-run State.

The Soviet Union was the final vindication of the precepts of a 'managed economy'. Through the exercise of complete control over external exchanges, over trade and finance, by allocating raw materials, capital and labour in physical terms within the domestic economy, by operating a system independently of relative external prices, the system seemed able to secure balanced growth and the full utilization of available resources, including labour. The relationships of the economy, it seemed, became 'technical' instead of competitive; engineering was a more appropriate skill for planning such an economy, as if the gross national product were the product of a chemical composition into which chemists could pour exactly the right technical elements, independent of relative scarcities.

The managed economies of the East also claimed a different relationship to capital. If the States of the West appeared sometimes like pieces of crust floating on a sea of international capital, then in the Eastern Bloc the State congealed its share of world capital beneath it, snaring its proportion of world productive equipment within its administrative reach. Ostensibly, capital and State were held in a fixed relationship. What surplus was generated by labour at home was accordingly retained within the territory of the State concerned.

There are a number of problems with this view, not least of which is an accurate account of the Russian performance, warts and all, in the thirties, the 'heroic period'. However, that would take this account too far afield. There is another problem with that group, called by the United Nations 'Centrally Planned Economies' and covering just under a quarter of world manufacturing employment and about 10 per cent of world trade. The classification is the product of political preoccupations rather than economic analysis, and as misleading as that other term, 'Less Developed Countries'. Indeed, there is an uncomfortable overlap between all the categories – with China, Vietnam, North Korea, Outer Mongolia and Cuba claiming membership of 'Less Developed' (and most curiously of all for Cuba, of 'non-aligned'). The group of centrally planned – properly so-called – covers the range of economic phenomena, and is not even politically united – from Yugoslavia to Kampuchea. They share only a common language of politics, of the aspiration to central planning, and images in both East and West reinforce this image of a common condition. Within the group – of sixteen countries where a Communist party of whatever name possesses a monopoly of power – there are nine which accept a common political loyalty, a common political relationship, if not to the rest of the world, then certainly to the United States. They accept also common administered elements in their economic relationships, embodied in the Council for Mutual Economic Assistance (C.M.E.A. or Comecon for short: Bulgaria, Czechoslovakia, Hungary, Mongolia, Poland, Romania, Vietnam, the Soviet Union, Cuba).

There is a second range of problems which underlie the Eastern Bloc version of the managed economy. For it is implied that a State can escape domestic effects of external competition; in some cases, can escape competition itself; that it can organize its domestic affairs to achieve a self-generating, self-sustaining pattern of growth. Now, in its extreme form, the proposition of 'economic independence' is clearly absurd, as absurd as the notion that a company could escape the market. It might be said that the analogy is false, for the function of the State is different. It does not depend for its survival on access to a market for the sale of goods. This is true, but only partly so; for the State depends for its survival upon creating or securing access to the social surplus generated in production, just as does a company. That necessity in turn imposes disciplines upon the State, and in so far as domestic production is governed by imperatives that are of the market, so State and market are linked.

However, that is not the most important element. States exist in part to defend their territory, to have what they hold, to protect their 'national independence'. That requires defence, military spending. There is no way of determining what is the 'right' level of defence spending; ultimately, one can be secure only if domestic defence preparedness is equal to or better than the best in the world, that of the greatest military rival. But the rivals are driven by the same imperative, so that no sooner does one State approach the military level of a second than the second endeavours to leap ahead – there is an arms race. The competition between States, the primary expression of which is military competition, is thus a direct result of defending 'national independence'.

Defence, however, is not merely a marginal addition to an existing economy. It was not so even in the 1890s, when Engels penned the words cited at the head of this chapter. Today, defence spending draws disproportionately on the core industries of a modern economy, on heavy industry, on metal-fabricating, engineering, electrical and petro-chemical industries. The arms race becomes a powerful factor defining the entirety of domestic activity – the more so, the more backward a country is. For the Soviet Union, contesting, world supremacy with the most powerful single national State, the United States, from a position of relative economic weakness, the imperative becomes very powerful indeed, shaping all other subsidiary decisions down to how much investment should be devoted to agriculture. The aim of national independence is not something achieved by simple declamation; it imposes continuing obligations, which in turn necessarily engage States in rivalries, in a competition, which shapes domestic relationships.

The priorities of investment ultimately affect the basic livelihood of the population. In Chapter 2, we noted the striking demographic changes in the Less Developed Countries which accompanied the great boom; indeed, the improvement in the average expectation of life at birth was described as one of the greatest achievements of postwar capitalism. If we apply the same criterion to the Soviet Union, it is startling to find that it is the only major industrial country where infant mortality rose and life expectancy fell in the decade of the seventies. In 1980, thirty Soviet babies died for every 1,000 born; in 1960, twenty-four died. In 1970, the average expectation of life at birth was seventy years; in 1980, just over sixty-nine. Alexander Smirnov, the deputy director of the demographic section of the State Planning Committee, who issued these figures, suggested the following as causes: a more efficient system of collecting data; increasing alcoholism (producing more children who die earlier and increased adult mortality, particularly among males); the effects of poor rural medical services; and a rising rate of abortion (affecting maternal health and so normal births).

The link between demography and the Russian system might be disputed. But there are other, less disputable, marks of the increasing difficulties experienced by the planned economy. Thus, despite the claims, fluctuations in growth are considerable, certainly equal to those in Western capitalism in the period since the Second World War. Furthermore, the high growth of the early years has tended to give way to steadily declining rates of increase. Like some of the Less Developed, some of the C.M.E.A. countries were able to offset world slump, but by the late seventies, most were beginning to falter. In the case of the European C.M.E.A. countries, the fluctuations were considerable – in Table 24, row 1 shows Hungary's rate of growth varying between nearly 7 per cent (1974) and −0.5 per cent (1980); Russia's between the average for the last half of the sixties, 7.6 per cent, and 2 per cent (1979) and, the most extreme case, Poland, varying from over 10 per cent in 1974 to negative rates in 1979 and 1980 (−2 and −4 per cent and the catastrophic −13 per cent in 1981). Only Bulgaria and Romania (up to 1979–80) were able to sustain relatively high rates of industrial growth. Furthermore, the gap between performance and plan – contained in the contrast between the unbracketed and bracketed figures of row 1 in each country section of the table – is itself an important comment on the capacity of the planned economy to plan.

Fluctuations in industrial output growth show lesser changes, although most countries show a falling off in 1979 (see row 2 of each country table). Investment, however, shows remarkable fluctuations, easily comparable to the variations in what are supposedly private capitalist economies in Western Europe (see row 3); note in particular the two distinct waves in Bulgaria's experience, with peak investment in 1975 and 1977, followed by an astonishing fall in the year following (0.7 per cent in both cases), and in the case of the second fall, followed by a year of negative investment growth (−3.1 for 1979); the two waves are apparent in the Hungarian case also, peaking in the same year, followed ultimately in both cases by negative growth (−0.3 per cent in 1976 and 1979); Poland and Czechoslovakia experienced the first wave but not the second. Given the impact of variations in these rates of investment on capital goods production, they must have produced changes in

24. *Real net material product (with plan target in brackets), industrial output and gross fixed capital formation (all, percentage rate of change); and balance of payments, dollars U.S. millions*[2]

	1966–70	1971–5	1974	1975	1976
BULGARIA					
1. Real net material product	8.7	7.9	7.6	8.8	6.5
plan target in brackets	(8.5)	(8.1)	(10.0)	(9.0)	(9.0)
2. Industrial output	–	9.2	8.5	9.9	6.7
3. Gross fixed capital formation	–	8.6	8.8	17.3	0.7
4. Balance of trade ($m)	–	(51)	−490	−716	−245
HUNGARY					
1. Real net material product	6.8	6.3	6.9	5.4	3.0
plan target in brackets	(3.7)	(5.7)	(5.0)	(5.2)	(5.3)
2. Industrial output	–	6.4	8.1	4.7	4.6
3. Gross fixed capital formation	–	7.1	9.8	14.8	−0.3
4. Balance of trade ($m)	–	(47)	−446	−889	−607
POLAND					
1. Real net material product	5.7	9.8	10.4	9.0	6.8
plan target in brackets	(6.0)	(7.0)	(9.5)	(9.8)	(8.3)
2. Industrial output	–	10.5	12.5	10.9	9.3
3. Gross fixed capital formation	–	18.4	–	14.2	2.2
4. Balance of trade ($m)	–	−659	−2,168	−2,256	−2,853
EAST GERMANY					
1. Real net material product	5.1	5.4	6.4	4.9	3.7
plan target in brackets	(5.4)	(4.9)	(5.6)	(5.4)	(5.3)
2. Industrial output	–	6.3	7.3	6.4	5.9
3. Gross fixed capital formation	–	4.7	4.3	6.1	8.4
4. Balance of trade ($m)	–	(21)	−898	−1.202	−1,835
ROMANIA					
1. Real net material product	7.7	11.3	12.3	10.3	10.5
plan target in brackets	(7.0)	(11.5)	(14.6)	(14.0)	(10.5)
2. Industrial output	–	12.9	14.6	12.2	11.4
3. Gross fixed capital formation	–	11.5	18.5	15.0	8.3
4. Balance of trade ($m)	–	(70)	−269	0	42
CZECHOSLOVAKIA					
1. Real net material product	6.9	5.7	5.9	6.2	4.2
plan target in brackets	(4.2)	(5.1)	(5.2)	(5.6)	(5.0)
2. Industrial output	–	6.7	6.2	6.7	5.5
3. Gross fixed capital formation	–	8.0	8.7	8.3	4.4
4. Balance of trade ($m)	–	(114)	−471	−728	−668
SOVIET UNION					
1. Real net material product	7.6	5.7	5.4	4.5	5.9
plan target in brackets	(6.8)	(6.8)	(6.5)	(6.5)	(5.4)
2. Industrial output	–	7.4	8.0	7.5	4.8
3. Gross fixed capital formation	–	7.0	7.1	8.6	4.5
4. Balance of Trade ($m)	–	(329)	2,511	−3,652	−942

1977	1978	1979	1980	1981	
BULGARIA					
6.3	5.6	6.5	5.7		*1. Real net material product*
(8.2)	(6.8)	(7.0)	(5.7)		*plan target in brackets*
6.9	7.0	6.5	4.0		*2. Industrial output*
14.5	0.7	−3.1	5.0		*3. Gross fixed capital formation*
−42	−170	−			*4. Balance of trade ($m)*
HUNGARY					
7.8	4.0	1.2	−0.5	1.8	*1. Real net material product*
(6.3)	(5.0)	(3.5)	(3.0–3.5)	(2.0–2.5)	*plan target in brackets*
6.6	4.9	2.8			*2. Industrial output*
14.4	5.5	−0.3			*3. Gross fixed capital formation*
−700	−1,590	−			*4. Balance of trade ($m)*
POLAND					
5.0	2.8	−2.0	−4.0	−13	*1. Real net material product*
(5.7)	(5.4)	(2.8)	(1.4–1.8)		*plan target in brackets*
6.9	4.9	2.8			*2. Industrial output*
4.3	1.0	−			*3. Gross fixed capital formation*
−2,353	−1,928	−			*4. Balance of trade ($m)*
EAST GERMANY					
5.2	4.0	4.0	4.2	5.0	*1. Real net material product*
(5.5)	(5.2)	(4.3)	(4.8)	(5.0)	*plan target in brackets*
5.4	5.4	4.8			*2. Industrial output*
6.8	3.0	2.4			*3. Gross fixed capital formation*
−2,310	−1,305	−			*4. Balance of trade ($m)*
ROMANIA					
9.0	7.6	6.2	2.5	2.0	*1. Real net material product*
(11.3)	(11.2)	(8.8)	(8.8)	(7.0)	*plan target in brackets*
12.5	9.6	8.0			*2. Industrial output*
11.7	16.2	−			*3. Gross fixed capital formation*
3	−830	−			*4. Balance of trade ($m)*
CZECHOSLOVAKIA					
4.2	4.0	−	3.0	0.2	*1. Real net material product*
(5.2)	(4.9)		(3.7)	(2.8)	*plan target in brackets*
5.7	5.0	3.7			*2. Industrial output*
5.7	4.1	1.6			*3. Gross fixed capital formation*
−875	−825	−			*4. Balance of trade ($m)*
SOVIET UNION					
4.5	−	2.0	2.0–3.0		*1. Real net material product*
(4.1)	(4.0)	(4.3)	(4.0)		*plan target in brackets*
5.7	4.8	3.4			*2. Industrial output*
3.6	5.2	−			*3. Gross fixed capital formation*
4,293	1,596	−			*4. Balance of trade ($m)*

domestic activity which were anything but the smooth trajectory of planned growth.

Furthermore, row 4 in each country table indicates that there was increased dependence on external activities through the seventies. Each investment boom seems only to have increased the deficit on the balance of trade which, for all except the Soviet Union and Romania, has been consistently in the red during the seventies. That is, the pattern of growth has an unmistakable resemblance to that which (as we saw in the last chapter) characterizes some of the faster growing Less Developed Countries. The propensity to import, whenever there is expansion, seems to be high and growing. In part, the deficits of the six East European economies are the opposite side of the coin to the surplus of the Soviet Union. Rising oil and raw material prices in the world are ultimately reflected in the export prices of the Soviet Union, the major supplier of these items to Eastern Europe, which are then in part funded by a decline in reserves and Soviet loans to its trading partners. This phenomenon produced a steady deterioration in the terms of trade between the Soviet Union and its six East European associates in the early eighties – the former's surplus jumped from 2.4 billion dollars in 1980 to 5.9 billion in 1982.

Another part of the deficit, however, is to the countries of Western Europe and the United States. In this case, the deficits have partly been covered by loans and credits from governments and from Western banks. By the end of 1979, the cumulative 'hard' currency debt (of the seven European C.M.E.A. countries and C.M.E.A. banks) was about 75 billion dollars, and by 1982 (including Yugoslavia), over 90 billion dollars. The burden of servicing this debt rose steeply in the late seventies, finally catching Poland in a near default. Even by 1978, interest payments were taking some 30–35 per cent of the export earnings of Hungary and Poland; for Poland, 54 per cent of its hard currency earnings was required to cover its hard currency debts in 1979, and 68 per cent in 1980 (Poland's external debt of 4.9 billion dollars of 1970 reached 24 billion by 1980, with debt servicing for that year of 7.2 billion dollars in comparison to the value of exports of 8.5 billion). By 1982, Poland was supposed to find 10 billion dollars to repay loans falling due that year as well as interest charges, in an economy essentially bankrupt. The banks were obdurate, but they talked; as one of their number commented in mid 1982: 'Poland has been de facto bankrupt for about two years. The sole purpose of the discussions now going on with the commercial banks is to prevent a legal formalization of this bankruptcy.'

The European Eastern Bloc countries are distinguished from the West European countries in one important respect: the scale of production devoted to accumulation, to investment, in the fifties and sixties. In the world figures, the share of light industry in total manufacturing output for the Centrally Planned Economies is said to have moved between 1955, 1970 and 1976 from 49.3 to 33.0 to 28.2 per cent (and for heavy industry, from 50.7 to 67.0 to 71.8 per cent, easily the highest share of any group of countries).[3] The shift in proportions has thus been particularly rapid in the seventies, despite a tendency to declining rates of growth. The disproportionate growth has affected the capital goods industry (metals, metal-working, construction materials) and basic raw materials (coal, steel, oil and gas), a kind of forced growth which, remarkably, has not produced higher rates of overall growth. On the contrary, it seems that it is precisely this disproportionate growth which has dragged down the rest of the economy and led to excessively uneconomic use of products, to waste. The Soviet Union, for example, is the world's largest producer of steel, but that supply of steel goes to service an economy which is considerably smaller than that of the United States; steel must be, by the most efficient standards of production, wasted on a substantial scale.

It is this problem which is one aspect of the underlying core difficulty in the East European States. They are driven by competition with the more advanced States to devote a very high proportion of domestic production to investment – at the cost of consumption of the mass of the population – but the investment is increasingly ineffective in generating increased output; for example, it is reported that five units of investment were required to produce one extra unit of output in East Germany in the first half of the seventies, but eight units in the second half. In the Soviet Union, an official journal noted in 1982 that the volume of investment required to secure an increase of one tonne in national oil output had increased by nearly 800 per cent between the two planning periods, 1976–80 and 1981–5; for one tonne of coal, the comparable figure was 21 per cent, and to secure an extra rouble's-worth of equipment, 39.3 per cent. The same complaints came from all the Comecon countries.

The result is that the planned expansion of investment becomes a kind of sporadic gamble, immediately producing severe bottlenecks in the supply of complementary factors and a sudden increase in the stocks of unused equipment; investment is then cut back to allow the rest of the economy to catch up. Such a procedure of advance on one front, followed by pauses, is a pattern of growth which is very wasteful, but may be the only method of moving a relatively primitive economy, based upon relatively abundant supplies of raw materials (from the Soviet Union) and labour (from agriculture) to produce a crude output (for example, steel). But in the sixties, it seems, Eastern Europe arrived at the stage of increasingly needing to expand the sophisticated quality of its output and, in the seventies, needing to economize on increasingly expensive energy and raw materials. The blunt instrument of the State and a monopoly of power, so effective, if so cruel, in bludgeoning crude output out of an obdurate nature, now becomes a powerful obstacle to growth; the physical planning targets which pay little attention to the relative scarcity of materials militate against economy; a structure of power that does not engage the profit motives of managers, let alone the active and detailed supervision of the mass of the population, makes economic modernization impossible.

The collision between the inherited political structure, designed originally for one task, and the developing economy, was compounded by all the more notorious features of the centrally planned system – what Brezhnev in 1979 called 'negligence, lack of responsibility and stupid bungling', or what the Cuban Defence Minister, Raul Castro, listed in 1980 as indiscipline, poor control, irresponsibility, complacency, negligence and 'buddyism'. The account of unfinished projects – power stations, hospitals, pipelines, factories, hotels, blocks of flats, coal mines (nine major mines in the Soviet Union each took eight years to build, or double the planned time) – of waylaid supplies, of wasted raw materials, of spectacular ambitions destroyed by foolish errors of coordination, is too long to be recited,[4] but they affect all sectors of the civil economy – from the phantom factories, officially finished but actually still building-sites,[5] to the 56 million pairs of defective shoes denounced by Brezhnev at the 1978 Party Congress.[6] On the collective farms, official estimates put the losses of feed grain as high as 20 to 30 per cent of the harvest, roughly equal to the 35 million tonnes of grain the Soviet Union was obliged to import in the crop year 1980–81; the diagnosis of the cause of the losses was that investment in agriculture was unproductive because 'profitability, efficiency and quality play virtually no role in the work of State and collective farms'.[7] World crisis and U.S. imperialism, Raul Castro argued in the case of Cuban difficulties, should not be 'used as pretexts to hide our deficiencies'.[8]

The chaos of actual bureaucratic planning stood in exact contradiction to the rhetoric of rational planning, making the 'anarchy of the market' not much different to the 'anarchy of the plan'. Furthermore, it added a special extra element of uncertainty to the reliability of the official statistics. There was another element here, a feature common, as we have seen, to both the More and Less Developed Countries: the black economy. Each surge in activity produces an increase in the demand for labour, and, where wage payments increase with output, a considerable increase in the demand for consumer goods. Yet the plan consistently seeks to direct investment away from consumer goods to investment goods. One of the first results in a Western State would be inflation in prices, but where prices are controlled, the same phenomenon is expressed through the physical disappearance of goods, through queues and forced or official rationing, and through wage-earners increasing their savings. Another result is a vast impetus to the unofficial supply of consumer goods, the black economy.

One of the most important elements here is private agriculture – whether it is the unofficial activity of private farmers (the major part of Polish land is in private hands) or the exploitation of recognized 'private plots' in Russia and China (that is, the gardens of agricultural workers or enterprising city-dwellers). Of course, the respective governments publish few statistics on how large this activity is; American sources have argued that nearly one-third of all the hours worked in Russian agriculture are devoted to private plots (a tenth of all the labour hours worked in the whole economy[9]); and there was scattered evidence from Chinese sources that, in the early sixties, the major part of the grain crop in some provinces came from private cultivation.[10] In the early seventies, it was estimated that some 50 million people cultivated 3 per cent of all the cultivated acreage in the Soviet Union to produce possibly a quarter of the value of the gross agricultural output (a result which arises because of the high value of intensive cultivation on private lands – potatoes, vegetables, fruit, flowers and livestock – as opposed to the extensive crops on much collective land); the output was sold in private markets at whatever prices the market determined. Sometimes the activity was illegal (using rent-free State land, stolen fodder, water, tools, transport, fertilizers) – sometimes it was not. To some extent, the East European governments have accommodated to the phenomenon as a way of increasing supplies and damping down inflationary pressure; thus, the Soviet Union has most recently removed legal limits on the private ownership of livestock.

About half the Russian population (and half the urban population) live in private houses, and something like a third of the new housing floor space constructed in 1975 was outside the State sector (built not only by individuals, but also by cooperatives and collective farms). The private housing sector proper, however, is partly supported by filched public building materials (which in turn jeopardizes public construction projects) and 'borrowed' equipment, and built by moonlighting building workers, aided and abetted by corrupt officials.

There is moonshine as well as moonlighting (that is, illegally taking second jobs). Between 20 and 30 per cent of the prodigious and famous consumption of alcohol by thirsty Russians was said to come from illicit stills in 1970 – and was traded illegally throughout the country.[11] Skills are illegally on sale for those able to purchase them, whether the skill is engaged full-time in the black economy (as with some construction gangs, the *shabashniki*), or only on offer out of official working hours – doctors, dentists, teachers, house or vehicle repair men, tailors. cobblers, and assorted artisans and craftsmen. The same is true in China, where, in particular, several million young people who have returned illegally from exile in the countryside to the cities are eager for odd jobs. The second-hand private market for goods is well developed, as also that for smuggled goods (particularly in the main port cities of Leningrad, Riga and Odessa[12]).

Indeed, there are reports in the Russian press like those from Italy, of illegal factories making garments, footwear, household articles, the survival of which depends on the connivance of party officials and police. For example, *Pravda* (24 December 1978) reports the sentence – after an eleven-month trial – of fifty-five people who had been for five years operating a knitwear factory behind the façade of a training workshop for the blind in Kazakh in Azerbaijan; the output was marketed in thirty-two cities of the Union, which shows an impressive retail distribution network.[13] In Romania, Gheorghe Stefanescu sold untaxed liquor, filched from State liquor stores with the connivance of bribed managers, and was thereby able to live for a number of years as a millionaire, according to the local press. (Sentenced with him in the autumn of 1978 were twenty accomplices, including the first secretary of the Bucharest eighth party district committee.) The Romanian ambassador to Bulgaria, Stefan Bobos, was sacked and expelled from the Party for building – for speculative purposes – six lavishly appointed holiday villas in Piatra Neamt, the mountain resort. And in the spring of 1980, some 200 officials in Moscow and Azerbaijan were arrested for selling to foreign dealers, over ten years, black caviar in tins labelled 'smoked, seasoned herring'; the dealers relabelled the tins, sold them at considerable profit, and diverted part of the proceeds to external bank accounts for the Russians; senior officials at the Moscow Ministry of Fisheries, including the Minister, were said to be implicated. In April 1982, the Deputy Minister, Vladimir Rytor, was executed.[14]

The cases can be multiplied for all the Centrally Planned Economies,[15] and in and of themselves are no more than the common occurrences of capitalist society. The distinction between what is black and white in all countries is within the determination of the law or, at least, of official recognition; it only matters in relationship to the claims of a 'managed economy', threatened by what a former British prime minister called 'the unacceptable face of capitalism'. Public recognition of petty unregulated capitalism is more of a problem in a Centrally Planned Economy because it jeopardizes the pretensions of the plan. In essence, it is a spontaneous self-reform, a compensation for the rigidities of bureaucracy; from the planners' point of view, it has the useful merit of 'mopping up surplus purchasing power' and introducing an element of flexibility in the achievement of plan targets (thus, factory managers can gain access to, for example, raw materials on the black market or skilled labour when the official allocation system fails to make legal supplies available in time for the completion of the plan). But it also rots the foundations of State power. The planners control less than would otherwise be the case; supplies and labour leave the known and manageable for the unknown sector, and the power of the State is thereby reduced. The standard response when that infringement becomes intolerable is the use of terror to drive it back, but that in turn requires that the Party is separate or separable from the black economy. Where incomes are unequally distributed, it is the better-off who have a vested interest in a black market, and in a Centrally Planned Economy, the better-off coincide most often with party cadres.

The alternative to brute force, with all its damaging results for the economy, is institutional and plan reform in order that the supplies provided by the black economy become available from the white. Reform of the plan, however, would require relaxing the effort involved in the competition with other States, particularly those in the West – diverting more investment away from defence and capital goods to consumer goods. While different governments have made sporadic efforts in this direction, none has sustained the effort long enough to make much difference except where crisis intervenes to force this result (as appears to be happening in Poland and China at present). Institutional reform, on the other hand, received much more sustained attention in the first half of the sixties. Proposals were formulated to 'decentralize' economic authority to the level of company or plant; managers were to be given the power to determine the supply of inputs and labour they required, to set the prices of output, all in competition with each other – their income was to vary in part with their success in producing goods of the quality and at the price which would ensure their sale; the sanction for failure would be a fall in income, and even, in some of the more radical proposals, their dismissal for failing to make an enterprise profitable. It followed from such proposals that price stability would end, and, politically even more important, so would guaranteed employment for all.

The reforms were not implemented, although Hungary went the furthest in making changes. Decentralization not only affected the inherited structure of power, shifting power from the State bureaucracy to managers, it also became indistinguishable from general 'liberalization' which, in turn, raised questions of the loyalty of particular East European States to Moscow. In the first case, as a former Polish Communist theoretician, Lezek Nowack, put it: 'They are bureaucrats (the cadre of the Communist parties) who express the interests of their class. They may desire reforms, but they are always confronted with the solid wall of their underlings.'[16] In the second, the evolution of Czechoslovakia in the mid sixties raised, for the Moscow leaders, a host of demons; in 1968, the Russian army invaded and ended all talk of reform not only in Prague, but also in Berlin, Warsaw, Bucharest, Sofia and, not least, in Moscow itself.

The central problem, however, remained. There was another remedy, but one which might have seemed – and in fact turned out to be – even more dangerous. This was to open the Eastern Bloc to world trade, endeavouring to use the world market to achieve the same upgrading of industry that institutional reforms had been designed to implement. Increased imports of high technology goods would, in theory, upgrade the quality of domestic output, economize on the use of raw materials, and make better use of investment; increased exports to pay for these imports would force at least exporting managers to relate their output to external markets. Thereby, the Eastern Bloc might stand an improved chance of competing with the States of N.A.T.O. on terms of reasonable equality, and do so without either shifting the pattern of domestic investment or disturbing the inherited structure of Party power and, thus, running the risk of undermining loyalties to Moscow. Furthermore, in the process of 'détente', increasing relationships with Western capital, perhaps some of the more sophisticated techniques of management might rub off on the Party cadres. The cautious words of a leading economist of a non-C.M.E.A. Centrally Planned Economy led the way for a comparable 'opening up' by the People's Republic of China:

> Methods of economic management in capitalist countries contain factors worth our study because the bourgeoisie of big companies ... consciously do things according to objective economic law, and doing such work over a long period, have accumulated quite a fund of experience and become proficient in applying these laws.[17]

Deng Xiaoping, deputy Prime Minister of China, gave a somewhat abbreviated version of the same thought during his first visit to Japan: 'We must absorb advanced technology and efficient forms of management from the outside world if we are to propel the nation forward.'

In the late sixties and the seventies, the change was almost universal among the Centrally Planned Economies, independently of their membership of C.M.E.A. The change indicated a common problem and a common opportunity. It coincided, as we have noted earlier, with a comparable shift in many Less Developed Countries from an 'import substitution' to an 'export promotion' strategy. The Centrally Planned moved from autarchy to, if not export promotion, then import-led growth. The participation of Western capital in Centrally Planned Economies became not merely acceptable but even highly desirable. Perhaps most dramatic in this respect was the behaviour of the Vietnamese Government. For, within a short time of coming to power, Hanoi was suggesting some of the most favourable terms on offer by an Less Developed Country to foreign investment (49 per cent foreign ownership in any activity except a list reserved for the State, and 100 per cent ownership for export activities; a State guarantee against nationalization for ten to fifteen years, with full compensation guaranteed thereafter; plus tax concessions and other incentives[18]).

Increased external involvement did generate domestic changes, but not necessarily of the kind the Party leadership desired. In the case of Russia, the changes were important, but still too slight to offset the increasing crisis that afflicted the ailing giant in the eighties. Then, increasing domestic weakness, growing external burdens, interacted with the impact of the second world slump to produce serious doubts about the long-term viability of the regime. The domestic weaknesses included four years of poor harvests, the poorest rates of industrial growth in the postwar period (far below the planned targets), and a necessity to match the increased military spending of the N.A.T.O. powers. The external factors included an expensive – and possibly disastrous – military occupation of Afghanistan, continued military threats on the western and eastern borders, a growing dependence upon imported grain, the need to support Poland with foodstuffs and hard currency, to assist the rest of Eastern Europe and Cuba as the cumulative debt problem forced them into slump, as well as maintaining extensive commitments elsewhere (for example, in Vietnam). For the ageing Russian leadership, it must seem that everywhere predators lurked, waiting only for the opportunity to despoil their decaying empire.

The problems of Russian agriculture epitomized the crisis, for after what was supposedly a spectacular record in terms of economic growth, queues for scarce foodstuffs remained a basic feature of Russian life. The 1981 Statistical Yearbook recorded the melancholy facts that in

1980 the average Soviet citizen consumed 2 lb less meat, 11 lb less fruit and vegetables, 11 lb less diary produce, and 7 lb less potatoes than in 1979; rationing had returned everywhere, but still could not guarantee supplies. In fact, given the difficult terrain, soil and weather of Russia, the long-term performance was not as bad as frequently portrayed, but increasing demand – arising from the growth of the urban population and from increasing incomes that changed household diets – constantly shot ahead of supply. The response of the Party leadership was always the same – to throw more money at the problem, and as a result, to lose more money. A backward industrial structure ensured that, despite major investments, the loss of agricultural labour to the cities could never be commensurately made up by capital investment. Indeed, each unit of increased output cost steadily more.[19] Nonetheless, extravagance in expenditure was designed to avoid radical reform. In May of 1982, as yet again reports began of a fourth harvest failure, Mr Brezhnev bravely committed the next Five Year Plan (beginning in 1986) to increase agricultural investment from 27 to 33 per cent of the Plan total.

The weakening of the Soviet Union jeopardized the position of all the much smaller Russian associates in Comecon. There, experiment in economic reform had gone much further. The changes were nowhere more dramatic than in Hungary which, for a time in the seventies, became the aspirant South Korea of the Centrally Planned Economies.

Hungary

The Hungarian Government began to introduce a 'New Economic Mechanism' in 1968, the year of the Russian invasion of Czechoslovakia. The process was reversed from 1972 in what seems to have been a wave of doubts among Party cadres, but then resumed once more from 1977, with the aim of equalizing a major part of world and domestic prices by 1980. In the interim, Hungary caught the switchback of world fluctuations in its upward phase. The actual Hungarian growth rate regularly exceeded the planned targets (see row 1 in Table 24 above, 1966–75) and persisted through slump in 1975. The following year, the process was finally checked sharply when the actual performance was only just over half of the plan target, but in 1977 the rate rose again, falling once more in the two years following.

The growth process was 'export led'. For a decade, Hungarian exports increased at a rate double that of the increase in national output. The value of exports began to approach half that of the national income (for

South Korea, the 1973 ratio was 40.5 per cent), taking a third of industrial output and some 50 per cent of the top ten sectors of the economy (pharmaceuticals, aluminium, telecommunications equip-memt, instruments, transport equipment, footwear, animals, poultry, fruit and tin).

The institutional reforms, however, were still powerfully tempered by the need to protect the party. In aim, the central proposed reform was supposed to create the independent authority of managers, and intro-duce the sole criterion of profitability for new investment. In practice, the State was fearful of the impact of any such change on employment; hiring and firing, and wage setting, remained the prerogative of the State. However, in the most profitable companies, 'incentive' payments could add up to 65 per cent to the basic salary. It was part illusion, for the State continued to protect unprofitable operations, to subsidize com-panies. The subsidies, to cushion the effects of reform, continued to grow; one official estimate has it that between 1972 and 1978 company profits increased by 14.3 per cent, but State subsidies increased by 17 per cent. Another source suggests that some 60 per cent of business profits were in fact State subsidies.

The State also protected consumers, offsetting inflationary pressure by subsidizing basic consumption. In 1977, subsidies reduced the price of meat by 16 per cent, of milk by 66 per cent, cereals 26 per cent, fuel 38 per cent and public transport 17 per cent. The State was also very slow in reforming the mode of external transactions: it did not introduce the convertibility of the Hungarian currency, the forint. Two exchange rates were permitted, with constant anomalies as a result; in some cases, the pricing of exports failed to cover the cost of imports which were con-sumed in producing the exports.

Slump challenged the process. However, as with the Newly Indus-trializing Countries, the choice was not a real one, for the known dangers of retreat were far more fearsome than the unknown possibilities of advance. When Western banks were competing to lend to a high export-growth economy, when foreign capital still appeared eager to expand production using Hungarian labour, the gamble promised the possibility of success. But to persist required the increasing 'flexibility' of the economy – variable prices, employment and the bankrupting of subsidized plants. In 1979, the Government tried to lay down that companies must make a 24 per cent minimum gross return on assets in order to secure bank loans. The great domestic monopolies were to be broken up into smaller competing units; the trusts governing wine, tobacco, sugar and confectionery were divided up. In the retail trade, private operators were given new opportunities to expand – the licensing of private artisans was increased, and State shops were available for leasing to private dealers (with the right to employ up to four workers). Direct financial relationships between foreign markets and Hungarian export firms were permitted, rather than State marketing agencies appropriating a monopoly of all external transactions. The Government set about lowering consumer subsidies while holding wages virtually frozen – the prices of foodstuffs were to increase by a fifth (with a 50 per cent increase in bread prices; 30 per cent on meat; 23 per cent on sugar; 20 per cent on dairy products); of electricity by 51 per cent; fuels 34 per cent; building materials 12 per cent; furnishings 18 per cent; and leather goods, 20–25 per cent.

The press began to prepare workers for unemployment increases, stressing that the 'right to work' did not mean the right to the same job. The 'aggregate wage system' had been introduced in the mid seventies; this permitted the wages paid out to remain constant as the workforce fell, giving an incentive to the majority of workers to accept the sacking of a minority. However, it remained formal up to the end of the decade, since the Government was not sure of its political effects. The 1967 labour code was redrafted to make sacking easier, and make possible the assignment of workers to several part-time jobs rather than one full-time one. Further efforts were bent towards increased income differences generally, an aim summed up in Janos Kadar's proclamation at the 1980 Party Congress, emulating an earlier statement by Josef Stalin: 'We should resolutely reject the appalling notion and easy-going practice of egalitarianism. Social justice requires the creation of bigger differences than the existing ones.'

By 1980, prices were beginning to reflect the changes. In the first quarter, the consumer price index was 12 per cent above that of a year earlier (the Hungarian National Bank estimated the rate of inflation in 1979 at 9 per cent[20]). But there was no clear evidence that unemployment had increased sharply, nor that companies were now seriously exposed to bankruptcy. By the time of the second slump, presenting a picture of iron-clad financial orthodoxy to the international banks (Hungary had the highest debt-servicing ratio of the C.M.E.A. group) added weight to the task of securing 'realistic prices' – 1982 saw an amazing surge of decreed price increases.

But, from the outside, it seemed the opposition to the strategy was slight. Perhaps it was that real incomes for many continued to increase rapidly enough to absorb the effects of price increases. Many must have been cushioned by the growth of the private economy – the officially recorded 90,000 private artisans; 10,000 private shopkeepers; 1.8 million private agricultural plots; and 35–40,000 private houses built annually (equivalent, the Government said, to the work of 120,000 construction workers). The black economy also seems to have flourished. The party daily, *Nepszabadsag*,[21] maintained that nearly three-quarters of all Hungarian families received some income from the black economy.

The changes flowed from Hungary's increasing integration in external trade, both with the rest of C.M.E.A. and, even more important in effect, with Western Europe. It was the trade integration which impelled domestic reform, rather than vice versa. Subcontracting work for foreign firms became important in the late sixties, particularly in textiles and garments. Hungary's textile exports increased in value from 84 million U.S. dollars in 1968 to 200 million in 1976; and garment exports from 92.2 to 270 million dollars. For some West German firms, it has been argued, subcontracting work abroad made possible their survival in the textile trades.[22] Much of the work was limited to a narrow range of operations, employing in the main unskilled, and often female, labour. But quite often subcontracting work involved more substantial lines in established firms – for example, the giant engineering company, Ruba (at Györ in Western Hungary), exporting about a quarter of its output, is contracted to supply truck rear axles to the U.S. companies, International Harvester, and Vauxhall in Britain.

Joint ventures between Hungarian and foreign firms gave Western companies access to the C.M.E.A. market at the same time as Hungarian companies gained improved access to Western markets. In some cases, such operations were part of integrated production lines spanning Eastern and Western Europe. Levi Strauss's Budapest factory exported 60 per cent of its output, much of it returning to Levi Strauss's marketing outlets in Western Europe. Biogal, the joint venture of a Hungarian company and Zyma, a subsidiary of the Swiss Ciba-Geigy, manufactured therapeutical liver products, half of which were repurchased by Zyma for its manufacturing activities abroad. Siemens took 30–40 per cent of the output of its joint venture in Hungary, Sicontact, for further processing in its West German factories. Thus, through 'intra-company' trade, intra-industry trade has become an important part of Hungary's external transactions. The process also goes in the opposite direction. Thus, Budapest Tungsram has set up a joint venture to manufacture electric light bulbs in East Brunswick, New Jersey (a phenomenon not restricted to Hungary – for example, East Germany's Carl Zeiss of Jena has been involved in joint ventures in Algeria and Central America).

Joint ventures are not restricted to manufacturing. In 1979, for the first time in Eastern Europe, a joint venture bank was set up. The National Bank of Hungary took a 34 per cent holding in the new operation, the other 66 per cent being shared among six foreign banks (registered in Austria, Italy, France, West Germany and Japan). The bank's operations were to be restricted to external currency transactions, with a special concern directed at raising petro-dollar funds for investment in large-scale energy projects.

The Hungarian Party leadership was constrained in its efforts to accommodate the country to external forces by the possible domestic and Russian reactions. Later, the fearful lesson of Poland in the early eighties seemed to vindicate their earlier fears. C.M.E.A.'s structure of exchanges impeded flexibility, although even here the changes were increasing (by 1979, about a third of C.M.E.A. trade was governed by world market prices, and the share was growing). Nonetheless, the Government was explicit in its aims if not in their immediate implementation, as this 1976 statement illustrates:

> Development and utilization of the productive bases already available in order to adjust to the demands of the world market are the main guidelines towards which policy in the field of the domestic pricing system, exchange rate policy, taxation and the system of central and enterprise management will be oriented. Fundamentally, our economic policy is one of increasing our orientation to exports. The interconnection between production and consumption, as well as the more complex system of interests, are to be aligned towards the expansion of exports to non-socialist countries ... In view of the insufficient amount of labour available, it is necessary to cut back the production of goods in the mechanical engineering sector which yield a lower profit margin ... Decisions as to which agricultural products to produce will be made in the light of extensive consideration of demand on the world market.[23]

Or, more succinctly in the words of Janos Fekete (deputy governor of the Hungarian National Bank) in 1982: 'We are a socialist planned economy under the control of the market.'

Budapest maintained externally an unimpeachable loyalty to the political standpoint of Moscow, and that preserved the Russian tolerance of its experiments. The Party cadres did well out of the changes. But slow growth and the black economy both threatened the future position. For the moment, however, the partial integration of Hungary's production with the world at large seemed, by the primitive criteria employed, a 'success'. By contrast, Poland was the awful warning of the potential for failure.

Poland

Poland is, in population terms, the largest of Russia's allies in Eastern Europe. It holds a peculiarly strategic position, guarding the most vulnerable marches of Russia by land, and by sea, sharing a long Baltic coast. The adventures Moscow might tolerate in Hungary would always attract more suspicion if repeated in Poland. The scrutiny of the Kremlin would be closer still, because of the well-proven capacity of Poles in general, and Polish workers in particular, to resist the proposals of the Polish Party leadership. Poland had been vital in the rebellions after Stalin's death; the leadership created by the movement of 1956 had then been popularly defeated in 1970, and there had been further explosions of popular anger in 1976.

Like the rest of Eastern Europe, there had been much talk of institutional reform in the first half of the sixties. The aspiration was crushed along with that of the Czechs in 1968. The problem was more pressing, however, precisely because of the much greater threat of rebellion in Poland. The strikes of the Baltic shipyards in 1970 underlined the need to reconcile high growth and improved living standards (or rather, at least to prevent a deterioration in consumption).[24] The new leadership, headed by Gierek, offered a reconciliation of a different kind – a spectacular gamble on accelerating growth so that the needs both of the plan and of consumption could be met without institutional changes. It was to be an export-led growth, fuelled by an expanding volume of imports, of raw materials and components, of technology, from Western Europe. And when slump intervened to threaten the process, then Poland – like the Newly Industrializing Countries – turned for succour to Western banks.

It might have worked if the first slump had been the only one. But stagnation scarcely allowed full recovery, and was followed by the second slump. Debts escalated with fearful speed. The Government tried to protect the basic strategy, the development of a diversified investment goods industry, by cutting consumption, or rather, by not meeting the growth of consumption that followed automatically on the boom (through the expansion in employment and the intensity of work). The revolt of 1976 was the first warning, but the Government still gambled on growth. In 1980, the popular discontent became insupportable, with the creation for the first time in Eastern Europe of independent institutions to embody the demands of workers. The trade unions of Solidarity threatened the Party's monopoly of power far more dangerously than would any of the reforms proposed in the sixties. Reform came whether the Party willed it or not. The only protection for the Party leadership became further borrowing abroad, from the common financial alliance of the Soviet Union, Western governments and banks. But in the event, even that proved too little and too late. In December 1981, the Polish army seized power, in much the same way as the Chilean army under General Pinochet had seized power in Chile eight years earlier, with the express aim of beheading the hydra, Solidarity.

By the spring of 1981, the cumulative Polish debt to Western lenders was estimated at 27 billion dollars (the fifth largest Government debt). From the staggering borrowing needs of servicing this debt, it was expected that it would increase over the following four years by an additional minimum of 10.7 billion dollars. The servicing payments for 1981 – 4.4 billion dollars to Western governments, 3.1 billion to banks – produced a grave threat of default, made almost inevitable by the collapse of Polish exports. A series of emergency meetings was convened to try to prevent this outcome, for a default would entail the suspension of the country's capacity to import, bringing much of the economy to a halt. To reassure the banks, Poland also began discussions to rejoin the International Monetary Fund; this would open the way to additional borrowing from the I.M.F. itself, as well as to I.M.F. inspection of the Polish economy and, depending on the loans required, supervision. The military coup only made matters worse, for the labour force were not persuaded to restore the fortunes of the State. Meanwhile, debt-servicing increased – the 1982 payments were to be 10.4 billion dollars, when hard currency export earnings were not expected to exceed 6 billion – and the obduracy of the banks became even more flinty. The Polish crisis, without apparent prospect of relief, could pull down the whole C.M.E.A. structure.

It was not until 1980 that it became clear how far the growth process of the seventies had integrated Poland's domestic activity with that of its neighbours in both East and West. As the Government tried to cut consumption, workers compensated by cutting production. In effect, the worker reaction wrenched the economy away from its heavy industry orientation, and what followed from the attempt to keep up growth, increased exports. The Government was forcibly obliged to cut heavy industry – 900 large and medium investment projects were closed or scheduled for closure – and divert funds to the expansion of agriculture. The damage was already done in the remarkable collapse of exports – coal exports to the West were halved in 1981 (they dropped 28 per cent in the first quarter, and 17 per cent to the C.M.E.A. countries). It was this which sent shock waves of panic through Western lending agencies.

Imports continued, of necessity, but it was in the field of foodstuffs, livestock feed-grain, agricultural inputs (pesticides, fertilizers, seed), in the field of consumption, not of subsequently increased exports. Scarce foreign exchange was not available for the import of industrial raw materials, semi-finished goods and spare parts. To the effects of strikes and stoppages was added a drying-up of the basic inputs. A deputy Prime Minister identified the impact of this on agriculture itself – a quarter of the available tractors were out of order because of the lack of spare parts (either because they were imported, or the factories manufacturing them in Poland were at a standstill because of a shortage of imports) during the spring sowing; so it was also with a third of the machinery for spreading fertilizers and lime.

The ramifications were not limited to Poland. Romania was obliged to use hard currency to buy coal from West Germany to replace its imports from Poland. East Germany formulated an emergency programme to convert furnaces from using Polish imports to local brown coal. Poland's exports to the Soviet Union – coal, sulphur, chemicals, industrial goods – suffered heavily, at just the time when the Soviet Union was obliged to offer increasing hard currency assistance to protect its neighbour. The crisis of Poland spread, like an infection, through the C.M.E.A. group. Western banks were likewise alarmed, and governments increasingly abandoned pretences of Cold War talk to rally round the beleaguered Polish leadership (but, of course, none was prepared to risk more than the others). There was a mild Austrian panic as it became clear that the loans to Poland were, per head of the population, highest for Austria, and the country had become heavily dependent upon electricity and coal imports from Poland.

A confidential report, prepared by the Polish Government for its meetings with Western creditors, for the first time laid out the severity of the crisis. It identified a set of 'mistakes' by the Government; it condemned the failure to reform the central planning mechanism, as well as policies which created industries which were not only heavily dependent on imports for their operation but which produced neither exports nor improvements in agriculture (as a result, Poland was increasingly dependent upon imported foodstuffs). The Government saw no possibility of rapidly restoring the situation, but proposed to continue to cut industrial investment and to favour agriculture. The document estimated that as a result of industrial contraction, 7–800,000 workers would lose their jobs; it was hoped that they would be 'absorbed' in employment in agriculture, services or an expanded sector of small-scale private enterprises (it is strange how the same fashions govern East and West), but, as the authors put it, 'We have to realize that a certain number of people will not be able to find new jobs.'[25] The D.I.W., the West German Institute of Economic Research, calculated that up to one million Poles would lose their jobs in 1981 (a figure which included nearly half a million school-leavers seeking work). Other estimates raised the figure to 1.5 million (out of 16.5 million employed, 5.4 million of them in the private sector).

The central problem would be made worse by the then stated intention of the Government to continue to seek increases in food prices – 'a very painful operation' as the Polish Report to Western creditors put it – while preventing wages increasing, a strategy that seemed positively utopian given the state of Polish opinion. Meanwhile, great efforts were to be made to restore and expand exports – special incentives were to be introduced, and companies earning hard currency were to be permitted to retain these funds for their own use rather than depositing them all with official banks. Improving 'incentives' in this way only further reduced central control of external transactions, supposedly one of the sources of the basic crisis; the Foreign Trade Ministry estimated in April 1981 that only just over 40 per cent of foreign trade still passed through its hands.

In sum, the bourbons of the Party were determined to persist. Workers might have yanked the country back from the excesses of the Government in the seventies, from its obsession with the capital goods industries. But the Polish Party leadership only awaited their opportunity to seek to resume the same process if they could. Something however had also changed, for Western lenders had had some effect in forcing Poland into a narrower range of specialization, into a more backward phase, and brutally terminating the attempt to diversify the economy, to build 'an independent national economy'. The process involved a measure of 'deindustrialization' and of an expansion of the private sector at the expense of the public.

The story, even after the coup, was by no means complete, for Western banks were still most reluctant to offer adequate long-term procedures to re-schedule the country's debts; Polish workers were in no way reconciled to paying from their own consumption for the gross errors of Government policy; and the Soviet Union was by no means reconciled to the dangers of any realistic remedies. Finally, the Polish Government was not at all reconciled to its new role – of improving agriculture and cutting industry. At heart, it admitted no mistakes of substance, only the bad luck of world slump. And in that judgement it was half correct. For the results were inevitable where a relatively poor State with all the means of production in its hands endeavoured to compete with richer neighbours by engaging in trade with them, at just the time when contraction became severe; it was inevitable that the rate of accumulation should be raised to excessive levels to the loss of consumption, and should impose on the economy an exaggeration of the fluctuations generated abroad. The 'managed economy' necessarily created unmanageability in such conditions.

Others

Both Hungary and Poland were members of C.M.E.A., and were constrained both economically and, even more, politically, by their relationship to Russia. Yugoslavia was not. It was Yugoslavia which pioneered the concept the Hungarian Government in part sought to copy, what became known as 'market socialism'. For the Yugoslav Government, all fields of economic activity were opened to foreign participation (except insurance, trade and public services), and foreign companies were active in numerous joint ventures (for example, Fiat in vehicle production; Dow Chemicals in petro-chemical production). The enterprise management has long been vested with considerable powers over the quality and quantity of output, its prices, the hiring and firing of labour.

Like the 'N.I.C.s' – indeed, in some classifications, Yugoslavia is included as one of the Newly Industrializing Countries – Yugoslavia kept up its rate of growth through the first slump and the years of stagnation (at about 6 per cent annually). But the costs of this exercise were also similar – a cumulative debt of some 18 billion dollars by 1980 (taking about a third of export revenue), 20.7 billion dollars by 1982 (requiring 5.3 billion dollars servicing and amortization out of 18.3 billion dollars hard currency earnings). However, given the 'flexibility' of the economy, other costs were absorbed in more traditional forms – a 13 per cent rate of unemployment (despite the exile of some 770,000 workers abroad – mainly in West Germany – returning about 3 billion dollars as remittances each year) – 800,000 had been sacked by the end of 1981, from a labour force of 7 million; a decline in real disposable income in 1980 of between 7 and 10 per cent, and in 1981, of 12 per cent; a 40 per cent rate of inflation. The banks were unimpressed – although the I.M.F. approved – and continued to force further cuts in imports which, in turn, reduced domestic activity further. As the stagnation of Common Market demand for Yugoslav exports set in during the second slump, the country moved to a closer dependence upon trade with the C.M.E.A. group – importing raw materials from Russia.

Yugoslavia's 'market socialism' and Hungary's 'New Economic

Mechanism' were extremes, and both undertaken before the period of slump and stagnation. Others left reform too late, and were then driven into it by slump itself. Cuba found itself trapped in the problems of external finance and trade in 1976, in what Fidel Castro described as 'the worst [slump] since the 1930s'; the £115 million loan arranged by some 200 Western banks could not prevent severe cuts in domestic consumption, of which the most vivid symbol was the reduction in coffee rations (from 43 to 30 grammes per week). North Korea was driven into default on servicing its debts to banks in Japan and eight other countries in 1976 and 1981; the drive to raise foreign exchange prompted its diplomats in one country to get caught engaged in smuggling.[26] In Cuba's case, the 1976 crisis did not lead to substantial changes of its planning aims, nor did it produce any substantial cuts in its overseas military efforts. But it did produce in 1979 the 'New System of Economic Management'. In China, balance of payments crises in 1974 and 1975 were duly followed by the spectacular ambitions of the programme of Four Modernizations. Although the targets were subsequently dropped sharply, nonetheless the core aim – integration into the world economy – continued; the world press noted the surprising innovations – Pierre Cardin invited to show his winter collection in Peking (to help upgrade the styling of Chinese textile exports), export processing zones, joint ventures, Coca Cola and McDonald Hamburgers for the delectation of American tourists. In 1981–2, the Government salvaged the external account by a remarkable increase in exports.

Even those left behind in this race felt the same need. The Czechs, still wounded by the savaging of 1968, faced the same central problems. At the 1981 Party Congress the Prime Minister, Lubomir Strougal, meditated that 'we cannot go on with the existing structure of production, with an excessively wide and diversified industrial complex which cannot be maintained at the required technological and economic standards'. The economy used raw materials, particularly imported oil from Russia, very wastefully. Czech production, the Prime Minister said, used between 20 and 50 per cent more energy per unit of output than that employed in Western Europe. 'The comparability of the standard of our output,' he concluded, 'with the world's top products must become the decisive yardstick.'

All were becoming increasingly obsessed with expanding exports, with expanding the inflow of foreign exchange. In East Germany, the flow of West German Deutschmarks in private hands was considerable. It led the Government to set up special shops to give a supply of imported consumer goods to those with foreign exchange; it was said that a quarter of the population purchased goods in the 'Intershops' at a quarter of the normal retail price outside (in response, some groups of workers demanded that part of their pay be made in West German marks). What were Intershops in East Germany, were Pewex in Poland and Tuzex in Czechoslovakia.

Almost all had, to a greater or lesser extent, made the choice to use the world market as a spur to domestic growth, a spur to develop a national diversified economy, with a disproportionately large heavy industrial sector. But the deal was a bargain, not a unilateral initiative. The whip to speed growth could as easily turn into a noose to strangle. The new capacity developed in the sixties and expanded in the following decade came on stream at the least propitious moment for exports to Western Europe and the United States. What had seemed a decade earlier proportionately small in terms of Western imports – the imports of Western firms from their East European subsidiaries or subcontractors, the results of earlier barter agreements (swapping exports of West European machinery for a share of the subsequently produced output of the machines in East Europe) – became scarcely tolerable when Western companies were fighting fiercely over no more than a marginal increase in the market. In a range of markets – steel, cars, shoes, textiles, electrical motors, ships – Western demands for import controls neatly coincided with an increase in anti-Communism.

The rapid expansion of East European chemical capacity – the Soviet Union doubled its share of world output between 1970 and 1977, increasing from 6 to 12 per cent (with the rest of Eastern Europe, including Yugoslavia, this made up 22 per cent of world basic chemical capacity in comparison to Western Europe's 30 per cent and the United States' 25 per cent) – caused increasing alarm among the giant companies of Europe. Of course, they had been a principal instrument in the expansion of East European capacity. In many cases, they had built plant in the East and accepted in part payment a return flow of the products, now entering increasingly glutted markets.

Western shipowners were comparably irritable at the expansion of C.M.E.A. fleets, taking by the late seventies some 35 per cent of the cargo trade between Northern Europe and the Mediterranean, 30 per cent of the European trade to East Africa, and 12 per cent of the movement between Japan and the United States. Big companies played both games simultaneously – using C.M.E.A. ships with one hand because they were cheaper, demanding the reservation of cargo space in 'their own' fleets with the other. Manufacturers were the same – making profits on exports to Eastern Europe (and on contracts to build factories) at the same time as demanding protection from 'cheap subsidized unfair Communist imports'.

In sum, the 'managed economy' in Eastern Europe, as its much slighter sibling in Western Europe, could be sustained only with declining growth, stagnating real incomes, with extraordinary waste and the rising threat of the black economy. In the 'dash for growth', the Centrally Planned Economies endeavoured to compensate for growing weakness at home with increased activity abroad – only to find that they were required to import 'flexibility' along with other things. The two 'offshore' worlds of private capitalism – the petty black economy at home and the giant world market abroad – squeezed the island of State property in the middle. At the same time, it blurred the edges, each subverting the sector between. The domestic structure was adjusted to fit the external role, and in doing so, began to import those familiar forms of 'flexibility' – unemployment and inflation.

The world market began to choose those items in the Centrally Planned Economies that it needed, and to bankrupt those it did not. It was forcing the C.M.E.A. group into a particular role, into a specialized function within a world division of labour. This necessarily involved some deindustrialization, some reduction in the disproportionate size of heavy industry, some narrowing in the range of diversity of production, and attempts to expand agriculture. Production and finance were being integrated across national frontiers, but at different speeds and mediated by different political crises. None of the East Europeans made their currencies convertible, although some non-C.M.E.A. members were moving in that direction; but all accepted the imperatives. At the end, subordination was advanced, but without even offering high growth. Nonetheless, the process had gone far enough to make virtually impossible sustained retreat. The States of Eastern Europe had become as captive to the system as those of the West or of the Less Developed.

Notes to Chapter 6

1. Frederick Engels, letter to Danielson, September 1892, in *Selected Correspondence of Karl Marx and Frederick Engels,* London, 1936, p. 498.

2. *Source*: up to 1979, national statistical yearbooks, *C.M.E.A. Yearbook*, Moscow, annual; United Nations, *Economic Survey of Europe*, Economic Commission for Europe, Geneva, annual; as compiled by Richard Portes, 'Effects of the World Economic Crisis on the East European Economies', *World Economy*, Nijmegen, 3/1, July 1980, Tables 7 and 8, pp. 33–5; 1980 and 1981 figures from data of the German Institute of Economic Research, West Berlin.

3. United Nations Industrial Development Organization (U.N.I.D.O.), *World Industry Since 1960: Progress and Prospects* (Special Issue of the Industrial

Development Survey for the Third General Conference of U.N.I.D.O.), United Nations, New York, 1979, Table III–1, p. 66.

4. For other examples, see report, *Financial Times*, London, 19 December 1979, and more generally the citations from official Russian sources in Hendrick Smith, *The Russians*, London, 1976.

5. Cases cited by A. Belyakov, director, Construction Statistics Unit, Central Statistical Administration, in *Pravda*, reported in *The Times*, London, 3 September 1980.

6. Reported by M. Binyon, *The Times*, 14 April 1978.

7. I. N. Buzdalov, Institute of Economics, Academy of Science, reported in the *Financial Times*, London, 7 May 1981, p. 3.

8. Report by H. O'Shaughnessy, *Financial Times*, 22 January 1980.

9. As calculated by Murray Feshbach and Stephen Rapawy, 'Soviet Population and Manpower Trends and Policies', in U.S. Congress Joint Economic Committee, *The Soviet Economy in a New Perspective*, U.S. Government Printing Office, Washington, 1976, Table 13, p. 138; see also Karl-Eugen Wädekin, *The Private Sector in Soviet Agriculture*, Berkeley, 1973.

10. For Chinese sources, see my *The Mandate of Heaven: Marx and Mao in Modern China*, London, 1978, pp. 48 *passim* and 132 *passim*.

11. See Vladimir G. Tremi, 'Production and Consumption of Alcoholic Beverages in the U.S.S.R.: A Statistical Study', *Journal of Studies on Alcohol*, New Brunswick, New Jersey, March 1975, pp. 285–320.

12. For details, see A. Katsenelinboigen, 'Coloured Markets in the Soviet Union', *Soviet Studies*, January 1977, pp. 62–85; see also J. S. Berliner, 'The Informal Organization of the Soviet Firm', *Quarterly Journal of Economics*, August 1952, pp. 342–65.

13. Report by P. Lendvai, *Financial Times*, London, 12 April 1979.

14. The latest instalment in the story, at the time of writing, is in the *Financial Times*, 28 April 1982.

15. See the works earlier cited; press coverage of the disputes of Solidarity in Poland exposed similar types of cases in other countries; for a report on the inner workings of the Chinese Party in the early sixties, see *Rural Communes in Lien-Chiang*, documents concerning communes in Lien-chiang county, Fukien province, 1962–3, trans. and ed. C. A. Chen, Stanford, 1969.

16. Cited by Leslie Colitt, *Financial Times*, 9 October 1980. For a more comprehensive account of an earlier phase, see Jacek Kuron and Karol Modzelewski, *An Open Letter to the Party*, 1965, published in *New York*, 5/2–3, and as *A Revolutionary Socialist Manifesto*, International Socialism, London, n.d. For the events leading up to the coup, see Colin Barker and Kara Weber, *Solidarnosc: From Gdansk to Military Repression*, I.S. 15, 1982.

17. Hu Chiao-mu, President, Academy of Social Sciences, Peking, 1977.

18. For details, see reported terms in *Far Eastern Economic Review*, Hong Kong, 13 May 1977, pp. 10–42.

19. See G. A. E. Smith, 'The Industrial Problems of Soviet Agriculture', *Critique*, No. 14, 1981, pp. 41–65.

20. Janos Bacskai, President, Hungarian National Bank, reported in *Financial Times*, 22 November 1979.

21. Cited in *The Economist*, London, 20 September 1980, p. 68.

22. The West German textile firm, Triumph, a large-scale operator in Hun-

garian subcontracting work, reported in 1977: 'Between 1965 and 1975, domestic turnover fell, with some fluctuations, from D M 375 million to D M 334 million: it may well have fallen over the last year [1976, N.H.]. At the same time, foreign turnover has increased from D M 116 million to D M 424 million. Foreign turnover is therefore not only higher than domestic turnover but is also responsible for the fact that the entire undertaking is once more growing in a contracting branch of industry.' 'Wandern die Arbeiterplätze?', *Die Zeit*, 25 February 1977, cited Fröbel *et al.*, *The New International Division of Labour* . . ., London, 1980, pp. 124–5.

23. Hungaropress, in *Cooperation* 2, 1976, Ungarische Sonderbeilage, pp. vii f., cited Fröbel *et al.*, op. cit., p. 100.

24. See Kuron and Modzelewski, *An Open Letter,* op. cit.; and also Chris Harman, 'Poland: Crisis of State Capitalism', Part 1, *International Socialism* 93 (old series), November–December 1976, and Part 2, ibid., 94, January 1977.

25. Report, *Financial Times*, London, 7 March 1981.

26. See reports, *Far Eastern Economic Review*, Hong Kong, 6 January and 19 December 1975, and 8 October 1976, p. 42.

SEVEN   **OF BREAD AND GUNS**

> Too little is produced ... that is the cause of the whole
> thing. But *why* is too little produced? Not because the
> limits of production – even today, and with present day
> means – are exhausted. No, but because the limits of
> production are determined not by the number of hungry
> bellies but by the number of *purses* able to buy and to
> pay. Bourgeois society does not and cannot wish to
> produce any more. The moneyless bellies, the labour
> which cannot be utilized *for profit* and therefore cannot
> buy, is left to the death rate.[1]

Two major sectors of the world system have been excluded from our
account so far, even though both are important threads in each conjuncture: the production of the means to live and the means to die. Both
stand in a rather peculiar relationship to the State, for States regard both
food and armaments as part of their central prerogatives. Food still finds
not only an international market but also an international system of
production. But arms remains the most extreme case of State-based
production.

   In profit terms, both sectors usually move in directions opposite to the
main cycle. Profits boomed in the food trade in the first slump of 1974–5
and, for a time, in the second, 1980–82. In armaments, the boom has
paralleled stagnation throughout the system in terms of trade; in the
United States, the second slump coincides with a return to boom in the
largest producer of arms. In the epoch of world crises, issues of life and
death come increasingly close to what is supposedly the placid tenor of
everyday existence.

1. Food

Food is, as economists like to say somewhat haughtily, 'an emotive
subject'. It is and ought to be so. For it is a subject close to the issues of
human survival, and therefore produces the most stark contrast between
the ethics we are supposed to believe – that human life should be
preserved, that the hungry should be fed – and the imperatives which
actually guide the world system – that 'market incentives', not need,
should govern production and consumption. Under the first regime,

world grain should belong to all who need it, not simply to those who grow it; under the second, those who have it should hold it unless those who want it can buy it. The market has no interest in the nature of the commodity – whether wheat or shirts or bauxite, reducible to a cash form; only the relative profit rate distinguishes one thing from another. If, therefore, people die by the accident of being unprofitable, then it may be regrettable, 'speaking as a person' (as people say), but merely an unintended accident.

Commodities are not distinguished from each other, so that it is no more possible to discuss foodstuffs in isolation from the world system than anything else. The weather determines the availability of grain only in the primitive sense that the demand for gold is determined by changes in gold-mining. Bad weather only produces famine in peculiar conditions, and it is the peculiar conditions which need explanation rather than the rainfall or lack of it. For in physical terms there is always food available in the world. In production terms, agriculture has done quite respectably since 1950 – annual rate of growth of 2.8 per cent, and even in the seventies, 2.4 per cent – when populations have increased by about 1.9 per cent. In principle, output and mouths could have been matched – the United Nations Food and Agricultural Organization estimate that the average person needs 2,354 calories per day, and the world produces about 2,420 per head. Of course, average figures disguise the occurrence of local scarcity, but the merit of a world system is precisely that, in principle, scarcity in one area can be met by abundance in another: distribution can flatten out the variations. That would be so if need, rather than income, the power to buy, determined the operation of the world.

Famine arises at the moment because the world economic crisis has removed from sections of the world's population the capacity to buy grain, and removed from their governments the will to buy food imports. Some of the Less Developed Countries were brought to market in the sixties; the obverse of the expansion in their manufacturing output was an increased dependence upon food imports – over half, for example, their consumption of wheat in 1979. Before 1939, only Western Europe was a net food-grain importer; Asia became a small net importer in the late forties, Africa in the early sixties, and Latin America in the seventies. By the seventies, only North America and Australasia were net exporters. The United States alone supplied nearly half the world's marketed wheat, about 42 of the 92 million tonnes marketed in 1980–81, a total roughly equal to what the Less Developed imported. Western Europe, defying weather and cost, had become the largest exporter of dairy products and sugar, the third largest exporter of wheat, and the second largest of beef. Western Europe and North America controlled three-quarters of the world grain trade – 'a more complete domination of this trade by the developed countries than the Organization of Oil Exporting Countries has over the oil market'.[2]

Importing foodstuffs is not wrong; on the contrary, food imports can often improve the diet of the mass of the population more swiftly, effectively and cheaply than reorganizing domestic agriculture; food has no nationality. Thus, if growth had been sustained, the growing dependence of the Less Developed upon the industrialized might have had important political implications, but it need not produce famine. Slump reverses the processes of integration; importers try to turn back to 'self-reliance' regardless of cost. Indeed, in the industrialized countries, the 'free trade' era of the fifties and sixties made very little impact on agriculture; the protectionist order remained intact, and the technical products of industry vastly expanded food output.

The first slump of 1974–5 illustrated the way famine as an endemic phenomenon had returned to the system, as the product of slump itself. The grain trade achieved the central function of slump, a 'reduction of capacity' – in this case, the physical elimination of part of the world's people.

From Rangpur to Rome – via Chicago[3]

(a) Rangpur

Rangpur was the province of Bangladesh worst afflicted by famine in 1974. The worst months were those of the 'lean' season before the autumn harvest was available. *The Times* (4 November 1974) compared conditions then to those in Belsen. The estimated number of deaths rose to fearful heights. Yet at the same time, the United Nations officials in Dacca, the capital, estimated that there was little physical scarcity of food-grains in the country. They said the central problem was hoarding, and smuggling grain (up to one million tonnes) out of the country to neighbouring India.

Whatever the causes, rice prices increased far beyond the capacity to pay of nearly two-thirds of the population. It was in striking contrast with the assurances of the new regime. During the 1970 election campaign, the man who became first President of the new Bangladesh Republic in 1974, Mujibur Rahman, promised to get rice prices down from Takas 40 (about 3.20 U.S. dollars) per maund (about 40 kilograms) to 20. By

August 1974, the price was over Takas 200, and in some cases, ultimately went as high as 400. Meanwhile the capacity to buy, even at the old price, declined. On the one hand, land was being redistributed, exaggerating the process whereby the proportion of cultivators without land had increased from 18 per cent in 1961 to 40 per cent in 1973. On the other, real wages for agricultural labourers declined by nearly a third.

Not everybody loses in a famine or a war. Some people make fortunes. Great estates were founded in the terrible Bengal famine of 1943–4 (when 3.5 million people perished). The same was true in the third quarter of 1974 in Rangpur. Lawrence Lifschultz[4] noted the process whereby these fortunes were created, in step with the stages of rural decomposition. In mid August of 1974, the poorer peasants and the landless labourers fled from the villages to the district towns in search of food. In the first week of September, the price of beef and bullocks dropped precipitately by a half, indicating that now the middle peasants were affected and driven to panic sales of their draught animals. Next season, they would have no animals for ploughing; they would, if they could, be compelled to hire them back from those to whom they had sold them. The future crop, still standing in the fields, was sold at a third of its real market value; the buyers would now scoop the profits of high rice prices when they sold, and those who sold the crop too early would be unable to repay their debts. Finally, in early October, there was a rush of land sales. In one district town, local officials estimated that not since records were begun in 1918 had so much land changed hands, and at half the normal price. Yet the cruel rice prices continued to rise. Those who could sold the rest of their belongings, blankets and clothes; with the onset of colder weather, pneumonia would be added to cholera and dysentery, the jackals that trail famine. In Bangladesh as a whole, perhaps as many as 150,000 died.

A lot of money, land, animals and belongings changed hands. As the flood level of the rice price subsided, it revealed a changed landscape. There were many more permanently destitute who, even if they had survived this catastrophe, would be carried off by the next. The people who ruled Bangladesh – the local politicians, rich farmers, merchants, traders, moneylenders and their gangster supporters, at that time organized loosely in the country's governing party, the Awami League – had made fortunes out of both hoarding and smuggling, then out of the resulting inflation in prices. Many of them must have found it an intolerable strain to avoid appearing to rejoice at their good fortune amidst the bad fortune of so many others, supposedly their fellow Bengalis.

Some of them gave in to temptation. In mid November, as the starving limped into Dacca, a most lavish wedding reception was held for 3,000 guests (including government ministers) in the fashionable Dacca Club. After all, a father cannot stint on the special day when his daughter comes to wed. The estimated cost of the marriage was 18,750 U.S. dollars. If the juxtaposition seems distasteful, we need only remember that an even more expensive sequence of banquets was being held at roughly the same time in Rome, in honour of the U.S. Secretary of State, Dr Kissinger, and other distinguished guests attending the United Nations World Food Conference. In part the Conference business included contemplation of the troubles of Rangpur; famine was the pretext for conferring.

(b) South Asia

The same picture was repeated wherever disaster afflicted South Asia. It was Mrs Gandhi, India's then Prime Minister, who declared that 'what food we have in this country is not far short of what we need, provided hoarded stocks are unearthed'. But the Indian administration, like its Bangladesh counterpart, is – at the level of the province where agricultural questions are determined – part and parcel of a society dominated by the interests of the rich peasants. It cannot be directed to attacking the interests of its kinsmen – which include its own interests. Indeed, as a matter of policy it has pursued the opposite course. For more than a decade, the Government has attempted to provide massive support to the rich farmers as the primary method of raising farm output. And with remarkable success; food output soared under this policy (associated with the so-called 'Green Revolution'). But the output was marketed at a price beyond that which most country folk could afford. Furthermore, the foodstuffs which were usually purchased by the mass of the rural population suffered as the result of the redistribution of farm inputs – water, fertilizers, pesticides, hybrid seeds – to the richer farmers.

A third of the population of rural India is without land. As in Bangladesh, in 1974 rural real wages declined. Late in 1973, daily wages in rural West Bengal (one of the provinces afflicted by famine a year later) were said to be 3 rupees; a year later, they were 1.50 rupees. At the height of the famine, the unemployed offered themselves in desperation at 1.35 rupees, but there were few takers (the rice price was around 3.30 rupees a kilo). Indeed, to conserve their grain stocks for better days still, the richer farmers converted their former payments to labourers from kind, grain, to cash, with the result that the labourers were even worse off.

The rich farmers had the whip-hand. A year before, they successfully destroyed the Government's half-hearted effort to nationalize the wheat trade (to curb prices) by withholding supplies to the market. Only the black economy continued to provide abundant food. The farmers have stifled every attempt at radical land reform, at lowering the guaranteed government wheat price, even at introducing some modest measure of rural taxation. Of course, the mass of poor farmers benefit little from these efforts.

The richer farmers complained that grain prices were too low to compensate them for increased costs of fertilizer, oil and pesticides. To add point to their complaints, they withheld supplies to the market until prices rose to a level agreeable to them. The famine was incidental. They could afford to do so because they had access, illegally, to credit to carry them through the waiting time. A West Bengal minister estimated that funds equal to 111 million U.S. dollars flowed into grain speculation from what Indians call 'black money', cash flows not declared officially for tax purposes.

(c) Chicago

The rich farmers of South Asia are only little men in this business. They measure their rewards in land and in thousands of rupees. Yet their relationship to the poor of South Asia is no different from the relationship of the great grain dealers of Chicago to the subcontinent. If the landless labourers are driven to mortgage their future just to survive, the poor countries of South Asia are driven to a similar course of action *vis-à-vis* the world. The 1974 global scarcity of foodstuffs was slight, proportionately much less than that inside India. In both cases, it was the price which put food beyond the reach of poor buyers. The grain market of the world, like that of Bangladesh, then as now, feeds very well those with large enough purses.

The poor were driven to market. Bangladesh's growing hunger – and its exchange rate – led many farmers to convert their acreage from jute, the country's main export crop, to rice. Output of jute in 1974 was substantially down. Foreign jute buyers were prompted to change permanently from jute as a packing material to synthetic fibres because of the scarcity, a loss to Bangladesh's future external earnings, and so to its capacity to import foodstuffs.

So it is, for many different reasons, for many Less Developed Countries. In 1972, for the first time for a long time, the raw material export prices of the Less Developed increased rapidly. Their share in the value of world exports, which had declined from 30 to 17 per cent between 1950 and 1970, rose to 27 per cent. The averages concealed many different performances – the average increase in export values was 40 per cent, but 55 per cent for the richer Less Developed and 18 per cent for the mass of the poorest. But in 1974, prices collapsed – with the exceptions among primary products of oil, foodstuffs and fertilizers. The export value of base metals, rubber, cotton and fibres halved in value in the second half of 1974. Far more exports were required to purchase the same level of imports, particularly because at the same time, the prices of industrialized goods were increasing rapidly. Debt servicing, as we have seen, only exacerbates the problem.

There was another factor. The last boom in the system sucked up prices generally in the industrialized countries; increased incomes bid up prices of foodstuffs. Increasing beef and mutton prices prompted farmers and governments to expand livestock herds. In Britain, for example, 2.7 million cattle and 2 million sheep were added, a 25 per cent increase in the herds. But there was little increase in pasturage, so the new animal mouths were fed from stocks. Fodder stocks dropped from over one million tonnes in June 1973 to 162,000 a year later.

The United States is one of the main exporters of animal fodder, but there also herds had been expanded as a result of the boom. The Government was therefore reluctant to jeopardize the survival of its herds by exporting fodder. When the maize and soya-bean crops were found to be less than expected in 1974, for a time the U.S. Government banned exports. There was panic among the buyers in Europe and Japan. They turned to any substitute to sustain their herds – milk powder, ground grape skins, and, of course, wheat.

The scramble for wheat was added to massive speculation as businessmen sought to get out of increasingly unstable currencies into commodities where prices were rising. The wheat price soared at the same time as, with the onset of slump, the demand for beef and mutton was falling. The poor of Bangladesh, of Eastern India, of the Sahel region of Africa, were sacrificed to the attempt to feed the extra cattle of Europe and the United States, whose beef would lack buyers. The 1.5 million tonnes of skim milk powder fed to those cattle in the industrialized regions was roughly three times the annual import of skim milk to the Less Developed Countries at that time.

In every thread of the cloth the same picture emerges. Take, for example, fertilizers, the condition of expanded food output. It has been estimated that the application of one tonne of fertilizer on good soil in a Less Developed Country will on average yield an increase of ten tonnes of food-grains; but in a More Developed Country, only three tonnes (because the land is already heavily fertilized). That would seem a strong case for redistributing fertilizers to where the yield could be maximized. Except that the price does not allow it. To build a fertilizer industry requires very substantial investment, energy supplies and technical inputs of a high order. It is therefore not surprising that in the early seventies, 90 per cent of world fertilizer output was manufactured in the industrialized countries. The Less Developed, with over two-thirds of the world's population, produced just 7.5 per cent (and consumed 15 per cent) of world output. Like other commodities, fertilizer prices increased rapidly in 1972. When other prices fell, fertilizers continued upwards. Meanwhile, the United States continued to use 2 million tonnes of fertilizer for non-agricultural purposes each year (for lawns, cemeteries, golf courses and so on).

In mid 1974, the United Nations (F.A.O.) appealed to the industrialized countries for fertilizer aid to the worst-off Less Developed. The British Labour Government, administering a country where 100,000 tonnes of fertilizer was used annually for non-agricultural purposes, made the princely offer of 5,000 tonnes – at world market prices (which were then three times higher than domestic British prices). The richer farmers of Europe and the United States were as unwilling as those of Bangladesh and India to jeopardize their profit margins.

However, the heart of the problem is not simply the rich farmer, but the system of which he is a characteristic representative. The American Government is not the creature of its farmers. It was deliberate policy by Washington to take out of grain production one hectare in every five during the sixties (land that, it is estimated, would have produced between 50 and 80 million tonnes of grain) in order to keep up prices. It was a policy which required high stocks to offset the possibility of prices going so high that buyers complained. The policy was to prevent 'surpluses' even though on a world scale there has never been a real surplus, only foodstuffs which could not be sold at current income levels.

When world prices increased rapidly, the U.S. Government saw a great opportunity to make much enhanced profits if output could be increased. U.S. exports could be pushed up, the external deficit reduced or reversed, and the decline of the dollar checked. Again as an act of deliberate policy, Washington 'freed' domestic farmers to grow as much as they liked and rapidly ran down stocks. Without those stocks, any quite small variation in world production could produce staggering increases in prices (and vice versa). A segment of managed capitalism opted to restore the old boom–slump pattern.

The United States has acquired control of a very large share of world grain exports, and this confers political power. As the former U.S.

Secretary of Agriculture, Earl Butz, concluded, food 'is a tool in the kit of American diplomacy'. And the crisis of 1974 provided Washington with, as the *Financial Times* (6 November 1974) noted, 'an opportunity to reassert its influence' in the world.

At the United Nations World Food Conference in Rome, the U.S. delegation was anxious to reassure the gathering that, 'With no acreage or marketing controls, and with strong price incentives, we fully expect that 1975 will bring a renewed upward curve in our breadgrain, feed-grain and soyabeans' (U.S. Secretary for Agriculture, Brussels, 4 November 1974). If the 'price incentives' were 'strong', then the expansion of output would not affect the problem of hunger; American farmers could double their output and still the Bengalis or Ethiopians would starve. The U.S. delegation recognized the problem by urging everyone else to pay, buying the grain at the going price and then giving it away to the hungry (provided this did not produce 'disorder' in the market, that is, affect existing sales). In particular, the American delegation was anxious that the oil-producing powers should pay the lion's share, thus in one move guaranteeing the U.S. farmers' market and recapturing part of what oil importers had lost by the oil price increases of 1974. The plight of the hungry became no more than a pretext to 'recycle' oil revenues and thereby cut down the power of O.P.E.C. The U.N. Conference newspaper summed up the American proposals as: 'You pay, we'll play.'

Few other governments in the industrialized countries emerged with much more credit. Protecting 'national interests' took priority over feeding the starving. Fred Peart, British Minister of Agriculture, suddenly discovered: 'I believe a lot of people in Britain are not eating enough. I do not want malnutrition to appear in Britain.' Britain therefore could not quickly reduce its herds for so lightminded a purpose as releasing grain to feed Bengalis. There were indeed people suffering from too little food in Britain. But neither Mr Peart nor the British Government would do much about that. The argument was strictly for the consumption of the Romans, not the English.

Much ingenuity was exercised in explaining the origins of the famine without referring to the price of food and the income of buyers. We were, it appeared, entering a second Ice Age. The weather had by accident been peculiarly poor. Raw materials were running out. The people of the West were universally greedy, and divine retribution would search them out. There were just too many mouths, and mankind really ought to be cut down to the size of available food supplies.

The real problem was smaller and larger. The weather was not the cause, but the pretext; famine was also a product of slump. The ingenuity of planners was devoted to diagnoses and policies which did not touch upon the problem of slump, of prices and profits. The Rome Conference was no different and therefore could have little important effect. The *Sunday Times* (10 November 1974) commented:

> When the widely predicted emergency comes and, because there are no adequate stocks in reserve, tens of millions of people starve to death, one trusts they will understand why.

The second slump

In 1980, every fourth person ate too little to be healthy. Every ninth person suffered from chronic hunger. And one in every seventy-three people died from the effects of malnutrition. Many more perished from diseases which occurred because of an inadequate diet. Some 12 million children died young because of protein deficiency in themselves or their mothers; a quarter of a million were blinded because of a vitamin A deficiency. And the old died in their legions, many of them because their food intake was insufficient to keep at bay cold or damp.

Newspaper readers had become inured to the pictures of spidery thin infants with bloated stomachs and eyes like saucers. It no longer mattered where the toddlers lived – in East Timor or Kampuchea, Somalia or Bangladesh, Haiti or Sudan: hunger wiped out the differences. The figures had come to people an unreal world, the fictional world of news reality. Thus can the instincts of compassion be blunted and diverted into the trivial.

In the second slump, the world seemed set to begin again the sequence of events in the food trade which produced famine in 1974. A run of bad harvest in Eastern Europe and the Soviet Union, a spate of increased buying by China (and famine in two of its provinces in 1981), a sudden fall in grain stocks in India (from a peak of 21.4 million tonnes in July 1979 to 10 million tonnes in mid 1981), all fuelled rising prices. In the United States it was a temporary relief for the Government, since the return to stock holding had produced high stocks (with heavy costs) at the same time as the debts of the mass of farmers were becoming increasingly unmanageable with low prices.[5] In 1979, with rising prices, stocks were run down quickly, such that by mid 1981, it was estimated they would be halved. The United Nations (F.A.O.) minimum stock target for the world is set at 17 per cent of world consumption (or forty-five days' supply), and by mid 1981, it was expected that stocks would be no more than 13 to 14 per cent (or thirty-two days' supply).

The increasing foodstuff prices occurred as the import prices (including oil) of Less Developed Countries were also increasing, and their export prices were once again falling as world slump contracted demand. Debt servicing also cut into export revenues. The effects were almost immediate in the poorer countries. Some 150 million people in twenty-six countries of Africa and two in Asia were noted by the F.A.O. as 'at risk' of famine in late 1980. But, again as in 1974, the size of the deficit was quite small – 2.5 million tonnes of grain for Africa; in 1974, it is said, a twentieth of the grain the O.E.C.D. countries fed their cattle could have saved the starving.

However, thankfully the worst was restricted to parts of Africa. It was severe there, but included what passed for manageable numbers. It was more by good luck – and good weather – than by good management. The threats for the moment receded. Grain prices fell – to the severe loss of American farmers. But it was temporary: if the slump persisted, famine could reappear with fearful speed. In the intervening years since 1974, nothing had happened to change the vulnerability of the poor. The managed economies still spent more to dispose of 'surpluses' than to feed the hungry. For the rest, the vagaries of the weather in an undercapitalized agriculture remained the ancient hope. Meanwhile, the industrialized heartlands of the world had become the world's bread basket.

Japan, the world's largest national food importer, nonetheless expended considerable sums to secure 70 per cent self-sufficiency in foodstuffs. The expenditure ensured high prices of output, the constant redistribution of funds from industry to agriculture, the reduction of potential consumption of all Japanese but with worst effects on the poor, without commensurate benefits to the mass of small farmers. Take prices: beef prices in Japan were about five times those in Washington, double those in London; butter was more expensive even than within Europe – and as a result, butter stocks constantly climbed to 'mountains', reduced only by massively subsidized exports to, among others, the Soviet Union; there was similarly a 'milk lake'. Of the 15 billion U.S. dollars expended each year on agricultural subsidies in the late seventies (equal to half the value of total farm output, or 2 per cent of gross national product), about half was devoted to subsidizing surplus rice production. The original rationale of the exercise had been that, because many factory workers owned small plots, high returns to cultivation would make possible lower factory wages, at the same time as Japan's conservative governments would have secure electoral bases in the countryside. But the anomalies became increasingly intolerable as slump stretched profit margins in industry. Keidanren, the business federation, consistently pressed for freer trade in agriculture on the grounds that the subsidy pattern jeopardized Japanese industry's capacity to compete. They offered as examples the case of confectionery makers, whose sugar costs, they argued, were between 40 and 70 per cent above those in Western Europe; of brewers facing barley prices five times the world level (costing consumers 62 million U.S. dollars in 1979); of dairy product makers, meat processors, cake makers.

The Common Market presented a comparable picture. In the late seventies, governments and the Agricultural Commission expended something of the order of £18 billion each year to dispose of 'surpluses' – equal to about a third of the gross value added in agriculture. Common Market prices for much of the time were two or three times the world level; and farm support spending increased by more than 20 per cent per year in the second half of the seventies. The effect was to cut consumption and increase output. The consumer thus paid twice over – first to subsidize overproduction, then to pay for underconsumption. It was understandable that in 1977 the only meat to show significant increases in consumption was outside the regulation of the Common Agricultural Policy – horsemeat. The mountains of surpluses were only curbed by massively subsidizing exports. But even that did not work, for the surpluses continued to grow. The common wheat stock, one million tonnes in January 1979, was 4.7 million tonnes two years later; butter stocks increased from a quarter of a million tonnes to 1.2 million; and beef from 254,000 to 5,104,000 (in total, all reserve food stocks rose from 3.2 million to 13.3 million tonnes).

The benefits did not accrue to the mass of farmers. Indeed, in 1980 and 1981 real farm incomes declined. If there had been benefits of substance, the numbers engaged in European agriculture would not have fallen from 16.3 million in the early sixties to 8.5 million in the mid seventies. In fact, farm incomes declined between 1973–5 and 1980 by 10 per cent in real terms (and by 22 per cent in Britain). The beneficiaries of the system were not the little farms, but a small number of large farmers, many of them companies, in relatively rich areas – about 25 per cent of Europe's farmers produce about 75 per cent of the output, and the household income gap between this group and the bottom quarter of farmers was put in 1976 at 20,000 U.S. dollars. Even the richer farmers did not gain as much as food processing, storage and transport companies. Of the 1979 Common Agricultural Policy budget, 35 per cent went on price subsidies to food processing companies, 48 per cent to traders for subsidized exports, and 14 per cent to storage companies holding stocks.

The export subsidies grew steadily; farm exports from Europe increased by 164 per cent in value between 1973 and 1978, but the subsidies soared even faster; between 1977 and 1982, the cost of export refunds (the subsidy) trebled again, and in total took 55 per cent of the Common Market farm budget. The exports had the effect of ruining the markets of rival food-growing countries which exported without subsidies. Countries with an advantage in food production – from soil or weather conditions – were thus prevented from earning an income. The scale of subsidy seemed without limit; for example, in May 1980, it was proposed to sell 20,900 tonnes of butter to the Soviet Union at a subsidy cost of £22 million; the gap between the selling price, £670 per tonne, and the Common Market buying price, £1,738 per tonne, was covered by a subsidy of £1,068 per tonne, or 30p per £ (the British retail price was then between 80 and 84p per £).

There were numerous other schemes to 'dispose of surpluses'. Indeed, government and Commission officials exercised considerable ingenuity on this question. Crops were simply destroyed – for example, the British Government paid farmers to destroy some 2,000 tonnes of foodstuffs in 1980. Products were recycled; dairy farmers were paid to feed skimmed milk powder to cows, wine was converted to industrial alcohol. Sugar, polluted with garlic to prevent it leaking back into the ordinary market, was fed to bees; when the product was found to cause indigestion in the poor bees, ground carbon was then added to relieve their tiny stomachs (regrettably, given all this effort, time and money, bees in Britain still refused to consume; their keepers were recompensed with another £125,000 for this trouble).

If the mass of farmers and farmworkers did not gain, nor did those employed in food manufacture, catering and restaurants. Such workers remained among the lowest paid.

All agreed, the system was a monster. It must be reduced. Yet, at each turn, it expanded. In the spring of 1981, prices were again increased. It was thought the cost might increase the agricultural budget by another billion pounds, and since there were formal constraints upon expanding the Common Market budget, the increase for agriculture might perforce eat into regional and social spending. The increases, along with the more and more elaborate and unpoliceable regulations, could only exaggerate both the economic absurdities and fraud. The press fell in love with the ingenuities that defeated the Commissioners – the eighty-five people accused of collecting the Common Market subsidy on tomatoes without growing any (and making 170 million dollars over a number of years); the Hamburg butcher who froze offal and called it beef, shipped it to Britain and collected the subsidy (with a benefit of £40,000); the enterprising traders who drove sacks of sand across the border between Eire and Northern Ireland, calling them cereals, or pigs or 5,000 cattle, in order to collect subsidies, before smuggling the items back again, and repeating the exercise (for cattle, the profit was £60 per animal).

How could such a system survive, constantly redistributing wealth from consumers and the mass of farmers to the agro-business sector? It survived first and foremost because of the interest of States in protecting, at whatever cost, their access to foodstuffs. In principle, the subsidy to agriculture should have been seen as part of the defence budget, part of the achievement of 'self-reliance', the price of international distrust. The State was unwilling to jeopardize its capacity to hold its population loyal by holding secure the supply of foodstuffs. Secondly, governments bribed their friends, the largest corporations who were engaged in food processing and distribution. Thirdly, parliamentary constituency boundaries usually gave the populations of large rural constituencies much greater electoral weight than the densely populated smaller urban areas, and conservatives frequently depended upon rural votes. The classic example was that of Herr Ertl, for many years West Germany's Minister of Agriculture. He was a member of the Free Democrat party, which held the balance between successive coalitions, and saw the farm vote as crucial for holding four of the nine Free Democrat seats; it was quite comprehensible that Ertl should therefore be the most intransigent defender of high prices in the Common Agricultural Policy. In France, the electoral contest between former President D'Estaing and his Gaullist rivals was said to turn in part on the behaviour of a handful of rural constituencies (particularly in the Limousin). In Italy, the Christian Democrats sought to prevent the growth of the Communist Party partly by maintaining the price for lemons, tomatoes, peaches and so on from Molise, Basilicata, Puglia, Abruzzi, Calabria and Sicily.

As in the case of industrial trade, all in part colluded in the breaking of Common Market rules to favour domestic agriculture – the outgoing Agricultural Minister of the last D'Estaing administration in France was twice reproved by the European Court for excessive subsidies to French agriculture. Nor was it simply direct subsidies; for example, the British complained that low energy prices assisted Dutch glasshouse growers to the tune of £6,000 per acre. To the jungle of white and black food economies was added overt and covert cheating by governments, all to defend their little acre.

In the other great segment of 'managed capitalism', the United States, it was not much better. For much of the period of the great boom, successive administrations were obsessed with the problem of 'surpluses'. It was this which produced the acreage limitation measures of the sixties which we noted earlier. As in Europe, the system did little to protect the mass of farmers. The 6.4 million farms of 1940 were down to 2.7 million in 1980. Of these, under 600,000 farms (or 22 per cent) produced four-fifths of all farm output; 2.4 per cent of all farmers produced nearly 40 per cent of American food output. Indeed, contrary to the political rhetoric employed in electoral campaigns, the effect of government measures seems only to have served to destroy the majority of small farmers, to increase the concentration of farm land in fewer hands, many of them institutional or company holdings. About a third of American acreage is owned by absentee landlords. In the seventies, as in Europe, the instability of relative profit rates, the pattern of subsidies and of taxes, all encouraged companies to move into agriculture either as a way of strengthening earnings or as hedge against inflation (the ratio of current income plus real capital gains to farm assets increased by 12.4 per cent in the first half of the seventies, and 9.6 per cent in the second; compared to the return to common stock in the same periods of −5.19 and 0.59 per cent, and to long-term bonds, 2.4 and 4.57 per cent).[6]

The second slump fell upon American agriculture with particular ferocity. The volume of debt (interest payments were 16 per cent of farm costs in 1981, compared to 7.5 per cent in 1971) and stagnating export markets pressed farmers – and their bankers – to the wall. Net farm income fell by nearly a third in real terms between 1979 and 1981, and was expected to fall by a further 25 per cent in 1982 to reach the lowest level since 1934. The decline produced a sharp contraction in capital investment (14 per cent in general, 40 per cent for tractors), spreading the contraction to the giant farm equipment and tractor makers. Good harvests pushed grain stocks high, simultaneously burdening the U.S. budget with the cost of support and driving down prices to below the average costs of production. For the farmers, searching for a scapegoat, President Carter's embargo on grain exports to the Soviet Union in protest at the Russian invasion of Afghanistan seemed an obvious target. Before the embargo, nearly 70 per cent of Russia's imports came from the States; after it, in 1981, about 23 per cent (Argentina and Canada showed greater market wisdom, quickly replacing the Americans as chief suppliers to Russia). It was hardly surprising that the great Western scourge of International Communism, President Reagan, should be suddenly so eager to negotiate almost unlimited grain supply contracts with Moscow, despite the events in Poland which were supposed to place a general embargo on help to the Eastern Bloc. The Russians, cannily, played hard to get.

As in the case of Europe, however, even in good times, the main beneficiaries of protected agriculture were the giant companies that dominated trading and processing. Their relationship to the Government ensured that the lion's share of the subsidies accrued neither to consumers nor to farmers.[7] But even the control of the land, of the crop, of the inputs, of processing and marketing was often not enough. Companies chiselled to get even more. In 1977, the Government of India sought to sue a number of leading American grain companies for shipping rubbish to India under grain contracts. The Federal Government was finally obliged to inquire into the matter and uncovered a vast racket to substitute dust or contaminated grain for contracted shipments. The companies sued included some of the great names in the grain trade – Continental, Cook, Louis Dreyfus, Peavey, Carghill. The companies were said to have made about £300 million over five years. Some of the dust was federally funded famine relief. One country, Honduras, said that grain sent to victims of hurricane Fifi under the U.S. 'food for peace' programme was so contaminated that it had to be dumped in the sea.[8]

In the United States in the late seventies, there were officially some 25 million people with an average family income below 8,000 dollars per year. It included some 12 million who were, according to the Government, 'starving or sick because they had too little to spend on food'. Possibly a majority of them were farmworkers. To their ranks must be added the vast unknown numbers of casual labourers, many of them illegal immigrants from Mexico in seasonal employment, as well as those other legions of the badly paid, employed in catering and food manufacture: none of these were beneficiaries of official largesse.

Agriculture has become part of large company business in the industrialized regions of the world. In turn, this has given the largest companies the springboard to invade the Less Developed. International companies control about a quarter of the processed food output of the Less Developed Countries, particularly in Latin America and South-East Asia. Gearing food output here to markets in More Developed Countries has the effect of expropriating part of local consumption for use overseas. The 'Green Revolution' had a somewhat comparable effect, as noted earlier, by redistributing agrarian inputs away from the production of the foodstuffs consumed by the mass of the population – millets and pulses in India, for example – towards wheat and other relatively high-priced products, many of them eminently suitable for export. This is part of the explanation for the coincidence of increased output and increased hunger[9] – in essence, the same phenomenon as in the industrialized countries. For example, in Brazil, about an eighth of the 11 million farmers (including company and institutional owners) is said to have benefited from the substantial Government subsidy system (valued at 18 billion dollars in 1978) to support high-valued export production; meanwhile, the mass of small farmers seek, increasingly poorly, to supply the elements of basic local consumption (rice, beans, maize, cassava, rather than soya-beans, wheat, beef and sugar).

Thus in almost all countries the picture is similar, even if at very different levels of household incomes. The imperatives of the market interweave with the competition of States and the resulting stress on 'self-reliance' independently of the incomes available. The fluctuations which produce increased hunger among the bottom quarter of the people of the industrialized regions produce famine in the same group in the Third World. The food is available, but not at a price accessible to the hungry. Only in the Eastern Bloc does the problem appear as a phenomenon of sheer physical lack of goods, and only then in the State shops (depending upon official tolerance, the private markets – at a price – boom).

The problem of 'surpluses' in the industrialized regions illustrates that the central question is not one of simple physical scarcity. Take the example of powdered skim milk. This is ideal for famine relief: light enough to be carried quickly by air, easily converted into a drinkable form, easily digestible for starving infants. The Common Market over-produces it – the mountain rose as high as 1.25 million tonnes under the stimulus of a subsidy equal to £100 per cow in the Community. In the United States, the dried milk mountain in 1982 was equal to 4 lb for every man, woman and child in America (and the butter stock, 2 lb, the cheese, 3 lb: all at a cost to the U.S. budget of a quarter of a million dollars per hour). The Japanese add impressive ranges to this monument to the productivity of cattle. But to release it would be to destroy those 'market incentives' which milk-processing companies require to produce; would even, it is now argued, stunt the capacity of richer farmers in the Third World to produce. Protection of 'market incentives' takes priority over the survival of the poor.

In the early eighties, the potential for a larger disaster than that of 1974 reappeared. In Eastern Africa, the danger had become reality. But contraction in the system helped to lower prices somewhat: insufficiently to give the Less Developed access to supplies, but sufficiently to suggest that American and European farmers might begin to reduce their output. For some countries, the picture was much more severe. Tanzania's foreign exchange reserves were exhausted, its cumulative debts for unpaid imports rising, its exports falling. The revenue with which the mass of Tanzanians might by purchasing foodstuffs keep body and soul together had disappeared. Only the charity of a remarkably uncharitable world could sustain them.

2. Guns

We become like the people with whom we compete. It's like
cannibals eating part of an enemy warrior to absorb his courage.
Crazy stuff![10]

We have travelled from one extreme feature of the system – the world of
fluid international finance, linked only temporarily and contingently to
national territories – to the other, the world as a set of national war
machines, strictly demarcated by territorial boundaries. Slumps and
famines may occur elsewhere, but in the military sector, there is only
endless growth. Here the achievements seem to dwarf all others; indeed,
when included in the total picture of the world system, they become so
impressive that we are tempted to conclude that the world system is first
and foremost a collection of war-making States, a global system of
production whose final achievement is auto-destruction. In idle
moments, we might entertain the illusion of universal peace, of humanity labouring cooperatively in a global economy: but war and its preparation nails exclusive nationality into our heads, nails us willy-nilly to the
tenacious struggle for power of the territorial State. As fast as internationalization has spread, it seems the shadow of national armaments
has leapt ahead of it.

War is still a global system. It is driven by an interdependent structure,
not by the eccentricities of one State or another. It is global in at least
three senses. In the first, competition between States requires at least
two to compete, and where two play, all are, to a greater or lesser degree,
also obliged to compete as the condition of their secure survival. The
people of Japan might, in weary memory of the savageries of the Second
World War, seek to bind their State never again to participate; but
Japan, covertly or overtly, is edged back into the competition (not least
by the pressure of its allies, whose civil manufacturing suffers disproportionately from the burden of investment in defence). In the second
sense, the technology of armaments now makes all lesser States dependent for supplies on the leading warfare States – pre-eminently the
United States, but also the Soviet Union, France and Britain. Third, the
nature of that technology now means there is no place left on the globe to
hide, nowhere safe from surprise attack, no locality shielded by sheer
distance or natural barriers. Indeed, as we go about our daily business
anywhere in the world, the military satellites of the Great Powers wing
their silent way above our heads, monitoring our actions. Nor is there

any defence against attack – the governments that still have Ministries of 'Defence' employ an archaic term for an obsolete concept. What is politely called 'Civil Defence' in Britain is no defence at all, but merely procedures of salvage after attack. The salvage is to be for those least in need, for 'Medical staff ... should not be wasted by allowing them to enter highly radio-active areas to assist casualties.'[11]

The structure of world power, of competing States, endlessly duplicates reactions. There are no starting points, no first causes, no single responsibility embedded in the voluntary 'aggression' of this power or that. Of course, each power cobbles together a rationalization for its actions. All present the image of injured innocence, merely reacting to unreasonable acts by other States. But this is merely part of the public relations work of governments, which, to be effective, may contain half truths, but certainly not the truth. Each State plays the same game according to a logic in which the criterion of success is not truth or moral virtue, but winning. It is of no concern who is right and who wrong. For in this sector, there is no semblance of control. No public opinion is available to soften the outlines of the most naked rivalries. What is called 'public opinion' at a minimum requires reliable information, but here there is secrecy, endless lying and concealment by august statesmen. The central issues can therefore hardly even be discussed by those outside the ranks of the few privy to the secret. The British Government decision to spend one billion pounds on the Chevaline programme to modernize its Polaris missiles was, as *The Economist* (22 November 1980, p. 17) put it, 'a project of questionable value which was never questioned because it was not announced until essentially complete'; three separate Governments of the two major political parties colluded in keeping the secret (even at the end, it was not clear whether the system would ultimately work).

In this field, all concepts turn upside down. Secret murder and maiming become noble, lawless destruction full of splendour, bribery and thieving part of national heroism. No rules must constrain the damage to be inflicted on 'the enemy', and the enemy is everyone beyond the national frontiers (and not a few inside the frontier as well). We are asked to admire those who kill by stealth if they are 'on our side'. Acts of arbitrary lawlessness evoke hymns of praise – the dismemberment of Lebanon, the United States occupation of Vietnam, the South African bombardment of Mozambique or Angola or Zambia, the Vietnamese invasion of Kampuchea or the Chinese invasion of Vietnam, the Russian invasion of Afghanistan, the meaningless destruction between Iraq and Iran, or the massive British naval mobilization to reclaim a group of South Atlantic islands to which the claim was doubtful and in which no interest had hitherto been shown. With such arbitrary, lawless and violent official behaviour, the efforts of private hijackers, rioters and rebels seem modest indeed.

Consider, in terms of truth, the spectacular lie of the 'growing threat of the Soviet Union', now the common currency of Western chancelleries. It is the mirror image of the 'growing threat of the United States' in the Defence Ministries of the Eastern Bloc. Undoubtedly, Moscow seeks to control the world as part of controlling its environment, just as Washington has, for much of the period since the Second World War. But the wish, the drive imposed on each major power by the system of competitive States, is not at all the same as the capacity to realize the wish. The Russian economy stumbles from one crisis to another, unable even to feed its people adequately without recourse to massive imports, particularly from the United States. Its armies, guarding 15,000 kilometres of border, face a ring of 2,400 military bases in thirty countries, containing 12,000 U.S. nuclear warheads (but Moscow has no bases ringing its adversary's territory). Its troops face in the West the most powerful military concentration in the world, the N.A.T.O. forces of Central Europe; in the East, it confronts the forces of the People's Republic of China; and in the middle, its military apparatus is bogged down in a hopeless war in Afghanistan. While Washington makes great play with Russian influence (and Cuban troops) in Angola, Ethiopia and South Yemen, much more impressive are Moscow's losses in terms of allies – first and foremost, China. Poland is in sullen rebellion; Romania's leaders of doubtful reliability. Cuba's African adventures drain resources from Russia – an estimated 8 million dollars per day. Egypt, despite amazing bribes (the Aswan Dam, for example), has exchanged Russian for American crutches. Those whom Russia backed in the past – from Sukarno to Nkrumah and Allende – are no more. Vietnam, the Russian client in South East Asia, is in principle bankrupt, and Russian intransigence over the return of the Kurile Islands in the East Pacific has produced a Tokyo–Peking axis. In Africa, Moscow supported Idi Amin in Uganda and Nkomo in Zimbabwe; neither won. In the Middle East, its flirtation with the Shah only alienated the heirs to power; its supposed allies, like Iraq, openly flout Russian wishes with impunity. And in Western Europe, two of the leading Communist parties, those of Italy and Spain, have long been known for spiritual defection.

Can this saga of defeat and humiliation for Russia's foreign policy really be construed as evidence of aggressive expansion? The truth was of little account when the N.A.T.O. powers decided that its arms must be technically upgraded if it were not to lose its lead. And by increasing the competition, N.A.T.O. thereby imposed an even more cracking strain upon the Russian economy in so far as Moscow seeks to match the Western bid.

One can make little sense of the arguments of each participant, except as simple – and often cynical – attempts to hold or recruit supporters, to provide a gloss on decisions taken for reasons not revealed. While the arguments clatter on, the military machines grow. By the late seventies, the nuclear stockpile of the two largest States was sufficient to destroy every city in the world seven times over, and equal to sixteen tonnes of high explosive for every inhabitant of the planet. World military spending has increased four times over in real terms since 1945; it reached 500 billion dollars in 1980 (70 per cent of this spending was by the powers of N.A.T.O. and the Warsaw Pact). The pace of growth accelerated in the late seventies, spreading the competition to all the undemarcated areas of the system: under the sea, the Arctic and Antarctic, and outer space (where 4,500 satellites were orbiting by 1980). The graph of the growth of military spending is, as Eugene Rostow, director of the U.S. Arms Control and Disarmament Agency, put it, 'a fever chart, recording the disintegation of world public order, and the consequent spread of anarchy, fear and panic in many parts of the world'.

Spenders and soldiers

The figures on arms spending are a minefield of methodological problems,[12] and cannot be seen as representing the total levels of expenditure: secrecy covers the field, and there can be no assurance that what is concealed is the same for each State. Nonetheless, perhaps some of the orders of magnitude represented by the available figures distantly reflect the reality. Between 1960 and 1976, cumulative military spending in the world totalled 3,325 billion U.S. dollars (compared to, for example, cumulative economic aid to the Less Developed over the same period of 162 billion dollars).

Between these years, the pecking order of largest spenders falls into some six groups (cumulative spending in billions of U.S. dollars in brackets), which can be compared to the earlier 'pecking order' of States by national product.[13]

1. United States (1,179); Soviet Union (966);
2. People's Republic of China (155); West Germany (125); France (117); Britain (116);

3. Italy (44); Canada (35); Iran (33); Japan (32); India (31);
4. Poland (26); East Germany (23); Israel (23); Czechoslovakia (22); Egypt (22); Netherlands (21); Australia (21); Sweden (21); Spain (20);
5. South Africa (16); Brazil (15); Belgium (15); Vietnam (14); Turkey (13); Yugoslavia (12); Saudi Arabia (10).
6. Fifteen States with between 5 and 9 billion U.S. dollars military spending; nine were part of the Less Developed.

The traditional distinctions, as we saw earlier, break down in terms of the ranking of absolute power – with China (given the awful problems of estimating its military spending[14]) appearing as the third largest arms spender, Iran the ninth, India the eleventh. Of the last three classes, thirty-one States in all, there are fifteen Less Developed Countries, and two more which might on some rankings count as members of that group (Israel and South Africa). The predominance of the European powers reflects not merely the size of their respective products, but also the fact that Europe has been the scene of the most sustained and dangerous competition since the Second World War. There are no African powers in the first five groups, and only one Latin American.

There are other measures of the relative capacity to kill. Firepower would be the best measure, but the problems of identifying a common measure, let alone those of obtaining the data, are too daunting to assess this. The numbers of men and women under arms is a clumsy surrogate. In the late seventies, there were some 23 million people under arms (paid by an estimated one-sixth of all tax revenue collected), or 36 million if we include those organized in paramilitary forces; in turn, they were backed by another 25 to 30 million civilian staff, a grand total of between 61 and 66 million. By way of comparison, the world employed in the late seventies 26.5 million teachers and 2.87 million doctors.

In manpower terms, the most powerful Warfare States then appear as follows, organized by region (with reserves and paramilitary forces in brackets).

Europe and North America

1.	Soviet Union	: 3.658 million (25.5 million)
2.	United States	: 2 million (243,000)
3.	Turkey	: 562,000 (545,000)
4.	West Germany	: 495,000 (750,000)
5.	France	: 494,730 (530,000)
6.	Britain	: 329,204 (194,000)
7.	Yugoslavia	: 264,000 (1.5 million
8.	Greece	: 181,500 (316,000)

Middle East
1. Egypt : 367,000 (384,000)
2. Syria : 247,500 (102,000)
3. Iraq : 242,500 (80,000)
4. Iran : 240,000 (475,000)

Africa
1. Ethiopia : 229,500
2. Nigeria : 146,000
3. South Africa : 86,050 (514,500)

Latin America
1. Brazil : 272,550 (735,000)
2. Cuba : 206,000 (208,000)
3. Argentina : 139,500 (254,000)

Asia
1. China : 4.45 million (5–15 million)
2. India : 1.104 million (540,000)
3. Vietnam : 1.029 million
4. North Korea : 678,000 (338,000)
5. South Korea : 600,600 (4 million)
6. Pakistan : 438,600 (622,000)
7. Taiwan : 438,200 (1.235 million)
8. Thailand : 230,800.

Now the pecking order becomes quite different, with China pre-eminent in terms of sheer numbers, and the United States coming third. India and Vietnam make up the others in the first five Warfare States, of which four are Asian powers. Indeed, in terms of manpower, it is the battle-scarred ancient homelands of the world in the Eurasian land mass that are the most dangerous places to be – wherever the sinuous frontiers of the Eastern Bloc thread – through Central Europe, the Middle East, Indo-China and East Asia.

The measure is most imperfect, for the firepower of the manpower is not self-evident. Another way of rating the States is relative to the proportion of gross national or domestic product which they devote to the means to inflict terror on others.[15] If we take States which spend 5 per cent or more on arms, then the European–North American picture for 1979–80 appears as: Soviet Union (12 per cent?); East Germany, Hungary, Britain (6.4 per cent each); United States (6 per cent); Turkey (5.7 per cent) and Greece (5.5 per cent). For the Middle East – excluding the small Gulf States – the figures jump dramatically: from Syria (43.9 per cent), Israel (31.7 per cent) to Jordan (14.2 per cent), Egypt

(13.2 per cent), Iraq (12.5 per cent) and South Yemen (11.2 per cent). In Africa, Somalia leads (22.4 per cent), followed sympathetically by the much larger Ethiopia (12.8 per cent), but with the impoverished Tanzania not far behind (7.8 per cent). In Latin America, the lead is held by Cuba (8.8 per cent), followed by Argentina (6.2 per cent). In Asia, the smaller powers, seeking to emulate their giant neighbours, emerge clearly—Brunei (17.6 per cent) to Laos (14.6 per cent), but followed not far behind by the medium-sized powers – North Korea (12.4 per cent), Malaysia (9.9 per cent), South Korea (7.5 per cent) and Pakistan (6.4 per cent).

The richer the power, in general, the less the share of its national product it needs to devote to arms in order to achieve the most deadly effect. Competition does not discriminate according to income per head, and in arms, there are no 'intermediate technologies'. It follows that those who compete most vigorously (or, what amounts to the same thing, feel themselves most threatened) and are poor will be obliged to spend the largest shares of current income on arms.

The figures are misleading in a further sense, for they do not show the alliances. States are induced to arm not simply by competition with each other, but also because they are allied to a Great Power. The most powerful alliance in the world is N.A.T.O.,[16] with nearly 5 million men under arms, covering a territory with a population of 572 million and creating a gross product of 5,098 billion U.S. dollars (or 8,909 dollars per head). Its *raison d'être* (and vice versa) is the Warsaw Pact,[17] with 4.75 million men under arms, covering territories with 375 million inhabitants and a gross product of *possibly*[18] 752.3 billion dollars (or 2,005 dollars per head).

The Allies

The power of N.A.T.O. is not enumerated simply relative to its immediate adversary. N.A.T.O. powers – pre-eminently the United States – maintain a network of bilateral relationships round the globe, particularly in Asia, the Middle East and Latin America, and now also in Africa. These relationships are sustained in part by the overwhelming domination of the United States in the field of arms production. It is scarcely practicable for the Soviet Union to compete effectively with a State so very much more powerful in terms of national production, but the Russians do seek to copy the Americans with a network of bilateral military agreements, backed with the gift or sale of arms.

N.A.T.O. and the Warsaw Pact, the members of which compete with each other as well as between blocs, extend smaller networks of alliance and arms distribution. For example, the aims of Russian foreign policy in Africa are partly prosecuted by Cuba, and the first Western rival for influence there is not the United States, but France. The Americans say there are 34,160 to 34,340 (a charmingly spurious accuracy!) Cuban military and civil advisers in ten countries (of which the bulk are concentrated in Ethiopia – 12,000 – and Angola – 21,000). The 13,595 French military advisers operate in twenty countries of Africa (1979). The Cubans maintained military specialists in Africa, but the French could call up French troop formations when required to support clients – as in Zaire in 1978. The effort was sustained by the fact that France was also the third largest arms seller in the world, and maintained the largest naval force of all in the Indian Ocean.

The N.A.T.O. powers were heirs to the global domination exercised by the European empires before the Second World War. The United States partly inherited and partly created a system of world control after 1947 that has been since then the starting point for world politics. Despite all the efforts made, the alliances, the supplies of arms to client rulers, the maintenance of bases and naval presences, it was never possible to control all. At different times, particular regions threatened to dissolve – North East Asia, the Balkans, the Middle East; some areas like Indo-China were endemically resistant to American stabilization; and there were areas well away from the border zones between East and West, in Africa and Latin America, which threatened to challenge the wishes of Washington. The attempt by the United States in the sixties to use its own troops to defeat the Soviet Union in Vietnam was among the more spectacular interventions; its defeat produced a slight withdrawal of American global power. It was brief. In the seventies, the problems of the Gulf and oil supplies provided the pretext for new intervention, the reconstruction of U.S. bases and creation of new client States.

The thirty years from 1950, two-thirds of it during the great boom, were the years of the United States' power. It was a system of domination, of the 'balance of power' similar in essence if not scale to the years preceding the First and Second World Wars. Then also a dominant power, Britain, controlled a major part of the globe, but was challenged on the margins by a relative newcomer to world power (Germany in both 1914 and 1939, challenging the Anglo-French world control). In fact, the newcomer – in this case, the Soviet Union – is not necessarily the cause of American efforts, nor the target of American action. Rather is Moscow the pretext for the maintenance of the power of Washington over a majority of the States of the world. If Russia did not exist, the United States would perforce have to invent it. Nor does it matter which power is dominant; their behaviour would be much the same whichever power it were, for the behaviour is determined not by an inner drive but by a structure of world relationships.

The West Europeans became increasingly sensitive to the underlying aim of American defence policy – to control Western Europe as much as Eastern Europe. Grave doubts were cast both on the validity of U.S. intelligence estimates of Warsaw Pact forces, and the paranoid fantasies built upon them. Nor was it the demonstrators who expressed such doubts. Brigadier General Krause, for example, former chief strategist to the Bundeswehr, argued that a correct appraisal of the balance of firepower suggested N.A.T.O. was slightly ahead of the Warsaw Pact; Washington must cease trying to panic Europe into higher defence spending on spurious grounds. The European response was to press for further détente with Moscow when it was already scorned in Washington, and to proclaim tirelessly the need for more disarmament talks. The second demand was somewhat pointless, since none of the past talks had done more than codify what was already seen to exist. The Europeans also dragged their feet on the question of meeting the targets for rearmament laid down by Washington; in some cases they resisted the siting of a new generation of weapons, the Cruise missiles, on their soil. Even the British, hitherto the most loyal defenders of American power but squeezed by the most severe economic difficulties, increased military spending only by the minimum 3 per cent per year – at the cost of the British naval contribution to the defence of the Atlantic sea lanes. The nuclear disarmers grew, and in the United States itself, there was a three to one vote in favour of a nuclear freeze in an opinion poll. But rearmament continued.

The structure impelled endless reaction by both sides, without any starting event. The 'fall of Czechoslovakia' in 1947 or the Chinese Communist Party's advent to power in Peking did not launch the Cold War; they were the pretexts. The Russian invasion of Afghanistan did not initiate the phase of increased hostility between the two dominant sides which marked the early eighties. The invasion was only one part of reactions to the 1977 N.A.T.O. decision to upgrade its equipment, itself a response to estimates of Russian power. The upgrading was part of a technical change which, for the first time, gave much improved accuracy in the use of nuclear weapons, so that it became possible to consider a 'first strike' to destroy an enemy's weapons rather than mere deterrence. To execute the general upgrading of weapons required a tangible threat, a role for which the Russians were naturally cast. Thus do the adversaries depend upon each other; so much so that if the other does not produce the required reaction at the required time, it is necessary to invent it.

War and the managed economy

The strategic aims – and games – of the Great Powers are not the sole element in the military field. Creating military power is also a system of production, part of the general system. The great size of military spending necessarily had radical implications for industrial economies.

For the United States in 1970, it was estimated that military spending sustained 8.4 per cent of civilian employment. The proportion was higher in particular sectors – 30.5 per cent of government employment; 27.3 per cent for transport equipment; 17.8 per cent for electrical equipment; 13.3 per cent for metal manufacture; 12.3 per cent for instruments; 9.6 per cent each for non-electrical machinery and primary metals; 7.0 per cent for metal fabrication; in four other industries, the employment share dependent upon military spending was between 4 and 5.4 per cent, and in another twenty-one, under 4 per cent.[19] In terms of raw materials, the arms budget was a prodigious consumer – it took 14 per cent of all bauxite used (for aluminium), 13.7 per cent of copper, 11 per cent each of lead and of zinc, and so on.

For economies smaller than the United States, maintaining a competitive performance in arms preparation imposed a commensurately heavier burden. In Britain in the late seventies there were estimated to be about 400,000 in full-time employment in the manufacture of military equipment or support work. The 1980–81 planned military expenditure was said by the Government to be likely to take a fifth of the output of the electronic industry, over 60 per cent of the aerospace industry, as well as lesser shares of metal manufacture, energy and so on. The White Paper waxed eloquent on the benefits contributed by a powerful industry manufacturing the means to kill, a good example of the absurdity brought to life in sober public officials by the irrationality of the system:

> . . . the ability to develop and produce arms is an important national asset. It ensures supply; it enables Britain to service requirements to be met in an appropriate and timely way; it provides domestic employment; it can be paid for in our own currency; it enables us to collaborate where that is our preferred course; and it offers the prospect of secure foreign exchange through sales. Above all, because of its contribution to our defence, it helps to maintain our security.[20]

Military spending has disproportionate effects for other reasons. It is more capital intensive than the average for non-military spending, with greater effects on the capital goods industries. It has a higher rate of price inflation. It is much more technically based, and this ensures that continued military spending tends continually to transform the technical basis of production. Some 80 per cent of all the research and development spending in the world is undertaken by the United States and the Soviet Union for military purposes. The cumulative world total for research spending between 1960 and 1977 was 336 billion dollars (an average of 30 billion per year), dwarfing all other sectors of research spending; it was, for example, eight times larger than spending on energy research.

The products of military research, like military needs themselves, shape future civil output in particular ways. Military priorities have been one of the most important determinants of aircraft technology. The concern with nuclear weapons has powerfully influenced the development of the nuclear power industry as well as an industry which is a 'spinoff' from military preoccupations, the electronics industry.

The large company is one of the main beneficiaries of the fears of the State. Increased military insecurity lifts share prices for those companies operating in the military field – those of Lockheed and McDonnell Douglas in the United States doubled in 1980 as the supposed Russian threat was officially developed. The new President, Ronald Reagan, raised target military spending for 1985 to 385 billion dollars – and over 25,000 suppliers and 5,000 subcontractors to the U.S. Defense Department rejoiced. Of the 1980 Pentagon contracts (valued at 48 billion dollars), 16.4 billion dollars-worth were awarded to six companies – General Dynamics, McDonnell Douglas, United Technologies, Boeing, General Electric and Lockheed. Ninety per cent of the contracts issued, it is said, were awarded without competitive bidding and in conditions of secrecy. This led some critics to argue that it was the companies who shaped American defence policy, not policy which determined company output. U.S. Congressman Richard Ottinger deplored the fact that American public opinion has 'swallowed the fiction that there is a weapons gap [with the Soviet Union, N.H.] . . . We are spending billions of dollars on weapons systems we do not need, cannot maintain and cannot operate.'

However, while some companies rejoiced at the abundance of defence contracts, increased military spending was double-edged. For the United States and Britain with a relatively weakened manufacturing base in the civil sector, more defence investment was likely to decrease the sums invested in civil production, divert scarce manpower, and increase pressure on raw material supplies, all tending to raise rates of inflation. The problem increased if it were true, as the House of Representatives Armed Services Committee complained in early 1981, that there had been 'an alarming erosion of crucial industrial elements, coupled with mushrooming dependence upon foreign sources for critical materials'. The Defense Department's call on aircraft could limit the capacity of U.S. airlines to compete with rivals overseas. What might increase profitability in one company could simultaneously deplete the strength of all – unless arms sales abroad made up for the losses in other sectors. In fact, it was here that there was a modest boom throughout the seventies, in the midst of slump.

The Third World

As the Less Developed Countries have begun to increase their share of world manufacturing capacity, of world manufacturing trade, it is appropriate that they should also increase their share of the means to destroy. In the seventies, the world arms trade increased three and a half times faster than in the sixties, indicating increasing capacity to buy, increasing insecurity and increased military integration world-wide. The oil exporting powers expanded their military spending by 15 per cent per year, South Africa by 16 per cent. What the Middle East achieved in the first half of the seventies, Africa and the Far East followed in the second. The market supplies were overwhelmingly dominated by United States for much of the time, although there was some doubt about the figures; thus, U.S. sources claimed that Russian arms exports to the Less Developed Countries (1978–80) were a fifth larger than American (with Libya leading the way as importer, followed by Iraq, Syria, Iran and Vietnam), but Moscow countered, not by denying the estimates of its exports, but by saying the American estimates of U.S. exports were grossly undervalued. However, in the arms trade, there were also an increasing number of expanding arms exporters among the Newly Industrializing Countries – Brazil (which claimed to be the world's sixth largest arms exporter), India, South Korea, Argentina, Yugoslavia (a power among the top ten arms exporters, arms revenue contributing a quarter of the value of its exports to Less Developed Countries), South Africa, Israel, China, Indonesia, Taiwan, and so on.

From time to time, the Great Powers made sporadic efforts to limit the export of some or all types of weapons. But their own rivalries, the need to expand exports and to bind buying States in loyalty to themselves, broke down any temporary barriers. Even if the leading States had bound themselves to restraint, there were always private operators prepared to break any boycotts of, for example, South Africa or the former Rhodesia. In the same way, world contraction in the nuclear power industry increased competition between the sellers of plant to secure contracts in the Less Developed Countries, and increased the need to 'adjust' informally the rules on controls over the proliferation of capacity to manufacture nuclear weapons. After all, if a potential British contract might be lifted by the French or vice versa, concession became obligatory. By the early eighties, a select group of Less Developed Countries were said to have access to the capacity to make nuclear bombs – China, Israel, South Africa, India, Pakistan, Brazil, Argentina, Egypt, Libya, Iraq.

There were no arms that could be outlawed in a lawless world. The market could at a price always supply whatever was needed. The anonymity of the world of international finance made controls impossible. South Africa could, through intermediaries, purchase a substantial holding in an American-Canadian military research company as easily as a newspaper in Norway or a couple of campaigning organizations to overturn a Senator in the United States. Pakistan could quietly purchase scarce nuclear weapons components through the innocent contracts of a tiny firm in Dubai, the Khalid Jassim Trading Company. Israel began construction of a secret nuclear research reactor in the mid 1950s with French collaboration. American sources suggested that the country might have possessed nuclear weapons by 1968. Mysterious fuel disappearances – 200 lb of weapons-grade uranium stolen from a plant in Pennsylvania in 1965, and more hi-jacked from a uranium shipment travelling between Antwerp and Genoa in 1969 – were correlated with the Israeli weapons programme.

If the constraints in direct production were difficult, there was always a contractor in an industrialized country willing to export relevant capacity. It was companies like the French Aerospatiale, Oto Melara of Italy, Belgium's F.N.B., Britain's Vosper-Thorneycroft who began production in Brazil, beyond any official supervision. The West German companies, Kraftwerke and Hoechst, exported the first complete nuclear fuel cycle to Argentina (in return for a secure supply of Argentinian uranium); in turn, Argentina made available supplies of nuclear fuels to Bolivia, Chile, Colombia, Paraguay, Uruguay and Venezuela, and built a complete experimental 10-megawatt reactor for Peru. The French Government, in search of security in its import of oil from Iraq (supplying a third of French oil imports) and of markets for a billion pounds-worth of arms exports, was persuaded to set up a nuclear research centre near Baghdad with three years' supply of weapon-grade fuel for the project; in reply, the Israelis are said to have organized a raid on the French plant to damage the reactor which was awaiting export to

Iraq (April 1979), to have murdered the leading nuclear physicist on the Iraq project, Yahia el Meshad, when he visited France in June 1980, to have had the finished centre attacked during the Iran–Iraq war and, finally, to have demolished it by air attack in 1981. The U.S. Government might protest, but nonetheless ninety U.S.-manufactured F86 Sabre jets duly arrived in Pakistan during the 1965 war with India (allegedly by courtesy of West German firms); prohibited arms arrived in Nigeria during its civil war over Biafra, in Rhodesia and South Africa under arms embargos; and uranium samples arrived in China, covered by forged West German export documents and facilitated by the connivance of West German intelligence officials.

Governments protested their virtue, urged controls – but always emphasizing that they could not sacrifice the 'legitimate interests' of the nation when other powers were cheating. For everybody, it was always the 'other powers' who provoked retaliation, who obliged the innocent to break the law simply in self-defence. At the end, it became surprising that, with such a daunting stockpile of the means of destruction, there were not more wars. It seemed impossible that war should not spread out of the 'free fire' zones of the Great Powers in the Less Developed Countries, the arena for fighting proxy wars. In Indo-China, the Great Powers had inflicted nearly forty years of continuous warfare; in the end, broken-backed States remained, with scarcely any other *raison d'être* than institutionalized savagery; but even then, they were not to be left alone: Vietnam as Russia's proxy, China as America's, continued the ancient duel. Idle chatter of 'socialism' or 'democracy' was no more than a cruel joke amid such catastrophes; the purpose of the terms was no more than to dragoon loyalties behind a continuation of the slaughter. The imperatives of mere survival had long since taken priority over higher ambitions, whatever the self-serving fantasies of Washington and Moscow, Peking and Hanoi. In a three-week campaign, China placed its most poorly armed troops in Vietnam to slog it out, not with Vietnam's front line troops, but with poorly armed border militia; 40,000 died as the incidental costs of the exercise.

At an expenditure of £432,406 per minute for the world as a whole, the role of warfare is a clear form of behaviour, whatever the talk. The world becomes not a place of people but of weapons. The embattled fortresses of the States confront each other, obsessed by the detail of the struggle, and mere people – whether officially 'their own' or those of the 'enemy' – are just so many sentimental distractions from the imperatives of the moment. The warriors feel themselves governed by urgent necessities, for they are the instruments of a world structure operating independently of any particular State. Amid the triumphs of production by capitalism, the closeness of its existence to self-destruction can only be a matter at which to marvel.

The world of food and arms shows the other side of the coin to the international integration of the system. Here the power of States remains supreme. While the growing of foodstuffs has internationalized, its 'distortions' are the product of State power. In arms production, internationalization also proceeds. But there can be no peaceful 'withering away' of the State as an international economy renders it obsolete. On the contrary, the predators grow more predatory even as their economic obsolescence grows.

Notes to Chapter 7

1. Frederick Engels to F. A. Lange, March 1865, in *Selected Correspondence of Karl Marx and Frederick Engels*, London, 1936, p. 199.

2. Melvyn Westlake, *The Times*, London, 8 January 1981.

3. Parts of this were originally published in 'Food, Development and the Crisis', *Contemporary Review*, Vol. 226, No. 1310, March 1975, pp. 137–45.

4. *Far Eastern Economic Review*, 15 November 1974, p. 16.

5. See Sada L. Clarke, 'The Farm Income and Debt Situation in Perspective', *Economic Review*, Federal Reserve Bank of Richmond, Richmond, Virginia, May–June 1978.

6. United States Department of Agriculture, *A Time to Choose: Summary Report on the Structure of Agriculture*, U.S.A.D., Government Printing Office, Washington, 1981.

7. On the large grain companies, see Dan Morgan's *Merchants of Grain: The Power and Profits of the Five Giant Companies at the Centre of the World's Food Supply*, London, 1979.

8. See report of the inquiry, 'The Grain Drain', *The Economist*, London, 22 January 1977, pp. 87–8.

9. On the Asian situation, see Asian Development Bank, *Rural Asia: Challenge and Opportunities* (Second Asian Agricultural Survey), A.D.B., Manila, 1978.

10. William Wharton, *Birdy*, London, 1978, p. 237.

11. Department of Health and Social Security, *Home Defence Circular*, 77/1, cited in letter, S. Dowling, *The Times*, 16 January 1981.

12. The figures cited here are derived in the main from the International Institute for Strategic Studies, *The Military Balance 1980–81*, I.I.S.S., London, Autumn 1980; the annual *Yearbook* of the Stockholm International Peace Research Institute (S.I.P.R.I.); and Ruth Leger Sivard, *World Military and Social Expenditure 1978*, W.M.S.E., Leesburg, Virginia, March 1978,

13. See page 000.

14. On the grave difficulties here, see *The Military Balance*, op. cit., p. 64.

15. The problems of method are compounded here because military spending is frequently concealed under heads of civil expenditure, national accounts are not necessarily comparable, and there are great difficulties in assessing real national products. Furthermore, the base figures, derived from *The Military Balance*, op. cit., compare the product of 1979 with the military spending of 1980–81, which gives an added inflation to the proportions.

16. The North Atlantic Treaty Organization, founded by treaty in 1949, with thirteen and a half members: Belgium, Britain, Canada, Denmark, Iceland, Italy, Luxemburg, Netherlands, Portugal, United States, Greece, Turkey, West Germany; France is the half member.

17. The Warsaw Pact was signed in May 1955 by eight powers: Soviet Union, Albania (which resigned in 1968), Bulgaria, Czechoslovakia, East Germany, Hungary, Poland, Romania.

18. The figures are almost certainly a considerable underestimate of gross product, since the value is translated to dollars at the quite unrealistic official exchange rate for the rouble.

19. The estimates are by Stephen P. Dresch and the National Bureau of Economic Research, for a mimeographed document for the United Nations Secretariat, *The Impact on the Economy of the United States of America of Compensating Alternatives to Military Expenditure*, U.N., New York, n.d., Tables 3 and 4, pp. 31–2.

20. Ministry of Defence, *Defence in the 1980s*, Her Majesty's Stationery Office, London, 1980.

Appendix   # THE END OF CAPITALISM
IN ONE COUNTRY

This account has covered much ground. A lot of it is littered with the barbed wire of tables and statistics. The thread of the argument and its relationship to the assumptions people normally make about the world has frequently become obscure. Here, we try to clear up some of the debris, even if this involves some repetition.

Capital and the State

From the time of Lenin, Marxists have assumed a complete identity between capital (companies, both industrial and financial) and the State. The State appeared as no more than an aspect of capital itself. The State was capital's instrument for the administration of territory and its inhabitants, for the maintenance of relationships with other units of national capital as embodied in their respective States.

The global system consisted of the relationships between geographically separate national capitals, each supporting its own State, its armed power. The State advanced and protected the interests of national capital at home and abroad. Capital itself could not survive without a State; there was no room in the system for the existence of agencies independent of one or other State (so that international agencies were always the instruments of the most powerful State or some coalition of powerful States).

Non-Marxists made similar, but weaker, assumptions. It was generally assumed that capital could invariably be identified by nationality, by a parent State. There was an *essential* link between companies and territorial States. However, non-Marxists did not assume the complete identity, for the State was ultimately independent of capital – in principle, it could control, supervise, guide or shape capital. Social Democrats based their political programme upon the idea that the State could represent the inhabitants at large and could reform capital, could supersede the market to the benefit of the population.

It followed from the assumption of an identity between State and capital that when the assets in one country were acquired by a company registered in another, this was an act of raiding by one national capital upon another (or, looked at in another way, foreign capital forced open access to the labour force belonging to another ruling class). War between States became essentially a battle between national capitals – to appropriate markets, assets, raw materials, labour, or to destroy the threat of a rival. While the propositions were expressed most clearly by Marxists, non-Marxists shared a comparable attitude – as illustrated in Servan-Schreiber's protest at the American 'invasion' of assets, labour or markets that rightfully belonged to French or European capital.

In practice, the discussion did not concern all States, only those which were dominant in the world order, encompassing territories with overwhelmingly the largest share of world capital. All other States were subordinate to these. Although they might possess the symbols of independent political power, they were essentially subsidiary agencies of dominant States, obliged to provide a stable environment to the capital of those States.

The period of the great boom, however, provided the material basis for the growth of greater independence by these subsidiary States. All shared the assumption of an identity with local capital, and therefore sought to police the frontier between national and foreign capital. Of course, in relatively backward countries, the distinction had much greater plausibility. Local capital was, at least initially, small, poor and backward, and needed the power of the State to protect it from international capital. It had, at that stage, little capacity to swim in the tide beyond the national boundaries, to compete. It could grow only by securing monopoly rights within its home territory, by growing within an import substitution programme. Of course, the more it grew, the greater became its capacity to compete, the more restrictive became the constraints of autarchy – national capital increasingly needed to merge with international capital if it were to secure access to the highest profit rates.

While many people assumed the identity of State and capital, there were always anomalies, companies that seemed Stateless. A well-known example is that of Bata, which began life as a Czech shoe company. The advent of Communist power in Czechoslovakia removed the company's home base, and, perforce, it was obliged to become an international company without a national home. However, the fact that this seemed such a rare case only seemed to confirm the general rule.

Furthermore, the rule did not exclude the possibility of a clash of interest between particular companies and the State, nor even all companies and the State. The specific interests of one firm could collide with the common interests of the collectivity of firms, and the State could make errors in assessing what was in the interest of the collectivity of firms. Nor did the rule exclude the possibility of disagreements between major sections of capital. For example, in Britain in the twenties, there was considerable tension between financial interests, embodied in the City of London and operating internationally, and industrial capital, apparently with much closer links to the British State and Empire. The State introduced exchange control and trapped British finance within the boundaries of the Sterling Area.

None of these cases – a 'Stateless' company like Bata, collisions between company and State or between sections of capital – invalidated the central thesis of the fusion of State and the collectivity of companies, the two constituent elements of national capital.

An independent national economy

There were, however, more substantial tensions, partly suggested in the British example of a collision between financial and industrial capital. The State was indeed fashioned by capital to prosecute its interests. But the State is wedded to territory, to the maintenance of the physical means to control and extend its territorial power; companies are not. The drive to defend involves a fine balance between striving for material self-reliance and extending power abroad; for extension of power abroad can produce a dependence on areas beyond the perimeter of direct physical control, jeopardizing the capacity of the State to survive independently of all other States. Being self-reliant requires a nationally independent economy, capable of producing the full diversified range of output, services and foodstuffs which guarantee survival and which match the pattern of output produced in rival States. An independent economy will include sectors or activities which, by the criterion of the market, are unprofitable, but are necessary both for self-reliance and to retain other activities that are profitable; the profitable and unprofitable are interdependent wholes, and the unprofitable is necessary to keep companies in operation which are profitable.

However, the economic system is not governed by the arbitrary lines of national boundaries. The process of the accumulation of capital is constantly driven to internationalization, towards forming the largest markets, serviced by the largest concentrations of capital. It seems now that the minimum optimum size for efficient production in many lines of output is well beyond the size of the domestic market of most States; the more specialized production becomes, the more that proposition becomes true. Thus, growth in the world system increasingly affects the relationship of State and company, affects differently the conditions for economic and political viability. In so far as the demands of profit maximization require international scales of output, the economic independence of the national State in the narrow sense is jeopardized, its capacity to control its environment, to remain a law unto itself. The State, the creation of capital, is reduced to wooing international capital, to straddling an unresolved contradiction.

The problem is not, in essence, new. For in the first phase of internationalization, the larger powers of Europe sought to encompass global empires, to match an economy that was becoming international with an imperial polity. These were small preliminary efforts in comparison to the global reach of the United States in the decade of the fifties. Even as decolonization was creating sundry new States, the political power of Washington went far beyond the earlier European ambitions. The attempt failed, just as it did for Britain and France. While the American State was busy policing the marches, its domestic economy decayed; or rather, the development of international capital pushed back the boundaries of American economic power. Capital, the major part of it American in origin, acquired many different nationalities, and so, in principle, none.

This in essence has been the preoccupation of much of this account: the contradiction between the national State (in the dominant industrialized zones of the world) and international capital. It involved some considerable over-simplifications. The first has been mentioned. It is not 'the State' with which we have been concerned, but that cluster of the most powerful States that control Europe, the North American land-mass and Japan, encompassing collectively the bulk of world capital. Here the divisions between the economies of different States have become very blurred indeed, but collectively, world capital is still tied fundamentally to this group of States.

The relationship between State and capital is not at all the same for all companies. A large part of capital still remains linked to a particular State. Large public sectors root an important section of private capital, particularly in construction, in defence industries, in railways, and so on. The protection of home markets, favoured treatment in terms of credit, public purchases, technical services, likewise complicate the simple calculation of potential profit and loss. Paradoxically, cutting public expenditure can increase the possibility of the emigration of capital. The external power of particular States – its capacity to protect and advance the interests of its companies – also influences the national loyalties of companies.

There is also an important difference between financial and industrial capital. Internationalization is at its most extreme in finance, for financial agencies require little in the way of physical location in comparison to industry. Industrial capital is fixed, at least for its life of production, fixed to one place. Here capital depends decisively on local physical attributes; it requires specific territorial location, protected by armies, police, courts and prisons of a particular State, on the provision of transport services and infrastructure, on a stable currency and stable means of transferring profits abroad. Once capital is in production, it is indeed very dependent upon the State. There are sundry other links which sustain historic locations – access to the local segment of banks and finance markets, and to the State itself (in so far as the company produces goods for the State or its agencies, for other companies whose survival depends upon public purchases or subsidy, or in so far as it relies upon local publicly sustained overseas aid programmes, credit schemes and so on).

Thus, there are great forces of inertia in the existing industrial struc-ture, and it would be wrong to exaggerate the potential mobility of industrial capital. However, over time, all old capital becomes new; factories can be transferred between countries only with difficulty, but profits with great ease. New industrial capital is not constrained: once in production, it also depends upon a State, but not a particular State. Company behaviour ultimately depends upon an appraisal of world market advantages of different locations rather than some overriding nationality. For new investment, businessmen shop around between

States just as they do between local authorities, seeking the best deal. The transfer of profits thus becomes the mechanism for the relocation of productive assets between different territories. Once the profits and company are operating beyond the boundaries of their original State, they are beyond its control.

This formulation might suggest that, if only States could control the movement of profits, they could restore their economic independence. But as we have seen, the integration of production renders any such response merely destructive – even if, in a financially integrated international system, it were in principle possible to identify accurately such financial transfers.

Thus, for part of new industrial capital, the link with a particular State, nationality, becomes contingent. It becomes a matter of convenience depending upon the local behaviour of the State and how far it is willing to water the flowers of production. At an extreme, companies in rapid growth with high rates of turnover of capital – as occurred in making micro-electronic devices in the last half of the seventies – have potentially high rates of mobility. Depending upon the local deals offered by the State, they could shift location every half decade or so.

Three features of the postwar world accelerated the trends. The first was the relatively long period of time in which the United States assumed the role of military defence of the Western industrialized powers, and made possible their integration. For war and the threat of war were in the past powerful factors in maintaining the separation of national capitals and the State's efforts to secure economic independence. The industrialized zones of the world, including the United States, were thus permitted to integrate economically, the basis for their increased penetration of the Less Developed, and in the seventies, the Eastern Bloc. The penetration was not, of course, one way; it also was a form of subsidiary integration.

War was the inspiration of the conception of a 'managed economy'. The postwar world saw the creation of a host of new independent States, each aspiring in a greater or lesser degree to create independent managed economies. In some cases, this involved the forcible alignment of State and capital through large public sectors and detailed national investment plans. To operate in such an environment, international capital had to operate with multiple nationalities. The more managed the national units, the greater the internationalization forced upon the international company – to the point where, in turn, international capital broke down the constraints of national management.

Third, and by far the most important, was the extraordinarily sustained boom, lasting for a longer period and encompassing more of the world system than ever before. The world market grew, necessarily internationalizing production, finance and the ownership of capital, incorporating and centralizing national activities beyond the national boundaries. Growth, increasing returns to the State as well as to other agencies, eased the development of international specialization and interdependence. If it had continued, it is possible that one or another of the More Industrialized States might have experienced rising income with an almost complete loss of manufacturing, becoming a 'Rentier State'. The ending of the boom, however, checks the process, setting the dominant States back into the task of trying to recapture an independent and self-reliant economy.

However, the prior integration blocks the possibility of pursuing this option. On the contrary, slump and stagnation in the seventies increased the degree of integration rather than reversed it. In terms of the orthodox wisdom, the reactions of capital were perverse. Increased centralization of capital there was, but not an increased degree of geographical concentration in the hands of the dominant States. Some of the more backward States which should, in theory, have suffered disproportionately in the period of stagnation, on the contrary accelerated, increasing their share of world production in important lines of manufacturing output. Of course, as we have seen, this process may not be sustained. But even if there is a retreat of international capital, it will not be to particular home States so much as to the collectivity of dominant States.

From the viewpoint of companies, the picture is much clearer. Each seeks to diversify its assets internationally as well as between different sectors (finance, manufacturing, trade, property, commodities, gold), in order to stabilize global returns. Increased diversification offsets the risks associated with dependence upon any one national market or any single sector. In the end, the company loses sectoral specificity (it becomes a conglomerate) at the same time as losing national identity.

In the heyday of European imperialism, some socialists saw the extension of empire as a means of eliminating war from the world. When all the territories of the globe were appropriated, matters of friction could be settled by diplomatic negotiation between a handful of imperial statesmen. In practice, the result of empire was the precise opposite. For with the globe controlled, issues of friction at any point could not be isolated. They became world issues immediately. In the event of collision between the dominant powers, wars became inevitably world wars, fought globally. And the forces of destruction mobilized by world empires ensured that the damage was commensurately greater than all earlier conflicts.

Some observers of the growth of multinational corporations have had similar hopes to those European socialists. Companies might grow so large that they could reduce the States to impotence: the State would, perforce, 'wither away', leaving a world governed by global companies lacking the means to inflict physical destruction on each other. However, the weakening of the economic foundations of the dominant States has the reverse result; it increases the elements of instability in the system. In so far as the State fights to retain the local share of world production, it jeopardizes all economic activity, including that undertaken within its own frontiers. Local high employment can only be secured through close international integration.

The State will not wither away, even if its economic foundations become increasingly unmanageable. While it retains access to part of the surplus produced by the world system, it can continue to convert this into weapons to defend what it holds. Unlike companies, States cannot be bankrupted – except in the limited technical sense of defaulting on loans. The liquidation of the State can be achieved only by its conquest, and so far international banks have been unable to mobilize sufficient power to wreak this sanction upon defaulting States (although in the past, when States and banks were closer, they could achieve this). The dominant States will fight to the end to prevent their individual decline, even at the cost of the world system. International capital possesses overwhelming power *vis-à-vis* any individual State, power to create production and employment in any particular country. But it has no power to stand against the physical and political domination of the State in the territories where it locates production. The State cannot control the world market which is the source of the economic activity within its boundaries; but international capital cannot control the States (even if groups of international companies control particular States).

The tension between capital and the State is paralleled by the conflict between the dominant States, each remarkably different from the rest. Britain is one of the least and Japan one of the most 'national' units (that is, by the degree of coincidence of capital and the State). The United States is so much larger than any other, it constitutes a special case, a kind of multinational State in terms of the old concept of national capital. The contest between the leading powers exacerbates the emerging division of labour – with, as we have earlier mentioned, increased centralization of key elements of manufacturing for the moment favouring Japan and West Germany, imposing upon Britain and, to a lesser extent, the United States, the role of rentier. The United States, like Britain earlier, seeks in part to prevent the change by using its overwhelming superiority in military power, at the cost not only of the world system but also its remaining share of world manufacturing. It also presses its competitors to accept common conditions, forcing the Europeans and Japan to spend more on military matters, to disperse more of their manufacturing capacity and permit improved access to their domestic capital stock. This is particularly important in the case of Japan in order to integrate Japanese capital in the common form of international capital.

To control capital, the State needs to extend its power to encompass the world. The same is true of labour. Despite the increased movement of labour internationally, workers remain divided in national units. The elementary needs of defending labour requires it to internationalize in pursuit of capital. International capital today is far more powerful *vis-à-vis* labour than ever before, not merely because capital has grown far faster than labour, but also because labour can no longer employ the State to curb its excesses. The ideology of the managed economy, sustained by Keynesians, Social Democrats and Communist parties as well as, for much of the time, Conservative parties, gave labour in the industrialized countries the illusion of control. It seemed that the national patch in principle could be controlled – full employment, rising real incomes and expanding welfare systems could all be attained by skilful direction of the State. The most extreme example of the ideology was in Eastern Europe, where workers were supposedly invited to exchange guaranteed material conditions (poor though they might be) for a complete withdrawal from any political role. The decade of the seventies was most instructive in showing why that guarantee could not be offered. Not only was 'socialism in one country' impossible, so also was 'capitalism in one country'.

EIGHT **ALTERNATIVES**

Wittgenstein . . . imagined some leaves blown about by
the wind and saying, 'Now I'll go this way . . . now I'll go
that way', as the wind blew them.[1]

The line between what people can do and what is done to them is
nowhere as clear as between wind and leaves. Indeed, the distinction is
false when applied to world society. For the winds, the 'blind forces' of
the market, are not at all blind. They are other people. Everyone is a
'blind force' for someone else. Furthermore, the leaves may learn; it is
within our power to understand the wind and ultimately to master it.

Yet the image of the leaves cannot fail sometimes to cross our minds in
contemplating the wealth of offerings designed to 'solve' this or that
aspect of the world economic crisis. For – to change the image – the
groaning bookstalls with their tomes on 'the energy crisis', 'the crisis of
development', 'the arms race', are in their turn symptoms of the disorder. And the detailed alternative proposals fade away into moods, a
feeling that the world cannot survive, that – in the words of a former
West German Foreign Minister in 1975 –

> Things cannot go on like this. No one with a clear head and a
> feeling heart should still be able to sleep calmly . . . We are stumbling
> in the dark.

Then radicals draw back in fear, and conservatives begin to demand
radical change; numerous distinctions that seemed to be eternal dissolve. For example, an O.E.C.D. 1975 blueprint for the future calls for
changes in the West in the following five years which would transform
the West to

> a model more akin to the Communist bloc countries, with emphasis
> on improving and expanding plant and equipment. This shift would
> be achieved in part through a reduction in real wages and limits on
> growth of living standards. One of the major tools to effect these
> changes would be a sustained level of unemployment well above
> postwar norms.[2]

The moods make difficult an appraisal of the plethora of alternatives
on offer. Nor is it always clear that proposals are alternatives rather than
cries of protest, suggestions for alternative life styles or even programmes of self-flagellation. There are few clear diagnoses to which one

can relate the proposed remedies. Many of the offers prove to be no more than familiar forms of special pleading, exploiting the pretext of the moment to advance particular interests – as we described the U.S. Government using the opportunity of the 1974 famine to seek to secure a larger share of O.P.E.C. oil revenues. Yet other pleas are flawed by 'tunnel vision'; each national villager can only see his or her own condition, not the general phenomenon; the epidemic is not a personal failing, and does not derive from personal or local sources.

The diversity of remedies indicates not only the level of anxiety but the range of interests that define our concepts and marshal the data. In most cases, the interests remain unspoken. We are invited only to consider the intellectual validity of the ideas proposed, and in doing so, align ourselves unknowingly with those interests. Steel men, grain men, supporters of this interest or that, tug our sleeves with arguments and remedies. Sticking to one's own perception of what is important at the same time as embracing a quite inconsistent set of proposals deriving from one or other of these interests is only possible with confusion. Above all, the debate is continually fogged by the effort to disguise the needs of capital as the needs of people, to bend the human agony to fit the purposes of business.

In general, it is not accepted that the problems of each sector – of arms or grain or cars or steel – are all interconnected, symptoms of a common problem. So there are many remedies for each sector. We look at some of these here, before considering the most important set of proposals for the world system as a whole. Finally, we touch upon the remedies actually adopted. The field is vast and the work undertaken often voluminous. We can list the remedies only superficially with a view to understanding not the detail but the broad practicality: what is the hope that things may, by conscious action, be improved?

Sectoral medicines

One of the most important range of reactions to slump and stagnation was frequently presented as 'remedial' when it was not: it did not end or reverse contraction so much as give order to the retreat. As we have seen, cartels became fashionable once more, and they were exactly attempts to organize reductions in capacity, to share stagnating markets, not to create expanding markets. In steel, Eurofer and the associated regulations of the European Iron and Steel Community aimed to achieve this result. There were similar measures in parts of the European petro-chemical industry, in engineering and shipbuilding. Efforts were made through the United Nations Conference on Trade and Development to organize world cartels – with buffer stocks – to stabilize the prices and traded quantities of primary commodities. In the grain trade, the International Wheat Council was set up to manage world stocks and prices; for a time, during Washington's embargo on grain exports to the Soviet Union, the United States sought to corral the world grain trade in a common agreement. The identification of O.P.E.C.'s pricing policy as the cause of world crisis prompted the United States Government first to threaten military occupation of Middle Eastern oil-producing States, and then to create a cartel of major oil-buying powers, the International Energy Authority. Finally, again under the leadership of Washington, there was an attempt at one grand cartel of seven leading Western powers, holding 'Summit Meetings' from time to time in the endeavour to coordinate domestic and external policies (without mentioning the earlier unofficial organization of the Trilateral Commission and its predecessors).

In general, organizational efforts foundered upon the impossibility of organizing all the relevant interests or of enforcing a common discipline on competing rivals. Effective cartels ultimately required political and administrative powers to impose sanctions upon rebels, powers that were the normal prerogative only of States. Yet neither within the Common Market nor in the world was there one State power that all would trust to implement the rules. So not even an orderly retreat could be organized. The more powerful States, like the more powerful companies, opposed regulation to protect the less powerful; the more efficient demanded the right to expand at the cost of the less. Thus, Italian small steel makers evaded the European regulations in 1979, and West German steel companies opposed the regulations in 1980. The States that were members of the International Wheat Council took six years of discussion to fail to agree on a renewed treaty to manage stocks and prices; the major 'surplus' countries tried to minimize stocks, since large reserves 'dampened' their selling prices, while the main importing countries tried to maximize stocks to lower their import prices; in the end, the producing countries – United States, Canada, Argentina, Australia, France – held the power to ensure there was no agreement.

In the oil market, the interests of buyers and sellers spread in many different directions. Europe – much more heavily dependent upon imports from the Middle East than the United States – eschewed all talk of military intervention, and discreetly developed a policy towards the Middle East quite inconsistent with that of the United States. Aid and arms were made available, and some European powers opened new relationships with the Palestine Liberation Organization at the risk of intense public friction with the United States' proxy, Israel. Separate policies of this kind made impossible the unified action that Washington had envisaged in the International Energy Authority.

Similar but more wide-ranging divergences of interest ensured that the much publicized Summit meetings merely summarized known disagreements or cast a bland gloss over the real issues in dispute. The basis for an organized stabilization of the industrial core of the world system did not exist. What divided the rivals in conditions of increasing competition (as the result of stagnation) was always more important than what united them. No one trusted his rivals sufficiently to risk any sacrifice that might merely be the gain of the others, and no outside power existed to 'bang all the heads together'.

So also it was with arms control. Militarily weaker powers were always in favour of controlling the weapons of their stronger rivals, but the rivals were less enthusiastic. Whatever the solemn agreements – starting at least with the 1899 Great Power agreement signed in The Hague – the stockpiles continued to rise, and were reduced only by the arrival of war. In fact, 'disarmament' talks were never about disarmament at all, but about controlling the rate of increase in national arms stockpiles, identifying levels of tolerable rivalry and seeking to keep newcomers out of the race. For much of the time, it was part of the common wisdom of governments that disarmament was important, that the arms race was madness; but governments, in their behaviour, invariably contradicted these sentiments. While whole industries of clerks, analysts, negotiators, grew up around the disarmament industry, while professional lifetimes were fully engaged in these labours of Sisyphus, arms industries grew even more rapidly. The talks were all to no avail, or rather, the effects were so modest that they were swept away in a twinkling by a slight shift of government policy. In the hypocrisy of the time, no State was willing 'to jeopardize the security of the nation' for the will o' the wisp of improving the chances of peace; arms in the hand were real, peace merely hypothetical. British Prime Minister James Callaghan, like his peers in other countries, had even lost his sense of inconsistency – in June 1978, he could put forward an eight-point programme for disarmament at a Special Session of the United Nations, while a few weeks later his armed forces were busily pressing arms sales upon the representatives of ninety countries (at the second annual army equipment exhibition, Aldershot).

The only constants were the expansion of world arms spending, the continued arming of the Less Developed, and the spread of nuclear technology. From 1977, the N.A.T.O. powers committed themselves to rearmament. The United States Government under President Carter initiated the most massive absolute expansion of military spending by any State in – supposedly – times of peace, an effort then capped by President Reagan's request to Congress for an eighteen-month military budget of 1,500 billion dollars. The new programme permitted once more an increasing flow of bribes to America's 'friends abroad' – Israel, Egypt, Turkey, Sudan, Thailand, Kenya, Jordan, Oman, Salvador, Spain, Tunisia, East Caribbean islands (in declining order of size of military grant).

The lavishness of the increases in American military spending stood in stark contrast to the relative weakness of the U.S. economy – and the likely increase in the weakening of civil production as a result of increased military spending. Like the British before it, the American State dedicated itself to seeking to recoup militarily what was increasingly slipping from its grasp economically. In that respect, Washington and Moscow behaved in identical fashion. The European States, however, as well as Japan, had their own game to play, a game in which their relative economic strength should be allowed to grow regardless of the difficulties of the United States. Some of them were beginning to question the European entanglement in the mighty American military machine. But the prospects encouraged no optimism, as the *Financial Times* observed (18 May 1981):

> A pessimist may fear that the next few years will be a surrealistic race away from rationality by both the U.S. and the U.S.S.R., with a pointless arms race which will further weaken both of them; under the worst hypothesis, it could be touch and go whether the United States succeeds in taking revenge for its humiliation in Vietnam before the Russians can bring themselves to reassess their real interests.

There were no institutions to control the contest of the two leading powers, no centre of authority powerful enough to oblige them to desist. There were no remedies on the table, and that fact rather weakened alternatives in all other sectors. For if the world were to be wrecked by the animosities of the two 'super powers', aided and abetted by much of the rest of the world, of what significance was haggling over steel or car prices?

However, this melancholy observation did not deter ingenuity in diagnosis and remedy in other respects. Some saw the world economic crisis as the result of a hiatus in the stream of technical innovations, a topic mentioned earlier in Chapter 3. New technology would therefore ultimately arrive to lift the world system back into sustained growth. It would make possible a new international division of labour – the old sectors of manufacturing, hitherto so heavily concentrated in the core industrial regions of the world, could then be relinquished to the Less Developed Countries, while the core zones regained full employment with the newest sectors of technology.

There are always 'new technologies', clusters of technical innovation which, if utilized, affect significantly the factor proportions of industrial or agricultural activity. The more research and development expenditure and the greater the proportion of such expenditure undertaken by large agencies, States and companies, the more continuous is the stream of innovation, slowly transforming the production process. Such changes were common features throughout the great boom. The problem is not the innovation itself, the diagram, the formula or the prototype, it is the reorganization of production that follows its widespread use. The use of innovations is a function of the expected profit rate of the innovators. Yet, as we have seen, slump and stagnation are precisely those periods when profits are least buoyant, when capital in general becomes most conservative in relationship to the risks of new processes. Not only is research and development spending sharply reduced to defend current profits, but also businesses become much more reluctant to risk the losses involved in trying out innovations.

There is no lack of clusters of technical innovation – in the fields of microprocessing and information technology, in new materials from the chemicals industry, in marine biology and mining, in solar and nuclear energy, and so on. In sum, the widespread adoption of such changes would transform systems of production. But poor profit rates in general deter innovation, deter the widespread adoption of such changes. Furthermore, markedly different profit rates, in the context of a low average, exaggerate the ferocities of competition that result from new technology. For example, Japan's profit rates in some sectors are high relative to its nearest rivals. As a result, there is a much greater propensity for firms in these sectors to utilize innovations. It was estimated in the early eighties that Japanese factories employed 60,000 robots, 'universal transfer devices', in comparison to 3,000 in American, 850 in West German and 105 in British industry. The result was much higher – and more rapidly rising – levels of productivity in Japan, thus exacerbating the economic warfare between the Japanese and the rest.

There is another problem with the 'new technology' argument. For many people confuse high rates of growth of output with full employment, when there is no such self-evident identity. Innovations may indeed slowly seep into the system, redistributing activity between sectors and countries, but the effect of this on employment may be merely to increase levels of labour productivity for a stable or declining workforce. In the period of the great boom, declines in manufacturing employment (while productivity and output continued to rise) were matched by an expansion in service employment, and while this did not help those sacked – unemployed ageing miners could not get jobs as central London secretaries – it kept up overall employment levels. But the innovations now proposed affect both industry and services, so there is no assurance that declines in one will be offset by rises in the other. In sum, the stagnation of profit rates deters or delays the introduction of new technology, and in so far as it does take place, it not only increases the difficulties of declining sectors and countries but also holds out no assurance of higher employment.

There is a different diagnosis common among those preoccupied with the development of the Third World. Here it is proposed that the problems of unemployment and increased social inequality in backward countries arise because the States there have pursued industrial growth too single-mindedly, and have done so at the cost of popular welfare. This is an odd case indeed, for while the neglect of popular welfare – except when reversed by rebellion or the needs of production itself – is fairly common, the pursuit of national economic growth single-mindedly is fairly rare. By and large, economic growth took place independently of the efforts of States; or rather, *despite* the efforts of States, which constantly burdened the process of capital accumulation with their tireless demands for more and more expensive armaments, for the symbols of competitive rivalry with other States, for perks and privileges for their own officials. It is the careless extravagance of States, their ceaseless devotion to ends quite inimical to economic growth, which is much more impressive than their preoccupation with expanding output.

Nonetheless, the diagnosis is the foundation for a programme to compensate for this alleged deficiency. A number of international agencies have promoted a campaign to urge on governments the need to formulate plans to meet the 'basic minimum needs' of their populations, to – as it were – insert a larger space for humanity in the spiky interstices of the world system.[3] The idea is full of good intentions, but least applicable when everywhere the crisis hammers governments into cutting rather than expanding their modest contributions to popular welfare. Even if it were not so, it is difficult to see how States, faced with such a network of urgent necessities, could indefinitely subsidize special unprofitable sectors, pensioning part of the population in perpetuity. Of course, the programmes assume that the sectors can ultimately be rendered profitable, but that is to neglect entirely the decision of the market. Without reorganizing the entire economy and existing distribution of income, it is most difficult to see how 'basic minimum needs' could be met except on a completely subsidized basis. And subsidies require an expansive income for the State, which in turn ultimately depends upon growth, the obsession that the programme was designed to offset.

A similar circularity emerges from a different approach to the programme; there is no use expanding the supply of 'basic' goods if incomes are too low to purchase them, so incomes must be increased. To do that, employment must expand; and that requires more growth. In practice, the 'basic needs' approach has been a useful stick with which the More Developed can block expanded access to their markets by Less Developed Countries; with supreme hypocrisy, Western negotiators can deplore the social inequality in the Less Developed, and refuse to offer trade concessions unless some of the returns to trade 'reach the poor' (an approach strikingly absent in the More Developed Countries).

The 'basic needs' approach places increased emphasis on the expansion of agriculture rather than industry, on expanded foodstuffs output rather than manufactured goods. This coincides with considerable shifts in emphasis by different governments to expand agriculture. However, the change is less to do with meeting 'basic needs', and rather to defend the external balance in conditions of rising import prices. Furthermore, stresses on agriculture do little to feed the needy, as we saw in the preceding chapter, nor do they do anything to help the mass of poor cultivators. Rich farmers, traders, transport companies and governments are the beneficiaries. Nonetheless, there has been a retreat from the tasks of industrialization in a majority of the Less Developed in the face of the increasing difficulties in sustaining it (that is, rising prices for industrial machinery and raw material imports at a time when arms imports are rising, debts are cumulatively high and so on), and the stress on agriculture is the ideological result of this necessity.[4]

The fashion for agriculture, for relinquishing any attempt to pursue the historical tasks of 'national economic development', has often coincided with another curious revival, the cult of the small-scale unit of production. Now it is not at all clear why size of unit should be a particularly important element; for the hungry and jobless, the size of unit offering employment is the least concern. Furthermore, it appears to be the case that large units of production tend to be capable of larger economies of scale, of cheaper output (in terms of costs if not prices), of more economical use of equipment and of higher employment potential. The evidence is admittedly patchy and sometimes contradictory, but it is sufficient to prompt doubts. Nonetheless the case is firmly advanced that large-scale modern industry has a disproportionate appetite for capital equipment, and a low potential for employment. 'Technology' should be adjusted to conditions of expensive equipment and cheap abundant labour working in small flexible units of production ('flexible' here means easily created or bankrupted). Perhaps the small workshop seems manageable, tangible, beside the global abstractions of giant companies and the 'tyranny of technology'. Whatever the reasons, the topic has been an endless source of day-dreaming in 'development studies', and is matched by a sudden awakening of interest among Western conservatives in 'small business'.

Day-dreaming it is. For whatever the ebbs and flows (and we have noted the growth of the sweated trades), large-scale production remains the core of the world system, and the hope that the world's peoples can be fed and clothed. The small survives in part because of the existence of the large. Small may be beautiful, but in a big world, bigger is better. The adulation of the small-scale sector is, like the retreat from industrialization, a sign of defeat – both in the struggle to master the large-scale sector, and in the aspiration to improve the conditions of work. For in South, North and East, the small workshops are where the most atrocious conditions of the system survive, where capital and labour are squandered with lowest efficiency. To fashion an ideal from such barbarities is indeed a defeat. It is also a curious throwback – in trial, capitalism returns for its fantasies to its earliest and most cruel days.

For many decades, the diagnosis of the ills of 'underdevelopment' in some quarters was a species of what is now known as 'supply-side economics', and stagnation in the world system has only increased the stress. Put crudely, the case is that if there is unemployment, this arises because there are too many people looking for work (not too few jobs for those in search of employment). This, it is said, arises because too many are born. The remedy is therefore to cut down the supply of labour, whether by birth controls or by encouraging (or enforcing) emigration. However, the general diagnosis is one thing; its policy implications quite different. Few of the decent liberal-minded people who advance such thoughts are up to the tasks of implementing them effectively. For birth control can collide with many other needs of poor households – for labour on their land, for those who will care for them when aged (since there are no pensions available). To secure a reduction in births may require more forceful methods, and even then would not affect the growth of the labour force for some ten to fourteen years (that is, the time a child takes to reach the point of entry to the labour force). No sudden increase in unemployment could be remedied by these means; only mass exile could, on this theory, achieve that. In Mrs Gandhi's Emergency India, forceful methods were used through the compulsory sterilization programme; in Vietnam, mass expulsions carried off the boat people; and in China, cruel structures of social control in the cities govern marriage and births. Few of the exponents of the 'population explosion' thesis were so brave as to follow their logic to these conclusions, any more than they could adopt – after the experience of Nazi Germany – its earlier version in the 'eugenics movement'. The savageries were in fact irrelevant to the problem, for the diagnosis was flawed. It is capital's demand for labour which determines the supply, not vice versa, and there is no level of population or labour force which can be tailored to fit the long-term demands of capital. On the contrary, the rate of population growth is partially determined by the demand for labour (although there are many complicated factors at stake here). If attention is required, it is to expanding capital's demand for labour rather than compounding the barbarities inflicted upon the victims of unemployment, using them as the scapegoat for the failures of capital.

The argument has a darker – and more honest – side. For the worry is not about the growth of population of the rich and educated, but rather the 'teeming millions' of the poor. No one is concerned about the numbers of rich, only about the 'profligate breeding' of the uneducated, the ignorant, the unskilled, a process in the past attributed to the poor's immorality, but today to the misfortunes of an advancing medical science. It follows logically that the rich should defend themselves against the hordes. Civilization, it is suggested, is a small lifeboat with room only for a few, those with the ruthlessness needed to defend themselves and fight off the pleas of the poor. The 'lifeboat theory' is, as we have seen, a rather childish misunderstanding (as well as a vicious and dangerous doctrine), for there is no separate 'lifeboat'. Since the world system is integrated, no corner can be isolated for defence; on the contrary, without the hordes of the poor, the incomes of the rich shrink, and their lifeboat sinks.

The arguments – sometimes explicit and detailed, sometimes little more than hints and moods – were rarely new. They had recurred whenever capitalism was in crisis, whenever the winds blew the leaves. They provided rationales for policies, for confidence, for cruelties, but none connected with the central problem; or rather, only some connected, and then with the result of tending to increase the severity of the problems. The cures were not cures at all, and often served to increase the chronic character of the illness. But what many of them did do was, regardless of the deleterious effects on output and employment, to preserve the existing social and political order. In crisis, holding on to what the Establishment held took priority over the restoration of the world system and the welfare of its peoples.

A strategy for the world

Not all who preoccupied themselves with the problems of the world restricted themselves to particular sectors. International agencies, perforce, were required to view the system as a whole. They did not agree on their diagnosis; indeed, some agencies identified the central problem as some relatively marginal adjustment by the main national participants.[5] On such views the world was not so seriously out of joint; it was a perception seriously at variance with the experience of the majority of States.

The governments of the Less Developed Countries turned to a different vision of an alternative world order. It entailed a kind of global Social Democracy, to achieve a 'New International Economic Order'. In the same decade when Keynesianism was being extirpated as heresy in some of the leading Western States, it found a new home in the struggle to create a managed economy for the globe: a managed economy without a manager, without a single world State.

The 'New International Economic Order' came to summarize a wide variety of proposals governing different aspects of the relationships between Less and More Developed, shifting the structure of world production towards the first by measures of increased access to the main world markets, finance, capital; by reforming the operation of international agencies, stabilizing commodity prices, increasing transfers of technology (but with curbs upon the activity of multinational companies); and at the same time, increasing self-reliance of, and cooperation between, the Less Developed. The programme was put together well before the onset of the first slump, but slump and stagnation sharpened the urgency of the campaign around the programme and changed its significance: before, the programme had been a question of justice for the poor countries; now, it became a programme for the future survival of the world system. Some of the proposals, the core, began as those of the 'Group of 77' countries at the first United Nations Conference on Trade and Development (Geneva, 1964); they were taken up and elaborated by the Non-Aligned Powers, and finally embodied in an International Development Strategy for the second United Nations 'Development Decade' in 1970. Since then, much has been written and spoken to detail the proposals and their central idea, a 'structural transformation' of the global system.[6]

One of the important driving forces behind the campaign for a New International Economic Order were those countries whose future depended upon increasing access to the markets in the industrial core zones, both for their manufactured exports and for finance. Another was the attempt to stabilize raw material export prices by countries which were mainly primary commodity producers. But by the second half of the seventies, it was becoming apparent that for the first time the More Developed had become more dependent upon the Less Developed, and therefore could no longer regard all proposals of the Third World as irrelevant or inimical to their interests. Less Developed Countries – in practice, as we have seen, a rather small group of them – doubled their exports to the More Developed between 1970 and 1980. More important, the Less Developed provided a market for nearly a quarter of the exports of the More Developed by 1980. Western Europe in particular had come to depend upon the Less Developed for nearly a third of its export sales. Furthermore, as we have seen earlier, part of the world banking system had become much more dependent upon a handful of the Less Developed; commercial finance and More Developed Countries exports were intimately related to official government-to-government aid programmes, and the decline in aid programmes in the late seventies jeopardized both activities together. The integration of the system obliged the O.E.C.D. group to pay rather more than lip service to the aspirations embodied in the New International Economic Order. The attention of the O.E.C.D. powers was directed to actual or potential economic collaborators, not to the incomes received by the mass of those living in the Third World.

The Brandt Commission Report, *North-South*,[7] was a brave attempt to straddle the gap, to go part of the way to meet the demands of the more forceful Less Developed States without losing a foothold in the More Developed. The Report set off from the assumption that the world was indeed in crisis and that the future threatened 'an unprecedented mixture of starvation, inflation, escalating unemployment, international monetary disorder, protectionism, major tensions, advancing deserts, over-fishing, pollution of air and water, and the arms race'. However, with a 'collective effort', none of the problems could not be overcome; the Report devoted itself to developing proposals supporting 'decision makers and appealing to the public on which they rely'.

The Commission outlined in each area sets of proposals. They covered:

(i) emergency measures to 'reduce poverty' in Africa and Asia (through water and soil management, the provision of health facilities, geological exploration, assistance to the development of industry, transport and infrastructure), financed through grants and concessional loans from 'lending countries';

(ii) improvements in agriculture, including land reform; the establishment of grain stockpiles and finance for famine relief; the 'liberalization' of trade in food and agriculture;

(iii) population control programmes; arrangements to protect migrant workers and refugees;

(iv) proposals to begin disarmament by the major powers, and to strengthen the military capacity of the United Nations (with provisions to tax international military spending and trade, the proceeds of which were to be devoted to development purposes);

(v) measures of reform in Less Developed Countries to secure improved social services for the poor; increased numbers of small-scale enterprises using 'indigenous' technology; more participation and administrative decentralization;

· (vi) measures to stabilize commodity prices with funds to finance commodity buffer stocks, and reduce restrictions on trade;

(vii) the development of an approach to the conservation of energy supplies and exploration for new sources of energy;

(viii) efforts to reduce protectionism, improve trade preferences, etc.;

(ix) arrangements to regulate the activities of foreign capital in the Less Developed Countries, while assuring foreign companies of the right to repatriate profits;

(x) a set of reforms in the international monetary system to increase and redistribute international funds towards the Less Developed, to ease the terms of borrowing;

(xi) proposals to strengthen the United Nations and other international agencies.

It was a most extraordinary list – and here, only a brief synopsis is given. It was remarkable not only for its length and detail, but because also it did not flow from any clear-cut diagnosis of the basic problem. Indeed, the length of the list partly related to the number of symptoms, rather than the nature of the problem. At most, the Report spoke of the 'world economy' crushing the 'Nations' of the world (rather than the other way round).

It was with 'nations' (that is, States) that the Report was primarily concerned rather than the inhabitants of the world. In the interests of courtesy, the Report said little that might be construed as criticism of the representatives of States. The approach was perhaps not unrelated to the distinguished membership of the Commission. For example, the

Commission Chairman, Willy Brandt, had been Chancellor of the Bundesrepublik in 1974 and therefore must have been only too familiar with the striking contrast between Common Market mountains of butter, beef, sugar, skim milk and the rest, and the famine in Bangladesh and the Sahel region of Africa. Indeed, it was his Minister of Agriculture who led the campaign for higher Common Market prices. The Report said nothing of the problem of high prices producing famine, only how to maintain emergency grain stocks (and, as we have seen, even that aim was in practice impossibly ambitious).

If the treatment of the grain trade seemed unsatisfactory, it was even more so with armaments. For disarmament talks had no credible successes to outweigh the endless tale of defeats – or rather, formal agreements to limit the growth of arms seemed invariably to coincide with increased arms stocks. Mr Edward Heath, also a Commission member, had earlier been the British Prime Minister who made the decision to spend some £1 billion on the Chevaline programme of new warheads for Britain's Polaris missiles. Mr Heath was in favour of disarmament, but the Report nowhere discusses this curious contradiction between action and aspiration – why people like Mr Heath continue to speak so vigorously of the need for disarmament while pressing on with rearmament.

The Report gathered together hosts of measures already proposed and pursued without success. But it also included some which were quite utopian – for example, a tax on the international arms trade. Yet which of the world States would trust any of their numbers to act as tax collector, or permit the creation of an authority with the physical power to collect taxes from traders?

Events, however, were harsh commentators. The Report urged more aid from the More to the Less Developed Countries at just the time when aid commitments were being reduced by the More Developed. The United Nations target for aid – 0.75 per cent of Western gross products – was not only not reached; there was less and less attempt to avoid slipping backwards. By 1981, the average for the O.E.C.D. group was 0.37 per cent. The contribution of the United States was down to 0.27 per cent (compared to a 1979 defence spending of 5.2 per cent); Britain to 0.34 in 1980 (0.52 in 1979); West Germany to 0.44. The new American President, Mr Reagan, aimed to cut U.S. aid by some 26 per cent in 1981, with further cuts later.

The Commission recommended reforms in the field of international finance and, in particular, in international financial agencies. Yet the decline in the International Monetary Fund continued; the size of its quotas relative to the value of world trade continued to decline (from

12 per cent in 1965 to 4 per cent in 1979). Increases in its capital were finally conceded, but too late to assist the Less Developed, and still the terms of later loans were hamstrung by the 'conditionality' clauses. For the I.M.F. to make up for the declining contributions of the More Developed by commercial borrowing would only increase the interest burden for its borrowers; and if it were Saudi Arabia which increased the funds of the I.M.F., it would probably do so only with concessions – that the United States relinquish part of its control of the I.M.F., and perhaps accept political settlements in the Middle East contrary to the interests of Israel.

In the case of the World Bank, the picture was similar. The United States contribution was cut so radically – and the other More Developed States failed to make up the loss – that the Bank's 'soft loan' agency, the International Development Agency, was effectively bankrupt by mid 1981.

High interest rates were an extreme addition to the cumulative debt burden of the Less Developed and external payments deficits. The Commission apparently had had no effect in this area. Indeed, national governments had no better success in curbing the interest rate war; as *The Economist* (13 June 1981) put it, somewhat unkindly:

> Expecting a mixed group of national politicians (or even their economically literate advisers) to produce a workable way of lowering Wall Street's interest rates is like asking the Mafia to write a sonnet. They will do it badly and with a lot of spilled blood.

The Brandt Commission urged an easing of the movement of private capital to the Less Developed – and government officials irritably repeated that there could be no tolerable interference in private capital markets.

The Commission proposed immediate and urgent action to improve world food supplies to the hungry. On behalf of the European Commission, Roy Jenkins greeted the Report with much enthusiasm. But there was no action to curb Common Market surpluses, to distribute them to the starving. On the contrary, administered price increases continued as before. The Report urged increased industrialization in the Less Developed Countries – at about the same time as the representatives of the United States and Britain (backed by those of Japan, Australia and Switzerland) publicly scorned the 'Lima target' of redeploying world industrial capacity so that by the year 2,000, a quarter of it would be located in the Less Developed Countries. Peter Baker, Minister of State at the British Foreign Office, affirmed that there was no 'way in which the free market economies could be directed towards any particular set of targets'. The United States representative, John McDonald, offered the official alternative to the Brandt Commission: 'The international trading system can best serve development if it continues to encourage the free flow of goods and services.'[8]

The Commission urged decreased restrictions on trade, particularly the exports of the South to the North. Yet everywhere the Less Developed Countries were the scapegoat for the domestic stability of the More Developed. Protectionism increased, and the More Developed in practice withdrew earlier promises of liberalized entry to their markets. The United Nations Conference on Trade and Development reported in 1981 that the Common Market was implicitly withdrawing preferences which had supposedly permitted an annual increase in imports from the Less Developed, a trend repeated in Japanese and United States schemes of preference. Furthermore, the 'voluntary restraint' imposed by the United States and Europe on Japan would affect the Japanese import of components from the Less Developed. Growing controls here contradicted the increasing advocacy of 'free trade' by the More Developed in other sectors. The United States was simultaneously the most passionate advocate of free trade and in practice one of the most protectionist of the More Developed Countries. At the World Health Organization assembly in May 1981, the United States representative was alone in opposing efforts to regulate the international trade in baby milk which was affecting breast-feeding in the Less Developed Countries (the vote was 118 for the proposed code, three abstentions, one opposed).

It was not just that the Commission was unlucky in its timing. It was completely out of touch with the real causes of events. Without an accurate diagnosis, its recommendations could be nothing but utopian. But then perhaps the Report was not intended to be what it claimed, 'a programme of survival'. Perhaps rather it was no more than a summary of brave hopes, a statement to sustain the morale of those who believed that the world was manageable when all around was the evidence of unmanageability. Perhaps it was a testimony that States were rational and well-disposed to the interests of the world's inhabitants, the best of all possible institutions in the best of possible worlds. Perhaps, the Report was more akin to the United Nations' successive 'Development Decades' or the 'Year of the Child' or the 'Year of Women', attempts at reform by simple declaration, without any agency to make effective the proposals.

The Report – like the discussions surrounding the idea of the New International Economic Order – has another significance. It may be seen as a symptom of the 'structural change' the proposals recommended.

Many observers detected a long-term shift of manufacturing from what had been hitherto the core industrial zones to the Less Developed Countries, and identified the increasing proportion of service employment in the More Developed Countries as evidence of this change. The More Developed, it was said, were becoming exporters of technology, not manufactured goods. West German Chancellor Schmidt declared as early as 1975 that by the year 2000 West Germany would 'essentially be exporting patents, process technology and blue prints'.[9]

It was said to be a New International Division of Labour. As an aside, we might note the intriguing prediction of the change in the early twenties during the debates on the 'colonial question' in the Communist International. The Indian delegate to the second Congress, M. N. Roy, presented an alternative set of theses to those prepared by Lenin; one of the issues in dispute was his contention that European capital was already at that time making the colonial territories its main centre of manufacturing, partly because of threats to its political security in its original homelands.[10] Lenin himself had made a similar point earlier when he described the conversion of the European imperial powers to the role of financing production taking place in the rest of the world; the Europeans had become 'Bondholding' or 'Rentier' States – 'the world has become divided into a handful of money-lending States on the one side, and a vast majority of debtor States on the other'. The Rentier States depended upon a flow of profits from their colonial dependencies, a flow which supported the entire population of the metropolitan countries and which 'set the seal of parasitism on the whole country which lives by the exploitation of the labour of several overseas countries and colonies'.[11] At the time and in the subsequent years, it seemed that Lenin was just wrong,[12] but on some of the evidence of more than half a century later, he might have seemed merely premature.

Did what Lenin called a 'Rentier State' – and others, more discreetly, a 'Servicing Economy' – make any economic sense? Was it possible for the Third World to capture much of the world's manufacturing capacity and, through the efforts of its workers, carry the whole world economy? In the seventies, it might have seemed possible, as the manufactured exports of the Less Developed expanded at remarkable speed. But the pace even then – as we have seen – was slow relative to the enormous share of world manufacturing output in the core zones. To close the gap in income per head was still a daunting task, as the World Bank's Robert McNamara noted in 1977:

> ... if developing countries manage to double their per capita growth rate while the industrialized world maintains its historic growth, it

will take nearly a century to close the absolute income gap between them. Among the fastest growing developing countries, only seven would be able to close the gap within one hundred years, and only another nine within a thousand years.[13]

Yet even then, by the early eighties, many of the top twelve Newly Industrializing Countries were beginning to flounder in debt, their imports constrained by growing financial limits, their exports hit by slump and increasing restrictions in the markets of the More Developed Countries. It seemed most unlikely that the Less Developed could repeat their performance of the seventies, saving both world profit rates and the More Developed Countries a worse fall.

A significant movement of productive capital from More to Less Developed Countries also required a revival of the world profit rate, of some courage and audacity. The main block of capital remained too intimidated by slump to run risks, and Western States were not tempted to relinquish quietly what they already held unless the proposed rate of return were high. Movement there was, but not on the scale required to revive world activity.

Even with movement, it required great faith to believe a financing and servicing national economy in the West could employ all the available labour force. While some happy commentators might discuss at length the problems of the 'leisure society', of 'post-industrial society', in a fiercely competitive profit-making system it seemed most unlikely that these dreams were realizable. Neither international capital, nor the national States it had created to administer the territories of its empire, would happily tolerate the costs of not only an unproductive labour force, but a non-working one as well. There would not be room for everyone in the new economy; as one Lancashire textile mill-owner, employer of middle-aged unskilled women, put it: 'Are they all going to become electronic engineers, physicists and astronauts?'

The system was not at all governed by the needs of the world's inhabitants, nor the needs of the poor, whether poor people or poor States. If the poor grew rich incidentally, all would cheer at their good fortune (provided they could gain access to the new market!). But without those accidents, no one would take time off from the main contest, the competition between companies and between States, to lend the poor a helping hand. Indeed, times of slump and stagnation were the reverse of those required for generosity, compassion and the helping hand. Charity increasingly began at home when the profit rate foundered. The Brandt Commission tried to create plans in the interests of the industrialized core that would help the Less Developed, but without confronting the growing rivalries between States within the industrialized core.

The real remedies

The world of States could not await the remedies of visionaries or technicians. There are always 'remedies', and, in this sense, no problem remains unresolved. Responses were found, regardless of whether their effect was to purchase temporary relief for one participant at the cost of more permanent recovery for all. And the remedies were cheered within the national villages. For here, the villagers diagnosed their afflictions as peculiar to themselves and remediable within the village. Of course, they blamed the low cunning or incompetence of 'foreigners' (whether the 'foreigners' lived abroad or in their midst) for much of their troubles, just as they reproached themselves for laziness and greed. But ultimately, all discussion was primarily determined by the need to strengthen the local State, and therefore involved an increased belief in the myth of national power, a national economy. The landless clung even more tenaciously to the land that did not belong to them, and did so with the fanaticism of true landowners.

This account has touched upon the 'remedies' undertaken by States, and here it is only necessary to remind ourselves of them. The States in the industrialized zones endeavoured to subsidize sectors of production. They sought to control their share of world production by increasing import controls, whether this was the imposition of temporary quotas (and in textiles, the 'temporary' rapidly became permanent), increased tariffs or through the hypocrisy of 'voluntary restraint' agreements. In so far as these efforts were successful, they reduced the income of those countries exporting to the More Developed, and so reduced their capacity to buy the exports of the More Developed and service their borrowings. Each More Developed State, however, hoped simultaneously to block imports while expanding exports on the basis of revenues earned elsewhere – dollars paid to, say, South Korea for exports to the United States, could then be appropriated by West German exports to Korea.

In the final days of the Keynesian 'managed economy' there were more elaborate measures. There were grants to employers to employ, subsidies, and the auction of bribes to international capital. However, such measures redistributed from profitable to unprofitable sectors (as well as from consumption to profits), so in turn exacerbating the central problem of stagnating profit rates. To electorates, it made sense to share a declining product.

It is perhaps for this reason, the innocent commitment of electorates, that it required a quasi-religious revival of monetarist economics to break the commitment. The technical argument – that the official supply of liquidity determined subsequent rates of inflation – assumed the existence of nationally separate and manageable monetary units, much as the Keynesians assumed separate and manageable units of demand and employment. Yet financial integration, the dissolution of national financial boundaries between the More Developed Countries, was the mark of the seventies. In fact, it was the political function of monetarism which was more important than its claimed technical merits. For the doctrine allowed, indeed recommended, attempts to organize a redistribution of income and wealth in favour of the rich on the shamelessly spurious grounds that this increase in 'incentives' would encourage the rich to work harder (it might just as well have encouraged them to work less, since less work now produced the same or greater income). It gave moral sanction to the proposition that there is always work available if incomes decline far enough; it was the greed of employed workers or trade unions who therefore were responsible for unemployment. Of course, it was true that much work would be available with declining incomes, but the incomes offered might well be far below those required for survival; in the classical economy, the death rate was not the responsibility of capital. The doctrines gave moral approval to a run-down of 'social expenditure', the welfare, health and educational spending of the State (but not, somehow, police and defence spending). And the whole, despite the claims to high theory, was infected by a moral self-righteousness, a sanctimonious tone, that indicated its real emotional basis in pure class prejudice. Nonetheless, it gave a messianic zeal to its protagonists; it was the last hope, apparently, of 'civilization as we know it'; as one of President Reagan's supporters put it:

> A sceptic might inquire: what if this new conservative political economy doesn't work? To which one can only reply: it had better work. It is the last, best hope of democratic capitalism in America, and if it fails – well, then conservatives can concentrate on nostalgic poetry and forget all about political economy. Someone else will be in charge of that.[14]

It was not only conservatives who remained committed to a refurbished State. Large parts of the Left were no less enamoured. In the Less Developed Countries, it was the vision of national autarchy, of State capitalism, which reigned supreme under the various slogans of 'national liberation' and socialism. In the More Developed, it was no less prevalent. Communist Parties in Europe championed the 'national interest' against the lurking 'foreign' sharks of multinationals, and proclaimed their ability to administer capitalism more efficiently than capitalists. In Britain, it was the Left of the Labour Party and opinion in the trade-union leadership which not only did not oppose import controls, but rather demanded their introduction as the most urgent priority. The power of the State must be increased, not reduced. The case, an 'alternative economic strategy', assumed that the State could organize a boom at home behind the barriers of import controls, that the State still had sufficient power over an economy sufficiently independent of the world system to organize full employment at home. There was little empirical support to justify it; or rather, what few examples there were seemed entirely to contradict other political priorities of the Left. The Soviet Union and Nazi Germany had both expanded during the thirties, both on the basis of dictatorship, one expanding from backwardness, the other through a drive to war. South Korea, Brazil and others expanded in the seventies, but at levels of wages and in political conditions far below those which, one would presume, the Left would be prepared to tolerate in Britain. Were these all the visions that socialism had left to offer a world in torment: increasing efforts by the British State to increase the ferocity of competition, of exploitation and possible war?

There were other problems with autarchy. The scourge of a capitalist system, the force which increased efficiency of production, was never the State. On the contrary, the political vulnerability of the State almost invariably jeopardized its economic activities. Limiting competition by protecting domestic manufacturing from foreign rivals could increase obsolescence, not decrease it. The evidence of the thirties stood witness to the results of national monopolies – without even the consolation of restored high employment. Where the State and capital united so closely, war almost invariably followed.

The economics of protectionism were simultaneously reactionary (they harked back to a world which no longer existed) and utopian (they could not be achieved). The *politics* on the other hand were vital for the ruling order, for they set country against country, not class against class. The problem became not capital and its propensity to employ, but foreign workers. So it was, in an even more extreme form, with the movement of people and the issue of immigration control. The physical supply of labour never determined its demand – capital did that. There was sufficient evidence that the immigration of workers in the industrial core zones of the system declined as local unemployment rose. To terminate the labour supply required no special measures by the State to reduce the flow of eager workers. Nonetheless, the endless, bitter and hypocritical debate over the margin of the labour force born overseas provided irreplaceable opportunities for the reaffirmation of national loyalties against 'foreigners'. Again, it was not simply conservatives who raised the issue. The American Federation of Labor (C.I.O.) led the campaign against Mexicans 'stealing American jobs'; it was M. Marchais of the French Communist Party who sanctioned a violent campaign against African immigrant workers in Paris; it was the British Trade Union Congress which pressed the Government to eliminate work permits for temporary foreign workers, instead of championing the demand to equalize the wages of foreign and native workers. The economic effects of immigration controls were trivial; but the political functions of the debate about immigration vital for the State.

There were politics in the air that were more honest: there may be no answers for the long-term future, but in the short term it behoved those with power and wealth to look to their defences. Any case would do for that purpose. Lurking behind the diagnoses of some of the Western press were familiar demons: the Communists of Moscow threatened Western civilization militarily from abroad and orchestrated the rebellion of the lazy and greedy at home. The selfishness of the working class was the source of the problem. Whether in the outrage of comfortable citizens at the feckless indiscipline of those less comfortable,[15] or the more measured tones of a German bank, the message was similar:

> The demands of German society have in recent years simply put too great a burden on the performance capacity of the economy. Indeed, admonishing voices were raised long ago. But warnings tend to pale when they appear to be refuted by reality for so many years.[16]

The mood revived any number of dormant prejudices, focusing them upon anything that was new, audacious and exciting (such attributes were to be restricted to capital alone). Education and morality had been too 'permissive'; people had been encouraged to scrounge off the State; pornography was everywhere, rotting the sexual disciplines that were the crucible of marriage and family; women had been given too much freedom; the young were no longer tutored when their mothers worked; prison and society were insufficiently nasty to stem the tide of declining work discipline; clothes and hair styles must be recolonized by the grey guardians of the past. In sum, the victims must be made the scapegoats.

If the State half toyed with such contentions, how much more violent were the reactions of its most loyal devotees. Whether it was the murder of an innocent Pakistani, the assault on women, or the slashing of the tyres of a 'Japanese' car, the slaves played back to their masters only an exaggerated image of official prejudice.

The 'freedom of the Individual' – against the shapeless threat of the grey 'masses' – could not be far behind. The concept had done sterling service to Western society in its hour of need. From the Individual as the cultured aristocrat and landowner of the eighteenth century, to the lawless audacity of the nineteenth-century entrepreneur, to the Führer of all Germany in the twentieth, such conceptions linked directly to the mysticism of the blood – and the debate about immigration. The Individual required the State and an end to the laws which might restrict it. Whether it was the popular slogan in the United States of 'Nuke an Ayatollah', or the demands in Britain to increase State discipline of prisoners or the young, the demand for official violence invariably increased unofficial violence.

The ruling orders of Western States were not united. The old dog of Social Democracy – and its intellectual parallel in the United States, Liberalism – still growled sleepily at the powers that be, and in France, more loudly, seeking the support of the poor without frightening the rich. It was an ancient tradition, described well in the nineteenth century by that French adept, Louis Blanc:

> . . . the question was to prevent the suffering masses from giving way to a movement of hostility against the more fortunate ones; and this was the import of these words, 'to plead the cause of the poor, is to plead the cause of the rich', showing that progress must be effected, not by the antagonism, but by the concord, of classes.[17]

Sixty years later, a British Liberal lamented that politics then failed to reconcile the ends of the equation:

> It is the abiding problem of Liberal statesmanship to arouse the enthusiasm of the working classes, without frightening the middle classes.[18]

The village, it seemed, longed to be led, still longed for the great Individual.

That was no more than the surface preoccupation. Below the surface, there were other remedies: silence, withdrawal, a decline in hopes and ambitions, a spiritual evacuation. In some places, it might be gambling; in others, drugs. Many people followed the Russians and Poles to an alcoholic anaesthetic, or the tired workers of Hong Kong to opium and heroin. Others found relief in clinging to old gods, in being born again as Christians or Muslims or Shintos. There were also those who packed the psychiatric clinics, or finally made an end of it, relieving the world labour market of their particular 'excess capacity'. Mental breakdown, according to the Japan Productivity Centre, was the favoured escape for one in ten of 12,000 Japanese workers surveyed; and suicide, for 340 managers in 1980.

The straws in the wind did not all point in the same direction. There were eddies and currents that blew the leaves in many different ways. But overall, there seemed little in the public world to give substantial grounds for optimism.

The officials had no firm hopes of revival, and no plans or proposals that promised to secure it. The efforts of each State to protect its interests nullified those of any combined efforts to restore matters. All comforted themselves that, if only they could hold on long enough, if no one 'lost their nerve', things would one day return to 'normal'.

Each of the threads – whether unemployment, inflation, famine or the arms race – led back to a central nexus, the ungovernable world market and the competition of the dominant States. There were separate symptoms, but one central cause. The structure of power was therefore the problem, not an instrument to overcome it. Proposals for change were generally considered on their intellectual merits, but validity was not the problem. Who was to implement the reforms? There seemed to be only States – or their somewhat nebulous shadows, 'public opinion' – and so the circle repeated itself.

It is a childish piety to say the world needs one government, a political order corresponding to its economic foundations as a global system. The thought horrifies most people; since the record of national government is so poor, how much worse would be an international equivalent. Yet just such an institution was the precondition for the effectiveness of many of the proposals for reform (leaving aside the question of whether, in sum, the remedies could have revived world boom). One world State might be able to mobilize sufficient power to bludgeon capital into some order. But it was an entirely utopian thought, since there was apparently no agency capable of defeating all to achieve this.

If the problem was not simply one of the programme, but the agency, of change, the cause of world reform seemed hopeless. Yet the two elements, what needed to be done and who was to do it, were related. Merely restoring the old world order was no longer enough, although this was the sole target of most of those who proposed reforms. Getting 'back to normal' included getting back to the Cold War, the Vietnam War and countless other barbarities. It included the restoration of work, rather than further moves towards the abolition of work. The times needed greater courage and audacity than boom, yet everywhere seemed to produce greater cowardice. At least, that is how it seemed from the crest of the mountain. Below that lofty level, the world presented a more contradictory image.

Notes to Chapter 8

1. G. E. M. Anscombe, *Intentions*, Oxford, 1957, p. 6.

2. *Business International*, 'Weekly Report to Managers of World Wide Operations', Business International Corporation, 7 January 1977, p. 1, cited Fröbel *et al.*, *The New International Division of Labour*, London, 1980, p. 1.

3. The foundations of the approach are outlined in some of the contributions to Chenery, Hollis, *et al.*, *Redistribution with Growth*, World Bank, 1974; see also International Labour Organization, *Employment, Growth and Basic Needs: A One World Problem*, I.L.O., Geneva, 1976.

4. The literature is daunting on the issue. But for one rationale see Michael Lipton, *Why Poor People Stay Poor: Urban Bias in World Development*, London, 1977, and the review by T. J. Byres, 'On Neo-populist Pipe-dreams: Daedalus in the Third World and the Myth of Urban Bias', *The Journal of Peasant Studies*, 6/2, January 1979, pp. 210–44.

5. For example, see the account of the G.A.T.T. (General Agreement on Trade and Tariffs) Secretariat: 'The State of the world economy can perhaps best be diagnosed in terms of the tension between its investment needs and potential on the one hand, and the insufficiency of the actual investment incentives on the other. To keep a sense of proportion, however, one should note the substantial volume of investment that is actually going on; the whole difficulty consists in raising its share in gross national products by a few percentage points ... The task of economic policy thus comes into clear focus. It consists in discovering or correcting those conditions in the institutional and policy framework of the economy which prevent the existing needs and opportunities for more investment being translated into effective investment incentives.' (Chapter 1, International Trade 1979/80, G.A.T.T. Secretariat, press communiqué 1271, Geneva, 9 September 1980, as published in *Comercio Exterior de Mexico*, Banco Nacional, Mexico City, 26/11, November 1980.

6. See W. Leontief *et al.*, *The Future of the World Economy, A United Nations Study*, United Nations, New York, 1977; Jan Tinbergen, *Reshaping the International Order*, Amsterdam, 1977; U.N.C.T.A.D., *Restructuring the International Economic Framework*, U.N.C.T.A.D., Geneva, 1979; U.N.I.T.A.R. (United Nations Institute for Training and Research), *Progress in the Establishment of a New International Economic Order: Obstacles and Strategies*, U.N.I.T.A.R., New York, n.d.

7. *North-South, A Programme for Survival*, The Report of an Independent Commission on International Development Issues, under the Chairmanship of Willy Brandt, London, 1980.

8. Second Conference of the United Nations Industrial Development Organization, U.N.I.D.O., New Delhi, January 1980.

9. *Suddeutsche Zeitung*, 24 January 1975, cited Fröbel *et al.*, *The New International* . . ., op cit., p. 164.

10. For the Theses on the Colonial Question, see the Second Congress of the Communist International, in Jane Degras (ed.), *The Communist International, 1919–43*, Vol. 1, London, 1971, and *The Second Congress of the Communist International, Minutes of the Proceedings*, London (New Park, 2 vols.), 1977; on M. N. Roy, see *Memoirs*, Bombay, 1964, and *Documents of the History of the Communist Party of India* (ed. G. Adhikari), Vol. 1, 1917–22, New Delhi, 1971. 1971.

11. 'Imperialism, the Highest Stage of Capitalism', in *Selected Works*, Vol. V, London, 1936, pp. 92–3.

12. For discussion of this, cf. Michael Kidron, Chapters 6 and 7, in *Capitalism and Theory*, London, 1974, pp. 124–67, and my 'Imperialism Today', in Nigel Harris and John Palmer (eds.), *World Crisis*, London, 1971, pp. 117–67.

13. *Address to the Board of Governors*, September 1977, World Bank, Washington, 1977, p. 7.

14. Irving Kristol, *Wall Street Journal*, 19 December 1980.

15. The response was not new. See the letter of the Webbs to *The Times* (6 December 1901): 'the complaints as to diminished quantity or energy of work and of the tacit conspiracy to discourage individual exertion, occur with curiously exact iteration in every decade of the last hundred years at least ... To give an instance only, we have found exactly the same accusation of the bricklayer limiting the number of bricks, and precisely the same belief that they were only doing "half as much" as they did twenty years before, in the great strikes of 1833, in those of 1853, again in 1859–60, and again in 1871.'

16. *Quarterly Economic Report*, West L.B. Information, 4/80, West-deutsche Landesbank Girozentrale, Düsseldorf/Münster, 1980, p. 1.

17. *1848: Historical Revelations*, London, 1858; reprint, New York, 1971, p. 139.

18. Cited by Bruce K. Murray, in *The People's Budget, 1909–10: Lloyd George and Liberal Politics*, London, 1980.

NINE OUT OF THE CLOSET

Sex, age, races, all that bullshit keeps everybody apart.
Competition gets to be the only link we've got. But, if
you've got to 'beat' somebody then you're more alone.[1]

... capitalist society, divided into classes, can only exist
when the mentality of labour peace is, so to speak,
universally valid; in other words, only when and as long as
the working class, this most important productive power
of capitalist society, silently 'consents' to fulfil the
capitalist function. Once this precondition disappears, the
further existence of capitalist society is impossible.[2]

Pessimism of the intellect; optimism of the will.[3]

What *is* the world economy? It is time to demolish the illusion that a
world economy exists as an entity separate from the inhabitants of the
world. The global system is not the heaps of implements people use –
from spades to steel mills, rowing boats to oil tankers, needles to dams.
All these without human beings to use them are merely heaps of junk. It
is as impossible for generals to fight wars without soldiers as it is for steel
managers to make steel without millhands. Nor is the system the heaps
of paper, from share certificates to banknotes; for such documents to
have meaning requires all of us to accept their significance. No, the
world economy is first and foremost workers, a set of global relationships between those who sell their labour power or cultivate the soil.
Their daily – if unknowing – collaboration, across thousands of miles,
ensures that the world's product is produced.

For much of this book, those who make the output of the world have
been largely absent, as if their daily routine could be taken for granted. It
is true that, for most of the time, the world's workers are astonishing
monuments of patience and discipline, of silence in the face of the
fantasies that dominate public existence. But in crisis, their patience can
no longer be taken for granted. When even their modest ambitions can
no longer be met from a lifetime of labour, the silent find voices.

In looking at the foundations of the system, we return to the national
village. For it is in specific localities that people experience the world
system. They may be unaware of the source of change – the village is
'false consciousness' – but in the tangible realities of the locality is 'true
consciousness'. It is here where people can resist, here that is the source

of compassion and courage, even if normally those feelings are frustrated by the walls of the State. The world system cannot be controlled except from within the localities where people are; no supranational authority can do it.

The numbers of the world's workers were vastly increased by the great boom. It created entirely new working classes in countries where urban labour had scarcely existed before, or where it had been entirely marginal to the social order. The boom expanded those working classes that existed, as well as transforming their internal composition. There has never been such a body of educated workers in the world before. Furthermore, the world system incorporated a much larger proportion of those who worked than ever before, both rural and urban. Fifty years ago, the world working class was largely a Euro-American phenomenon, although there were important working classes in the larger backward countries – Argentina, China, India and so on. But today, it is everywhere, the great helot class whose labour constitutes the world system, whether it be the growing of rice or cotton, the making of missiles or sewing machines, the provisions of soldiers or servants.

Those who labour in the great concentrations of world and national industry are the basis of the system. They hold the power to change it. In their concentration – in numbers, in units of production, in localities – lies their access to the levers of power upon which the ruling orders depend. It makes them, in principle, the most powerful class. Paradoxically, they are most powerful where countries are less developed – here, the strategic power of a relatively small working class is much greater than comparable groups in a fully industrialized country.

You can hear echoes of that power in almost every industrial dispute. Take for example the Ford worker in São Paulo in Brazil in May 1977. Strikes were illegal when the car workers struck, when one of them commented:

> When we first stopped work and listened, it was all silent. All the factories were silent. I had never heard that quiet before in all my life. I suddenly realized how powerful we were.

There was another echo of the same feeling in the words of an old labour leader, standing on a hill high above the coastal steel plant at Wollongong in Australia: 'I feel proud when you see twelve or fifteen iron ore tankers lined up in the harbour; then you know there's a strike in the plant, and *we* control how much ore is landed.' No doubt a similar thought crossed the minds of oil workers on Kharg Island, the main Iranian oil terminal, as they saw the lines of giant tankers queuing fruitlessly for crude in November 1978; it was a symbol of their power to stop the flow of oil, of their power to break the back of the regime of the Shah of Iran.

That sense of power is a revelation of the real world beneath the abstractions that dominate most people's heads. It is not a real world only in what is called 'capitalism', the West, or in the Less Developed. Beyond the iron and bamboo curtains where, supposedly, the working class runs the State, workers occasionaly experience the exhilarating and liberating sensation of power. Polish workers broke the regime of Gomulka in 1970 and of Gierek in 1980. The party leadership were obliged to listen as they would never otherwise have done when the docks of the North and the mines of the South stopped. The strikes in May 1980 in the car plants of Togliatti and Gorky, the Kama River truck plant and the Chelyabinsk tractor factory suddenly conjured meat out of a meatless Russia, some of it filched no doubt from the stockpiles accumulated for foreign visitors to the Moscow Olympics. President Ceausescu was obliged to negotiate personally with the 30,000 miners who closed the pits near Petroseni in Romania's western carpathians in the summer of 1977.

The illegal literature of the East bears witness to the common essential condition of labour there as well as in the West and South. Wages, housing, holidays, all differ, but the yoke of wage work is the same. Whether it be Hungarian,[4] or Polish,[5] Russian or Chinese, the refrain is common: what is called 'socialism' is a fraud –

> According to the Marxist theoreticians, under socialism, the masses hold all political power. Go and ask Chinese workers: 'Apart from the wretched pay which you are given every month, just to prevent you from starving, what rights do you have? What power do you have? Whose masters are you? Alas, you can control nothing – not even your own marriage!'[6]

Polish miners drew similar conclusions: 'You miners understand well', a 1980 Solidarity bulletin in Silesia proclaimed,

> that our system has nothing to do with Socialism: it is state capitalism in which there is not room for concern for workers' well-being. Miners are not important: the only thing that counts is the coal that can be exchanged for dollars.
>
> The Red bourgeoisie profit by your sweat, your injuries and often your lives at the expense of working people. They build themselves palaces equipped with modern gadgets imported from the West. It is they who build the luxury Party houses at the cost of one thousand flats, for which you have to wait years.[7]

The workforce of the world economy may be its most important element, but there is grave difficulty in identifying the rhythms of its activity. Volumes and values of currency transactions and commodity movements are recorded, but not the world class struggle. The forms of opposition – from strike to riot to guerrilla warfare and civil war, from absenteeism to countless demonstrations, large and tiny – against the Bomb, against pollution, the oppression of women and racial or religious groups, against rent increases and food shortages – are not recorded in a form where we can quantify, where we can plot the temperature reading of the world body politic. The forms of forceful 'participation' are screened out to protect the illusion of a great silence below stairs, a silence which rulers can infer embodies approval.

There is an additional problem. Each incident of class collision is seen by the participants on both sides as uniquely related to local and specific circumstances, just as each capitalist sees no more than his or her specific interest. Like the participants in the market, few understand the causes of their action, only the immediate pretext; nor the ultimate results, how each pursuing what seems to be a unique end nonetheless conforms to a general movement. The issue here in Cracow is a shortage of meat and milk, and an abundance of corrupt Party officials; here in West Virginia, it is the hoodlums employed by the mine management; here in Calcutta it is the price of rice and the wage cuts that squeeze the life of jute workers. Yet meat and milk and rice, corrupt officials and hoodlums, are all interwoven in one system. The pretext is not the cause, nor is the effect simply a local settlement. A strike in São Paulo interacts with one in Warsaw, and not merely because the same banks have lent to the Governments of Brazil and Poland (and for the bankers, it is all the same); the São Paulo labour leader, Sr Luis Inacio da Silva (or 'Lula'), is known as the 'Lech Walesca of Brazil'. In sum, as the world profit rate drifts sickeningly downwards, stomachs and heads are squeezed, and the working class bangs against the walls of each national ghetto.

The struggle to master the system is thus not a matter for cosy discussions between the leaders of the world, whether at the United Nations or at summits. It is an unremitting daily matter. Through the years of the long boom, millions of heroes and heroines in almost every factory and workplace, farm and plantation, struggled to win a little more space to be human, to curb the foreman or the line speed, to extract a mite more for selling their labour, to make room for a tea or a lunch break. Their efforts are unrecorded, almost never surfacing to the public world.

Despite all the rhetoric in the core zones of the system, power and authority remained obstinately resistant to change, as did the symptoms of power, social inequality. Take the mute comment of the demographic results of inequality in Britain (Table 25).

25. *Standardized mortality ratios for males, by class, England and Wales*[8]

	1949–53 (aged 20–64 years)	1970–72 (aged 15–64 years)
I. Professional occupations	86	77
II. Managerial and lower professional	92	81
III. Skilled occupations	101	104
IV. Partly skilled	104	113
V. Unskilled	118	137

If society remained firmly resistant to social change, its production unit was impregnable to the seductive sounds of the permissive society. And with reason, for it is here in the basic building block of the world system that the foundations of the world social order are revealed:

It is always the direct relationship of the owners of the means of production to the direct producers – a relationship naturally corresponding to a definite stage in the development of the methods of labour and thereby its social productivity – which reveals the innermost secret, the hidden basis of the entire social structure, and with it, the political form of the relation of sovereignty and dependence, in short, the correspondingly specific form of the State.[9]

The spectacular collisions of the world system were restricted during the great boom to those points where it was weakest, the Less Developed Countries. And in general, it was not the new working classes who fought, but students and groups of peasants. The fight reached the stage of armed warfare, most bitterly in Indo-China and the former territories of the Portuguese empire. The tempo of battles reached a crescendo in the second half of the sixties, the warning signals of the seventies. In Indonesia in 1965, the social order collapsed in a welter of slaughter. In South Asia, a seismic zone of the world system, elements of disintegration emerged in the late sixties – the Indian State was paralysed in its eastern provinces, Pakistan fell in half, and Sri Lanka experienced the revolt of its youth.

These were the years when the main components of the world system were moving into synchronization, and revolt was also partly synchronized. The years of the first slump – between late 1973 and 1975 – witnessed the most widespread rebellion across the globe seen to that time. The statistics are less than reliable, but national strike rates in many countries ran at record levels (in particular, in Italy, Australia, India, the United States, Ireland, Britain, Japan, West Germany, Norway). If we take the average of days lost in disputes in industry per 1,000 employed, for fourteen of the More Developed Countries, the figure rises from 450 (1964–6) to 611 (1967–71) to 687 (1972–6).[10] In Burma, Malaysia, Jamaica and southern Africa (in South Africa and on the Zambian copper belt), there were major skirmishes. In Chile, the development of revolution was bloodily put down. In Nigeria, a public sector strike intimidated the military regime into conceding a 30 per cent pay increase.

At least three authoritarian regimes collapsed before the onslaught. The national liberation wars in Mozambique, Angola and Guinea-Bissau produced the fall of Portuguese fascism under Caetano, followed by the rapid radicalization of Portuguese workers. It became impossible to hold intact the authoritarian regime that succeeded Caetano's. In Ethiopia, the general strike of Addis Ababa workers broke the long-lived order of Emperor Haile Selassie. And in Thailand, mass demonstrations and strikes dispatched the military triumvirate; it was the first time strikes – and workers – had played a role in Thailand; annual man days lost in disputes, running at below 18–20,000 between 1956 and 1972, rose to half a million in 1972, and nearly three-quarters of a million in 1974.

Students played an important role in precipitating events. And interwoven in each revolt was the rebellion of other groups – of peasants and cultivators in southern Portugal, in north and north-eastern Thailand, in northern Ethiopia; of those defending a religious or cultural identity as in the Muslim revolts in the southern Philippines and southern Thailand, the Eritrean struggle in Ethiopia, the Tamils in Sri Lanka, Palestinians, Northern Ireland Catholics and Kurds. It is as if three vital sociological seams of the system – worker–employer, peasant–landlord, ethnic and religious groups relative to 'majority' cultures – each began to tear under the impact of world contraction. It became clear that the seams had not at all been soldered tight in the years of boom.

Ancient issues of oppression re-emerged – or rather, those oppressed came to rediscover that they were oppressed and that something could be done to remedy it. In the turbulence of industrial Thailand, three of the five factory occupations in Bangkok in the spring of 1976 were by teenage women. Even in the midst of South Korea's accelerating boom of the seventies, it was a group of women textile workers in the Dong Il factories at Inchon who demanded – as Christians – respect for their human dignity. Their battle through much of the decade for trade-union rights, in the face of fearful opposition from the alliance of employers, State and trade-union leadership, was one of the rivulets that joined many others – like that of the miners who seized the town of Sabuk in 1980 in order to get a trade-union leadership independent of the State – to bring the temporary collapse of the Korean dictatorship.

The ruling orders recovered from the shock of the first wave of revolt between 1973 and 1975. They did so in different ways. Some permitted more popular regimes, Social Democrats in Portugal, Britain and Jamaica (Prime Minister Manley suddenly discovered the virtues of 'Jamaican Socialism', backed by the Gun Court, an Industrial Relations Act and a wage freeze). Latin America moved sharply to the right; Chile was the harbinger of appalling slaughters in Argentina and Uruguay. Mrs Gandhi hammered down the lid in her Emergency. President Ceausescu moved the army into the mines to arrest the militants. Others moved more precipitately, copying the Latin American lead, with military coups in Thailand and Ethiopia. Everyone was older and wiser.

In due course, even where the advent of Social Democracy seemed to promise something better, as we have seen, ruling orders moved to beat back the tide of discontent. Monetarism provided the rationale for an employers' offensive to re-establish 'managerial authority', to intimidate the mass and separate even further trade-union leaderships from their membership.

In the years of stagnation, there was no repetition of the synchronized movement of the first slump. But major collisions there were – general strikes in Sri Lanka, Egypt and Nigeria. In Pakistan, a wave of general strikes swept away the popular regime that had salvaged the ruling order in 1971, that of Mr Bhutto; only to have a military dictatorship replace him. In Brazil, the labour movement, cowed in the military coup of 1964 and the repression between 1968 and 1972, began to revive, and so also, after a much shorter time, did that in Chile. In Turkey and Jamaica, armed street warfare threatened the dissolution of all society. In South Africa, the continuing civil war flickered into sudden major collisions, and the strike rate trebled at the end of the decade. In Central America, civil war also paralysed regimes, overthrowing one (that of Somoza in Nicaragua), decimating others (Salvador, Guatemala) and even affecting that hitherto model of Social Democracy, Costa Rica. In China, rumbling discontent periodically burst out, with the demand, in one strike, for 'the right to decide our own future for ourselves' and to 'break down the rusted door of socialism'.[11]

Possibly the most astonishing event was the collapse of the apparently impregnable order of the Shah of Iran, suddenly alerting the world ruling orders to the possibility of world war over the Persian Gulf. No less fearful was the answering echo from Poland, the most massive worker rebellion in any country of the Eastern Bloc, and threatening the foundations of the world order.

The tumult appeared universal, but without any unifying perception. Events were diverse symptoms of a common phenomenon, but reports isolated each occurrence in the peculiarities of one place, whether the status of the Shah's commitment to Islam or the meat supply in Poland. Furthermore, when the cries subsided, the victims were buried or bandaged, the system remained intact. Even the victories were converted into local occurrences, with Islamic or People's Republics. The ruling order retained considerable resources for survival. Its most powerful weapon was precisely that the rebels each pursued a separate thread, each unaware in the main of either the world at large or the generality of revolt. The women who occupied the Harra Jeans factory in Bangkok knew nothing of those fighting at Dong Il in South Korea's Inchon, nor, later, of those women occupying the Lee Jeans factory in Greenock in Scotland. Indeed, mere knowledge alone would not have helped them to fight.

The rebels needed knowledge but also organization. They needed knowledge of each other and of a programme to transform the condition of their own subordination, the world system. Most of them fought, not for a new world, but in defence of the old; or at best, for the chance to create a new regime in one country. Yet as we have seen, the condition of the emancipation of one national village is the emancipation of all – or at least, of a sufficient number to constitute an independent force. At best, in such circumstances, the rebels could achieve only temporary amelioration, even if they persuaded themselves that this was a fundamental triumph. Too often, the victory proved no more than the prelude to a more fundamental defeat. The workers of Karachi and elsewhere defeated Mr Bhutto, but General Zia inherited power. The mass of Iranians overthrew the Shah, but one section of the Ayatollahs inherited. The mass of Vietnamese battled, but at the end, it was the Party which remained supreme.

The demand for an 'independent' organization rose almost everywhere in the spontaneous movements, independent of the local State. Any such organization needed independence, but it also needed politics. For it was the politics which failed in the revolts of the seventies.

Those who might once have been thought able to provide those politics, the Left, the socialists, were in disarray. Some of the most dedicated were governed by a conception of socialism in which everything had become its opposite, the result of the appalling experience of Soviet Russia. Now it was not ordinary people who were to be liberated, but only the State. The State was to own all, subordinating all to its competitive drive with other States. The core of socialism, human freedom, had been subverted by the doctrines of worship of the State. The alternatives of the Left – like so many of those considered in the last chapter – depended entirely on the institution which was one of the central problems of the system, the State. This was part of the explanation as to why, so often, the Left made little contribution to the movements of the seventies, so often was no more than those who trailed behind movements, attempting without success to capture them (despite the invariable allegations of the Right that all movements were fomented by politically motivated conspirators). For, to exchange bureaucratic State management for a class of private employers was hardly worth a great commotion; and even if achieved, it constituted no act of emancipation for anyone except the officials of the State.

Thus, there *was* an agency, a force for social change, and one that was, in principle, both independent of the State and of sufficient power to master the States. Yet the participants had no awareness of themselves as a social force, no common programme for the transformation of the world, and no party capable of fusing their enthusiasm with the discipline and clarity required to conquer State power. The disintegration of a tradition of revolutionary socialist thought left the rebels unprepared and unarmed for the great contest. Despite the obstinate and bitter efforts, each movement was deflected or defeated. In the end, each State could rely on the fear of the outside world to corral its inhabitants, and thereby ensure loyalty to the world system.

The stalemate between the world classes, created and sustained by the stalemate in the world of capital, blocks any resolution of the central problem of a world in slump. Catastrophes ebb and flow, whether as famine or sporadic wars between States, leaving the mass of the world's inhabitants watching, waiting, hoping, victims of an order beyond control or influence. The experience of the last breakthrough – the Russian revolution of 1917 – sours all hopes. For the Russian regime was subverted at home, became the mirror image of its main rival abroad, and in turn reduced a generation of Communist workers to no more than faithful fellow travellers of the Russian State; when reform once more became possible, the Eurocommunists broke with Moscow only to embrace yet more varieties of local nationalism.

Yet the rebellions will continue, for a world in slump and stagnation impels States to purchase their survival at the cost of their population, which in turn impels even the sceptical to attempt to defend themselves.

It also impels the States closer to the brink of war. If we follow the analogy of 1917, we can see that a breakthrough in one national village is the precondition for the creation of an international alternative to begin the process of spreading revolution. Such social change is the precondition for the reconstruction of the world system on the foundation of popular control, on the basis that those who labour shall hold the power to determine the system, that the needs of the majority shall govern growth and change in the world's output.

It is not at all a new view. In the handful of years before the Communist International was subverted by the Russian Government, it saw its purpose as the formation of the first party of the world working class. The second Congress dedicated itself:

> to fight by all available means, including armed struggle, for the overthrow of the international bourgeoisie and for the creation of an international republic of Workers' Councils as a transitional stage to the complete abolition of the State. The Communist International considers the dictatorship of the proletariat the only way to liberate mankind from the horrors of capitalism.

The task remains, many years after those at the Congress thought it would have been accomplished. It remains not because of some commendable virtue in an 'ideology' or a set of 'ideals' – only the foolish opt for hypotheticals except under the pressure of overwhelming events – but rather because of the fearful alternatives facing the world's peoples. The world economy, the skills and disciplines of its workers whether at the bench, on the land or in the laboratory, has never before achieved such miracles of production. In principle, the world's workers can, with obstinate dedication, feed and clothe the world's inhabitants, can protect them from the ravages of disease and accident, can assist them to create an environment they choose and govern. Yet in practice, the organization of the present world – a profit-making system and a set of competing States – makes for the opposite reaction: sacking workers, cutting production. And the shadows behind these elements of the foreground are of war and famine. It is the alternative to socialism, barbarism, 'the common ruin of the contending classes', which is the most powerful case for world revolution.

Notes to Chapter 9

1. William Wharton, *Birdy*, London, 1978, p. 193.

2. N. Bukharin, *The Economics of the Transformation Period*, Moscow, 1920,

3. Romain Rolland; a phrase adopted by Antonio Gramsci; cf. *Selections from the Prison Notebooks*, London, 1971, p. 175.

4. See, for example, Miklos Haraszti, *A Worker in a Workers' State*, London, 1977.

5. Jacek Kuron and Karol Modzelewski, *An Open Letter to the Party*, 1965, published in *New Politics*, New York, 5/2–3, and as *A Revolutionary Socialist Manifesto*, International Socialism, London, n.d.

6. The Chinese citation is from Wei Jingsheng, Canton Big Character poster series, 1971; for more details of the Chinese dissidents, see my *The Mandate of Heaven: Marx and Mao in Modern China*, London, 1978, p. 132 *passim*.

7. The Solidarity bulletin is quoted by Denis MacShane in *Solidarity: One Year On*, London, 1981.

8. Sir J. Brotherstone, 'Inequality: Is It Inevitable?' in C. A. Carter and J. Peel (eds.), *Equalities and Inequalities in Health*, 1976.

9. Karl Marx, *Capital*, Vol. 3 (Moscow, 1959 edition), p. 772.

10. Calculated from Table 4, 'Comparison of working days lost through industrial disputes in mining, manufacturing, construction and transport, selected countries (Britain, Australia, Belgium, Canada, Denmark, West Germany, Finland, France, Ireland, Italy, Japan, Netherlands, New Zealand, Norway, Sweden, United States)', in David C. Smith, 'Trade Union Growth and Industrial Disputes', in Richard E. Caves and Lawrence B. Krause (eds.), *Britain's Economic Performance*, Brooking, Washington, 1980, p. 109.

11. Citation from the *Taiyuan Daily*, reporting a strike at Taiyuan steel mill, by Agence France-Presse, *The Times*, London, 6 February 1981.

INDEX